Corona-affected Economy and Treatment Procedure! (World business scenario - Before and after corona)

Finding a way out of the corona crisis

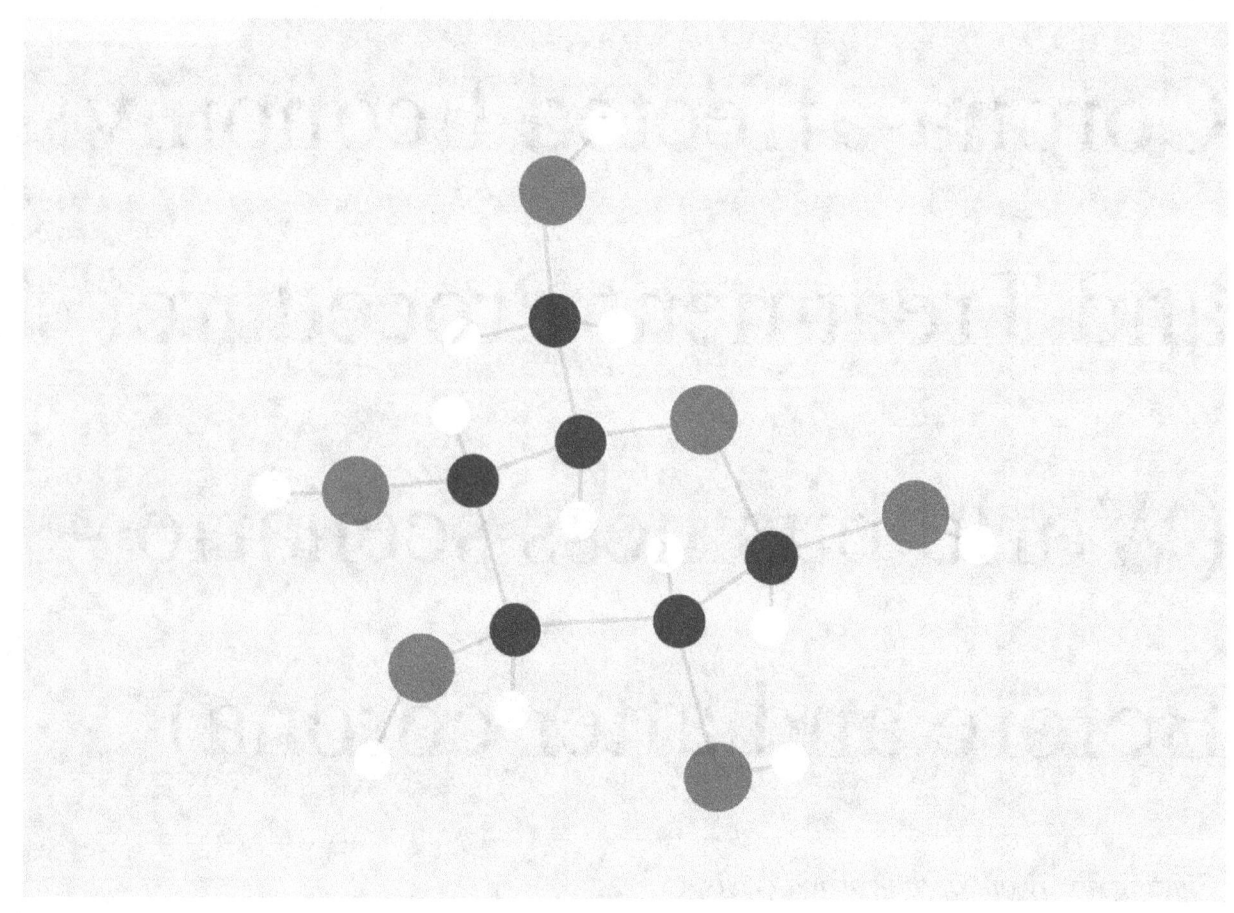

C V Madhavi

&

Ch. S Rajagopal

2020

Acknowledgements

I am immensely grateful to my mother who is ever supportive and encouraging by taking care of everything to let me think free while working on the book.

I would like to thank my father who readily agreed to be my co-author. He has devoted a lot of time in multiple reads and repeated editing to give the final finish on the book.

We are thankful to the CXOs who spared time to give inputs in helping us write the book. The saga of corona is not splattered in the pages of the book but a simple yet elaborate procedure for economic revival is proposed for the post-covid-19 industry 'warriors'. We thank all readers in advance, for motivating us to bring out this piece. Any shortcomings are our mistakes and would be corrected in future editions on valid suggestions from Learned Readers taking them as inputs!

Backdrop - CORONA fears

Lincoln believed that people of any country can handle any crisis if we provide true data and facts. The WORD corona (Tables 1, 2) should stop scaring WORLD -industries and governments across the globe. Let's treat corona like a sandal that has to be stamped by our foot. The virus with a short lifespan is able to end our life span of decades because we are not able to appreciate our greatness as against the insignificant existence of the virus. We can not talk to viruses to tell us not to infect such long struggling human health because it does not deserve to stick to us in stature. Thinking of corona viruses as cruel outsiders ruining our nice armor of immunity and health can let us take care and precautions in staying away from unhealthy habits because the truth remains that we are suffering due to the diseases spread by these pathogens. Still hope and courage are needed to thwart the ill effects of corona as curable by research originating new alternatives in the field of medicine. Nevertheless collaboration, opportunities, readiness, optimism, nimbleness, altruism are saviors demanded by the corona infected economy. As global citizens we must ward off the fears of corona and help others overcome the same. The Senior citizens all over the world serve as our teachers. Successful recovery of the corona patients over 90 years of age, teaches us to be wise in our daily habits to be free of the fear of falling sick. Their interviews reveal that they know how to face the struggles of life, they all eat in moderation, nor detest family atmosphere, all of them live with the grandchildren and celebrate life without running behind worries.

Table 1: List of Likes of people

Likes				
Free	New	Discount	Onlineshopping	Gift cards
Extra	Offer	Sanitizer	Coupons	Selfie

Table 2: List of Dislikes of people

Dislikes				
Corona	Discussion	Call holds	Price hikes	Maid holidays
Covidpositive	Compliant	News	Hand-washing	Eat at home
Lockdown	Complaint			

Global health concerns

The fear of infection and social proximity leading to the spread of ailment cannot be removed from people's psyche unless sincere attempt is made to deviate efforts to tasks that we don't otherwise normally perform so that we can shift our concentration in learning a new thing or execution thereof rather than intuitive chores not refreshing our brain with new inputs. People like sanitizer and innovative equipment like ones spreading aromas and scanning your home devices but we're not sure how to get used to repeated washing of hands. Social media marketing research (conducted by Tietoz in June 2020) response results reported that we don't like washing hands though we would do it as a health measure. Above are some common words we would like to hear from newsreaders, sellers or to read online. The second group is the list of things and words we don't like. People like the word 'new', and everything 'new' but not news, understandably so, for apprehensions of learning about bad news more than good (Tables 1, 2).

Another interesting find is that most of us don't like to deal with complaints though we end up making complaints or resolving issues or getting victimized by others. It's pretty common that we don't like to be complying with rules for more freedom than restriction.

Children like this concept of lockdown though adults are not much in favour, response is highly appreciated, with kids getting to spend time with the family in the home vacation and naughty kids are becoming more uncontrollable with parents pleading for silence and solitude.

The fears if cannot be eliminated being natural to human beings must be managed well by framing protective policies for one and all in the economy without letting the culprits off the hook by taking shelter under the new economy formative reformatory steps. The quintessential life with all essential safety and hygiene items would now be applicable to be led by not just the rich but all segments of the society that have thus far been deprived of high quality healthcare. The entire economy belongs to the same social segment without room for disparity between man and woman or rich and poor, the well-to-do's must ensure well-being of the remaining people otherwise lack of social progress could hamper an otherwise even global economic development track, as argued in the kindred works by scholars and economists like Adam Smith, Milton Friedman and John Miller. The calloused economy due to corona crisis must be healed by wise economic growth and wealth creation for avoiding the deterioration of people's health or wealth by a bollockery of unimplemented rosy promises of government or companies becoming mook in the pretext of pseudoscience or exclaiming bleugh on social networks as if genetically predisposed to participate in online protests when the productivity is already falling to pieces.

Global workforce issues

The employees are fearing loss of pay or job or personal belongings due to failure in payment of loan instalments. The fear is true where the employees are not able to show output to employers who would otherwise search for a reason to answer personal crisis fears by firing the employees as the closest option to solve the scary company failure. Another is the fear of getting relocated and stuck in foreign countries. MNC employees are not able to stay back nor travel to home nations in the corona lockdown. It teaches governments to formulate policy to give and take brain drain of upto 10%. Not more than 10% of our population should travel out for foreign employment and residence status. There should be no restriction on intermingling tourists and business visitors but not more than 10% of our population should be composed of foreign immigrants and workers. Refugees and illegal migrants should be handled by separate policy. Rotation of foreign immigrants could ensure an even opportunity for all eligible citizens. Every nation should follow sons of soil at national level so that we have a home in time of crisis.

The economy can grow globally if concentration of resources does not happen in a few countries. All talented people from different countries are doing well in the USA that enables and motivates people to study, stay, work and do business. Hence the USA is the most important and powerful economy of the world. In a crisis, a single wrong decision could send negative influence on the rest of the world because the other countries are not able to stay focused on filling the gap created by brain drain clogged by other nations to get the latest local growth advance. The world is divided by religion though leaders proclaim equal opportunity society. The population of all religions should have own country in which we would be able to stay and bring growth, Muslims and followers of Islam (>25% world populace) have their nations in middle East and Arabia mainly but 25% of the world cohabits them with more than 30% population of every nation belonging to Islam. Followers of Christianity have their nations in the western part of the world. Followers of Buddhism and Taoism have China, Sri Lanka and other countries. Followers of Hinduism have Nepal, Mauritius and India though the population of 1.2 billion Hindus forms more than 15% of the world population. The crisis should teach us to manage nations like companies. We would not clutter employees of a given department in the corner of office, by discriminating against those of another, by bossism and other superiority domination tactics later blaming the same for poor performance. Colonialism of the past should not have discriminatory effects on people of any country because this would impair the world growth as is witnessed now. The complete revival of economy is required now and global revival is not possible without realising and correcting the mistakes of the past that deprive certain countries of growth. Governments of every nation should have enough resources for growing in the world past covid-19.

Corona lockdown should teach us not fears and phobias but cooperation and understanding. The world should follow the uniform goals of saving every life as best as possible, *supporting the children* who are sharing the most part of risks instead of rights, at a tender age, and *rethinking about restoration of environment* to the core (rebuilding animal habitats due to unusual forest fire activity in the world; afforestation, water bodies, pure air, birds, and other bio resources reaching enervating depletion). Strategy of reducing fears is by facing and mitigating them by becoming leaders ourselves in guiding others out of fear instead of waiting for others to lead. We can then see how small or irrelevant our fears are when we realize the difficulties faced by others. Helping others helps us know how to help ourselves and crisis situations are confiners of freedom including that of thinking. Fear of fear can be conquered easily if we understand the situation of others in contrast to ours. One can see how others are facing times of turmoil; two things are possible, either we learn from their patience and way of dealing with problematic times, or we can understand the situation and possible options to get out. In the first case we have been helped by someone else; in the second one we have to help others as a token of gratitude. Fear is managed thus in the process of collaborative growth as we cross the hurdles together instead of sailing alone. Often we feel that we cannot grow unless others stop growing. That's not true. We cannot grow unless others also grow. The crop field does not have some plants obstructing the growth of others but healthy growth means that the field sees equal growth of all the plants present therein. Collaboration and growth are not far but near as we master our fear.

INTRODUCTION

JF Kennedy said that the word crisis in Chinese script, comprises two characters or symbols, one represents opportunity and other...danger.

Corona is a disease that is affecting the health of the people as well as the economy all over the World.

Thank the professional people wearing the caps and the capes of doctors, security guards, cleaners, police, administrators, nurses, nutrition experts and other professionals who have been in the process of taking care of others like us searching for a way forward amidst the wilderness of widespread panic that has changed the Economy of the world from the best to the worst of its 'un'kind in less than an year.

Economic revival and continued development of all nations' health is now the topmost priority because we won't get food unless the economy grows. The economy can only hope for production with the renewed collaboration of primary, secondary and tertiary sectors. The three interdependent sectors largely thrive on manual functions that is feasible by multi exponential agricultural leaping rise by supporting farmers with new technology to help them grow food in exemplary productivity strides reflecting our global health. The responsibility rests with the entire world, not limited to Europe, Asia, India or Africa, as native of one particular continent we may consider a group of countries as translocal but the industrial and financial growth disparities are irrevocably challenging the whole world to resolve before progressing to the next generation of technological modernism.

Health is Wealth, America, Japan, Germany, have to become big brothers for India, Australia, Singapore etc who would then guide the economic revival of Africa, Brazil, Europe and other regions. No country is backward or third world, some countries got luckier in one or the other thing, others want to add it to their strength. Heads of Government from various Friendly Countries should assemble periodically to discuss, review the economies; and weaknesses have to be corrected for overall Health of the GLOBAL ECONOMY! Thus we would be able to revive the global economy to its best by championing the cause of the certain nations that are left behind in the global race badly affected by the pandemic. Certainly, Global economic growth is no race but a continued exercise in solidarity based on the "GLOBAL VILLAGE Concept " in its real perspective! There are three segments that the Nations hitherto ranked e.g. Developed, Developing and Under-developed/poor. The Corona crisis has not yet disturbed the sustainability of Developed nations except eating into their past surpluses but sickening their economic prosperity which in due course of time land them into the List of Developing countries status , so long as Corona pandemic continues. Similarly the upcoming or Developing Countries are thrown farther away by the crisis in terms of reaching near becoming the category of developed countries.

The category of poor countries (African, Bangladesh, Pakistan, Burma, et al) has probably the richest natural heritage and lineage than any other region in the world, can they hence call the developed nations like the UK backward or less developed? No. The category of developing nations like Asia, including China and India, has a right to claim cultural, spiritual and Divine heritage (can Lord Rama, Lord Buddha and other millions of deities put the rest of the globe in the backseat? No.). In the present state of economic collapse we would not make a mistake by grouping Japan, Canada and USA in the world leader category because Japan could be creditworthy, and almost ignore corona, and not let the virus from touching Japanese health. Japan has done it by including technology, government and people in the same loop with the same stead. Japan's collaboration lesson is for all nations to learn 3Ps, patience, prevention and persistence. The country did not create any vocal protests blaming anybody but developing its own awareness and tools to prevent the spread of the disease. It developed machines to monitor the presence of pathogens in the air around us so that they could be exterminated wherever born. America could control the spread though after a few million gone. The learning is visible in the way the Americans are supported by the government through all trouble. Canada is no backbencher in doing the best for citizens to keep off the virus. The UK is trying but it has lost some say on the international dais due to its wavering presence at Brexit issues. Economic revival nevertheless requires equal participation of all countries regardless of the current performance in the world (corona, GDP growth or foreign relations). The productivity has fallen more in Australia, China, India, Singapore, notable because they have been growing most strongly, it's not intended to criticize any country but to provoke fast pace development that we have to accept reality and face the truth staring strikingly in the face of the world. The gruesome fact is that corona lockdown has brought the global economy to a standstill and to 'our' knees because we are part of the global economic health. Now is a time to motivate the weak by showing them the strength, and simultaneously challenge the strong to rise further by picking out their faults. Brazil is worsted by corona and more devastated than other regions of the global economy. Industry growth rate will slow down further in Europe unless techniques are quickly put in place to propel a manual intervention free function, operation and management. It may seem next to impossible but we have to imply that learning sabbatical is for the global community where machines take over the primary and secondary sectors, partially tertiary sectors because we don't need to forgo the important human interactions factor in the personalized or customized services. First, it has to more than make up for the losses due to the global lockdown. Second, men & machines have to recover the space surrendered by us to corona. Third, there does not seem to be any other better alternative. Companies assure that the work didn't stop despite the lockdown, work from home is no less than desk work at office but we are still human or we would not be scared of corona and stayed at home. The corona fear will come to affect the quality of work because our creativity is no free of- what if I lose job, how should I be normal, why is the vaccine still not in the market, where is a customer losing satisfaction, when is a competitor going to give market signal and a score more stupid things add up. If you find a company asking for cost cutting measures, it means that the firm is deliberating on the global cost of corona in the current world of business crisis. The cost including opportunity cost, BAU (business as usual) income, contingency cost, and other customer losses would become all-impending expense of corona that is hard to quote in number because the global economy has definitely lost what it cannot fathom and there is no other planet against whose species we can compare to know the global advancements that could be made during the lot of time and space lost in corona lockdown or afterwards. The world will wobble for support after this lockdown period comes to an end. Demand and supply would behave like dotted lines, markets would be anything better than dashes and the worst flowing would be the company cashes neither enough to start new ventures nor too low to be motivational for further improvements. You should not seem stupid in comparison to the virus but you would seem, and we all seem to be stupid when we lose our jobs due to a micro-organism, when the stock markets topple without warning and when the health companies fail in their tests of new drug. We have to identify the hidden opportunities in healthcare and technology besides other sectors for the virus to become irrelevant to times.

Acknowledgements	2
Backdrop - CORONA fears	3
Before corona (BC)	12
After corona	16
Procedure for corona crisis management	24
Customer	27
Agricultural Economy	30
Post Pandemic Growth of Services Sector	34
Modern Education	36
Changing employment contractual models	40
Our Responsibilities	43
Government	48
Industry	53
Sport & Fitness industry - Health is wealth	57
Global apparel and textiles	62
Shift in Global transportation industry	65
Entertainment & Media	68
Information technology	71
State of Energy sector	74
Electronic future	78
Semiconductors and memory storage	82
Insurance	85
Banking	88
Real estate parody	91
Kids industry segments	94
Data analytics	97
GDP (Genetics, Diagnostic and Pharmaceutical)	101
Total transformation in FMCG	104
Global Payments industry	108
Markets	116
Investments	119
Taxation	122
Procedure to revive the economy	125
Organizational inertia	129
Entrepreneurial benefit	135
Rethinking strategy	139

Supply chain management	143
Networks and transaction cost models	146
Way to Innovation	150
A special mention of Quantum Computing	153
Corporate ethics after corona lockdown	156

Business administrative transition (Bat to hit the crisis)   160

Marketing, sales, advertising	165
Financial twists	168
Management tantrums and Corporate revival	171

CSR   **178**

Competition Strategy   **181**

Technology Risks or digital wars	186
Organizational Resilience	189
Leadership in post crisis world	196
Cross border Collaboration	203

Population - Boon for Economic Revival   **206**

GOD   **209**

Eco-friendly Revival	216
Post Covid Knowledge Economy Transformation	219
Failures of the decade and impact on post pandemic economy: Company closures (Covid-19 Positive Corporate Cases)	222
New Opportunities (Covid-19 Negative or Immune Industries)	226

CONCLUSION   **233**

REFERENCES   **237**

Before corona (BC)

Man is measured by the response to... challenge and controversy... but not ...in moments of comfort, as suggested by Martin Luther.

The stock of affairs and the state of mind has been extremely focused on what to do with the most flexible and affordable terms of business to make out of the market crisis initiated in 2008. The slowdown is expected to catch up with the lost momentum of mortgage goof up but only to be slowed down slightly more by the virus under the carpet. It will not be pleasant to reiterate the millions of deaths caused by corona especially when they have been pointed out by the newsreaders continuously over the last few months of lock down globally ranging from a minimum of 10 days to 100 days to even further down the year as expected in various areas of the world. The first thing that we need to do is to bring a perspective to be able to help organisations with the identification of the lost ground and increasing threat of flooding with the growth challenges due to the chain of changes inundating the governments, communities and other participating institutions in building control over the next generation of business systems that can provide support for safety of the users and sustainable success with the process, product and service, all three of which are now in the state of transformation. They will also need to ensure the information on containing the debacle of corona and forecasting similar or different types of data modification arising from the future global economy growth. Doing away with the problem of creating a new business model is a great dream for many Companies that offer the best tailored services to the customers in establishing a successful winning team and working stakeholder relationships with the market agents.

The World of 2020BC (and pre 2000BC *BC = Before Corona) has been growing most satisfactorily if not great or worst. Asia is at no worse than 5-6% growth, now too if optimistic handling is supposedly relied on. Americas could achieve 6-7% for the North and 5-6.5% for its Southern dip. South America is now a loss hub for corona afflicted economic slowdown. Europe with 4-7% growth can be a huge ground for leaders, laggards and learners. Poor countries would have to wait for catching up with the world because it figures below the world average of 3-5.5% growth rate. Australia is on track of improvement with mining on the top of 4-5% growth. The other things like innovative business ideas, profit making international collaborations, new technology introductions or other industry growth concerns have occupied prominent slots in the history of global economic development programs. Agriculture, engineering, services and many sectorial participants are facing only one question as to how to sustain in the global collapse.

One question leads to the other and companies ask about how to dive out of corona to drive back on the old strategy of success or as to create a new one or what if they go bankrupt or what the future will look like. The future is bleak, the world is no sonnet to change tunes in favor, the world is going to be the same, viruses are going to be on the planet. Can we invent a vaccine like that for smallpox or chickenpox? Trials for combatting SARS virus from corona are not paying back so a more fervent effort is required in the different or more effective direction because the world could see even 8% rate economy in BC pre-2000 years. India or China or both were expecting to see 8-10% GDP growth. Medical, financial, management or business miracles are needed for the world immediately and instantaneously or instantly to go with the previous jest and harmony across the globe.

Pre-corona economic trends of developed countries and developing countries further suggests that world trade almost doubled from $10trillion to over $18t during 2005-14. Both the USA and India faced brutal trade deficits with China. The era witnessed fall in manufacturing output, rise in unemployment in the manufacturing sector, cheap imports, and pressures of automation in advanced economies. The global economy's immune system was compromised by allowing free trade for long at ignoring the rising costs that were more than offsetting the benefits of liberal trade. Economic disruption resulted in the journey from doing away with protectionism to embracing technological progress. Both the national governments have since hailed 'make' out of make or buy rule with India insisting on the Make in India principle and USA working with pro-business policy for the citizens. Pre-Covid period of low or negative interest rates is expected to land the global economy in deflationary state even with the impact of monetary policy, structural policy and fiscal support in the post- covid19 world. The cost of living is lower in the pre covid stage than the post Andropause world. Two of the green industries of the BC (before corona) have turned red ever since the corona lockdown - restaurants and out-of-home entertainment. Flourishing travel and transportation sector has now seen more than 80% decline in revenues. Consumer price indices globally, are set for a decline in the post covid world. Cost of living and salaries have been higher in the pre-covid times than later. Changes are minor in both directions with some nations seeing a rise and others witnessing a fall in the prices.

The world of knowledge economy has been growing to guide the needy towards the trend of education followed by employment, and intellectual property accumulation so as to sum up individual growth towards national development leading to a cumulative global economy in the pink of health.

Countries have been confirmed to improve their tourism industries, foreign relations, local heritage, anti pollution results, literacy levels, standard of living , employment growth, foreign currency reserve, foreign investment, business competition, anti crime initiatives, healthcare (for infant mortality reduction, women hygiene, senior citizen care, poor people), gender parity, racial homogeneity, gay rights, drug addiction reduction, trade dumping reduction, to space debris reduction and extra terrestrial space research. The globe is in the huge network of to-do lists. We have to fulfill the most important ones but we don't need more problems.

Now is a job to remain focused while solving the new troubles because we should neither ignore corona nor get bogged down further but unitedly fight against the same to be able to solve the old troubles failing which is a soup we would dip into and will be made slaves to chance when we are trying to establish some control over the key discrepancies (manmade and natural) of our world. Of course, the economy needs to understand that we have to overcome tests of time to prove ourselves worthy of the next advancement otherwise success loses its charm and excitement.

The ups and downs are part of all forms of development but if something goes wrong and out of control, then fire engine protection has to be brought on. Still if we can not bring normalcy with the help of water, calmness, running around, escaping, blaming and wars may erupt, the given economic loss throws similar gauntlets.

We would have to imbibe the best lesson and strength of pre corona (BC) strategy in better continuation of economic energization by entrepreneurial boosts, global cooperation and healthy competition. Small mistakes and some things get accepted by the time, but not deliberate big errors repeated across times whether by country level or at individual end or group slips.

The first case of corona attack in China in 2019 is not in the control of anybody but the mistakes of entering into the border on India side and attacks on 96 soldiers should have been controlled, corrected and punished or now penitent China has to cooperate with the rest of the world in developmental policy implementation. Otherwise we have to ban chinese participation in international growth initiatives.

Any policy announcements related to the US economy affect the economic performance in the other countries. The FED chief has to think of the globe before administering a more profitable strategy for the US economy.

Our reactions and responses in times of adversities define our nationalities and economies. It is true that nations are trying to help one another, with India sending medical supplies for Chinese aid, similarly China reciprocated with Alibaba's CEO Jack Ma supplying masks and ventilators to India, but it needs to scale up across all the nations in a way mentioned broadly in the book, but not as formation of some groups or alliances discussing broadly on the crisis and doing nothing to mitigate the effects. The global coalitions or the Coronavirusfacts Alliance or the UNCTAD chaired meetings would only add to the expenditures because corona needs grass root level solution and not 800-feet level propaganda or conferences establishing the same known problems in repeated discussions and arguments revolving around facts, weaknesses, loopholes, mistakes or comments about other nations without result -fetching -measures to resolve the impending issues.

It is time to get collaboration of all countries in fighting against the corona epidemic.

After corona

A Vacant Park in Hyderabad, India, Courtesy: Corona

According to Biocon empress Kiran Mazumdar Shaw , the greatest lesson taught by covid-19 is that all humanity is in this together.

Covid19 is a lesson taught to us by nature. Before Corona we used to mingle with nature but after the arrival of corona we have to distance ourselves from nature. Or in other words, nature seems to mock and move us away now just as we mocked at nature until now.

Earning is no priority because health is wealth.

Billions of dollars have been redirected towards the crisis of corona and many other issues arising from the same. The dilapidated state of the global economy is further dented by the corona fever. The global concerns on illicit trade, poverty rate, unemployment spikes, illiteracy issues, crime scenes, substance addiction and other things undermining our economic growth or productivity have got another added to the list of threats. One new tactical miracle is a sought after dream to get the globe out of all disturbances but it may take even a hundred years to shake off the entire muddle before it becomes a Bermuda triangle and starts consuming our economic strength and creativity. The state of the world is disturbed by a single virus that we can not even see with naked eye. Schools, colleges, offices, shopping malls, public transportation, and all forms of activity have been grounded for months in different parts of the world. Production has stopped and series of new problems have stemmed up globally, related to migrants agonies, job retrenchment, spiking mortality rate, though we cannot ignore the benefits in reduced pollution levels, freedom provided to birds and animals, new family time attained and space for self reflection from the constant daily rat races or cat fights without really understanding our responsibility for the next generation people, industry or environment. True, we are all doing our best in the given limitations but a single virus could win because of certain flaws in our way of life. So far we could not mend the personal habitat, earth, because we did not want to change but now we have to. Hen, chicken, cows, birds, dogs, snakes and now bats are on the list of food followed by the disease. Plant is no dead creature even after eating, as explained in the ancient relics, it is meant for food, granted by our caretaker, nature, and we have to still avoid questioning if we wish to see more of the wonders of time and nature. The topic is discussed because without human health no industry growth is a possible idea. Next, education if followed by healthy occupation can generate healthy brains for understanding our mistakes and achievements for further development of a healthy economy. It sounds a bit. But we can't ignore any of industrialism, socialism, spirituality, environmentalism or idealism to save ourselves because we are all sheltering these and many other 'ism's under some influence or the other. Now we are on ground zero and we have to be more open minded to accept reality, mistakes and change. The industry growth won't get positive unless healthy people start working with new ideas and we have to resume interactive classroom-online education to bring out new graduate groups while training the people with workplace skills. The general trends are mentioned below to extrapolate post lockdown situations-

General trends

1. People are not willing to invest in the betting room for free windfalls but looking for surest measures to avert permanent damage caused by the disease. We would buy a vaccine

with a hope whether it works or not but an effective medicine is our current need. Companies must not try to commercialise the trend by selling anything or everything in the name of covid-19.

2. Lot of time has been spent on the deliberations and other natural outcomes of cross border allegations. The global economic damage has to be reversed by the government collaboration between the different countries wholeheartedly and without further doubt. In the sense that as Corona addressed the Globe as a whole with no prejudice, now the Global Countries should unitedly fight against the Corona affected Economy (i.e. Global Economy in Toto) for necessary treatment with solidarity. It is not one Country's loss but of all ! Thus Corona unites the Globe (the entire victimized mankind) which should be optimistically a positive benefit to all Countries! Thus, Consequences of the current economic situation will not support a healthy economic climate until shared by the entire global community.

3. Products are the best recipient to corona impact. The major change is bound to happen in the beverage industry by falling demand followed by a rapid falling consumption of all forms of drink except the water and milk both of which are probably going to take a steady increase in the world dietary intake. Water will certainly be the best cleanser for the toxins that bolster the viruses and other natural benefits as advocated by the doctors who are sincerely motivating us to drink more hot water in fighting against the disease. At least 50% of the world population is a consumer of boiled water, distilled mineral water and refined water by an increase of at least 1-2 litres of water per day per person thereby increasing the amount of water consumption by more than 100 billion litres per month that will last longer than a year. Regardless of your lowest price range of the beverage, milk will be a good option for future use as a special immune system enhancer. Milk may not have much rise in consumption because of the cost and quality issues, earlier in the era we had the capability to consume more than a litre of milk per person per day but not now as we are vulnerable to digestive disorders leading to diarrhoea. Today a litre of milk is served to 3-6 people. One billion litres of milk will be a good thing to see a rise per day globally.

4. Another important sector is the hygiene and hand washer solutions in liquid and vaporizer are perfect for seeking a comfortable market share. We're not unaware of any of the methods. We have followed them with a freedom of hygiene and the need for prevention of corona has emphasised on the way more fervently than a commonsensical

need to be clean.

5. We are straightforward and all we want is a medicine or vaccine for handling corona threat. Russia hopes to give the world a vaccine not before August 2020. Let not the companies use the situation for generation of profit by false promises or fake promotions. The things like masks, gloves or sanitation kits should be free of cost and made available at least to the poor but stores are selling at different price ranges and qualities to show the best interest in entering into the new business segment opened up by corona.

6. We are better off in using the post lockdown period as an opportunity to educational furtherance for the mindful handling of any such international epidemic in the future. Training kids and old people in steps to be self caretakers, without depending on others, can help tackle health crises. Training groups of working people in ways to stay fresh and work without loss of productivity can boost output quality in the post turmoil world.

7. Governance mechanisms for both office and teaching institutions should change to preferring a more individual than team achievement, though the group ethics can be taught by intermittent online seminars or gathering in sterilised environments. Individual contribution should be recognised at all levels of work if we want to continue with the safe WFH MODEL (Working from Home) in the quarantined world of 2020. Otherwise productivity will drastically fall.

A new battle is waiting in the post-corona world. Before moving on to the future we have to save people in India (Assam, Bihar and Arunachal Pradesh), Nepal and China (as of July 2020) that are under floods to add to the problems. The evacuation and rehabilitation services for the residents have to be conducted in full swing by NGO vehicles, the government and us. Efforts are needed to save the natural fauna and wild animals that may be in the list of endangered species soon. Auto alert weather systems should be installed in future, for getting advance warnings about such calamities so that we can help the people by advance evacuation before the inhabitants get victimised by the nature's furies. A flood disturbs the entire ecosystem and displaces a lot of things like education, employment, property, or local ties amongst other things like health imbalances and sense of belongingness. Moral and material support must be shouldered by us in showing concern for the victims by providing basic necessities to families of rehabilitated residents. We have to make accessible food, water, medicines, clothing, blankets, mobile shelters (at safe distance from flooded areas, government should arrange for mobile homes for relocating such victims of natural disasters, to save time in constructing new homes), and start working with the victims on resettling and reconstructing cities after the end of monstrous calamities. Corporates and governments should treat these people as customers and voters, and help them out now for securing vote banks and business sales in future. It would then be real politics and ethical business, winning out battles before they are fought.

Gut of War

Modern day warfare is with no risk of real battles of tough fight in the soils but in the business changes brought in by different sources in different directions.

The cause for the rut is the customer confusion with so many options and preferences provided by the companies. On so many occasions in the past also the product space has been filled up with rivals competing on close yet differentiating characteristics. Today all companies and products operate with common customers who have no need to commit or subscribe to a single one for any duration given the consumerism and commercialism free from monetary involvement most of the times thanks to the technology pampering the customers without a condition or term but for a mere presence of customer in their business (website, blog, audio, video, and all forms of content). Making money is no more a criterion of measuring profits but views, visits, clicks, referrals, data (email, name, phone) and finally purchases if any measure success of an offering making it profitable for existence or shutdown. In future this very model will remove the last industrial growth phase of stagnation or maturation not because all companies would make profits but every company will have at least one customer and that will make it attractive to competitors and markets for acquisitions or buy-outs. The charges for the e-businesses would be met out of charitable venture capitalists and intellectual properties generated out of the contributors for business (employees, customers, partners) who would all be sharing profits in the business in several forms including monetary, voting, representation or other management decision making rights. It would be the gut driving future businesses without any cold or pricey wars except for the understanding that would trigger different competitive moves and responses in the markets by the different global players.

Companies are ever competing mainly as they see markets saturating and the dearth of ideas pokes them into poking the rivals for hints or responses inciting new avenues for the management progress with customer alignment. Customer alignment happens when a firm replaces competitor product with their own but technology is disabling customer alignment with informed products to the total profit of customer as monetary low price and total benefit of company in loyalty terms thus shifting the entire game of business in the favor of customer according to the theory of business management, corporate truths and principles while not ignoring the company profits at the same time get rewarded on customer trust and reward of adherence to the product for a given time or at a point in time. No more startling on business woes resting on Strategic planning, companies are able to mend their instant strategies even to the extent of customising preferences on-the-spot for customer demand at that time. Varying preferences create diversified set of needs that are distributed by the markets amongst the different players as per their capabilities and weaknesses thereby throwing challenges and opportunities at the same time but with immense scope because each user can generate million products based on her differing needs at different points in time buying in the company loyalty and stake in one way, selling the customer ideas and participating in the business decision-leading on the other side. Though companies have strict policies on decisions and implementations, the key driver of any decision arising from a requirement turns out to be user of the business product, service, solution, output or business space. Days are gone when a company used to innovate for years experimenting, testing and correcting the solutions with the customers eagerly waiting on the products without of course knowing about any such business ventures most of the time. Today a company has to reveal its budget, timelines and scopes much ahead of the customer even getting the product but the advantage is that it reduces the time lags for implementation given the continuous pestering by the customer inspired by latest technological developments backing user comfort and confidence levels on the higher anvil.

Can we wait for another technological revolution? Given the high speed of innovation taking place on the consumer side and higher turbulence generated by the global issues lacking a visible solution there is the highest chance of getting technology whipped by the world organizations probing for answers to the environmental degradation and human regression in the current century? How many Einsteins and Newtons can we see in the next century? Their research is not joke but jolt for mankind to understand the hidden issues of environment and life in general because of the unique paths adopted by their brains and work to lead out the humanity towards the path of overall improvement rather than self-centered progress in lifestyle as propagated by the Technological Tete-a-tata bidding bye to core intelligence of man. Elon Musk may fly us around Mars and even build a home office or two there but can that involve solving the problems or is it escaping them in a bid to find alternative solutions that is always a welcome path to buy time because unsolved or half-solved problems can but lead to half-baked progress finally succumbing to the very problems. What is needed is not a great leap to the moon on space, meteors or asteroids. A simple truthful commitment to Earthly issues from every individual with the proper awareness will not deviate us from the goals serving one another's existence along with the planet's (White, 2013-14). It may be tough preaching vehicle pollution safety norms and ensuring their adoption by every individual but that is the light of the day for us to enable the planet to support our sustenance.

Photo Illustration: A lonely deserted park in India (No kids, no birds, no animals, no adults) during Covid Lockdown

Procedure for corona crisis management

Corona battle begins with detection of symptoms and diagnosis of intensity of virus activity followed by the treatment of every affected person to avoid further spreading of the disease. The second half of quarantine management deals with the invention of vaccines or adherence to the daily hygiene program (washing, physical distancing and sterilization) for prevention of the covid-19 mutiny. In the absence of any kind of medicine and vaccines the world is resolving issues thrown by corona by following lockdown methods and with the help of safety techniques for the conduct of most essential business and services that we can not live without.

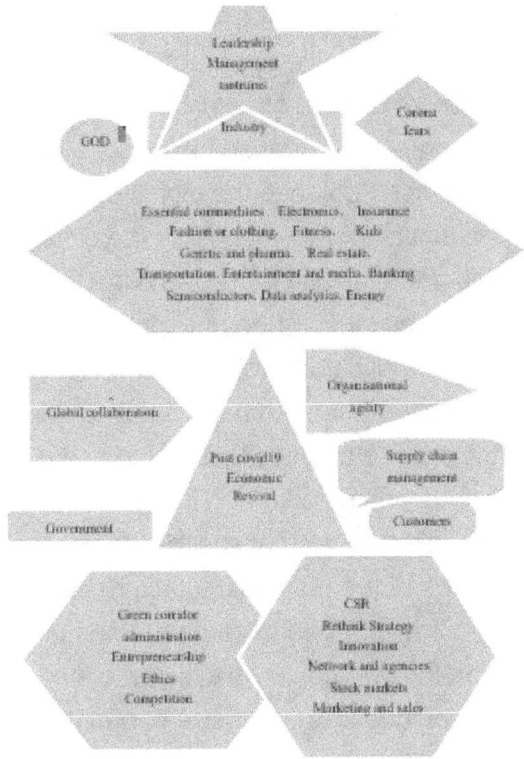

Fig1: Outline of Procedure for corona crisis management

Industries and professions are not able to stay unafraid and are playing on and off by resetting productivity goals and objectives for the employees. The world is full of energy drain, chaos, change and chance games, and other things that don't enable us to proceed with growth in crisis. The current situations demand that crisis and effective methods ought to be followed by management of systems, investment, and expectations of customers, governments, and industries for successful business administration and economy management for achieving the goals with best results in different countries. The combination of - updation of technology, with use of existing capabilities - skills and wisdom of the most recent and old times - best and successful - ways of thinking, doing, working, examining and resolving issues- with the help of resources and research, could bring a check on the crisis and may contain it to lead to a better crisis management system without trying to laws and regulations because some freedom can grow better ideas for handling crisis situations where rules fail to give results. The objective of the present process of crisis management is to revive the economy. The result will be reflected in the world getting able to save people from becoming victimized by the crisis generated by corona viruses. The what ifs and how abouts are described in multiple ways till the end of this book starting with the process (Fig1) that first details world crisis management for industrial and governments entities working with customers' problems in the different sectors. Some of the sectors addressed are - energy, electronics, clothing, consumer goods, sports, pharmaceuticals, media, real estate, banking, analytics, software, transportation, insurance and other things needed for kids. Next, the procedure for economic development is elaborated with focus on key areas of improvement, important for winning the covid-19 battle. Inclusive approach is advised for working with changes to fight organisational inertia, imbibe innovative structure, handle competition strategy, follow ethical standards, promote entrepreneurs, cleanse business administration, deal with marketing upscaling, protect environment, balance the digital age costs, cross country collaboration and other management aspects to give a boost to the global economy. World can take the assistance of quantum computers to devise a precise crisis management strategy for handling the complex covid-19 curse because quantum computing could generate solutions in 200 seconds in Google for some complicated problems that the super computers could solve in 10,000 years. Google has claimed quantum supremacy for its quantum computer Sycamore. A lot needs to be done in the area to achieve leadership and it might not be before 2050 that the use of quantum computing becomes common in institutional and research activities with more applications possibly in the extra terrestrial space to understand the potential of resources and life on different parts of the planets. It could be further refined to generate quick forecasting algorithms for weather, traffic or health care to prevent the unfavorable events. Instant warning and superfast protection triggers could be system related developments with the application of quantum computing techniques. Present size of quantum computers might be reduced in the future with the innovation in the space of nano materials. The combination of some of the technology innovations like superconductors, ultracapacitors and nuclear fusion power could generate miracles in the area of energy and computing both of which are the drivers of the technological world. Innovation in storage of such power with its sources could revolutionize the adaptation to different types of products right from the palm size smart phone to the space shuttle travelling to the Moon or Mars or Sun or another celestial body with equal ease and flexibility. We could see the next century equipped with capabilities to replicate the Earth on another planet to regenerate alternate options for life. If we cannot control the bulging populaces we have to move half of them to another Earth. History might repeat the colonisation and other earthly acts for building our confidence because we are used to a certain kind of life here. We must step out of our comfort shells and gauge the changing world of technology, environment and mindsets. On one hand technology is flying high with rapid and disruptive innovations, but the environment is fast deteriorating with no scope for improvement even in the long run, there seems no stopping the minds from redefining the facts when people want more comforts at the cost of the factors of self sustenance. All these im-balances need us to step to another level of economic growth planning with room for conservation of natural energy sources supporting the existence of ours and generations to come.

Customer

JRD Tata believed that money was like manure, to stink when you pile up but it would

grow on spreading.

We end up spreading infections if we don't spread money. Customers should enquire about the benefits of a wide array of different types of business solutions instead of getting confused in the disturbed situation with new limitations created by corona lockdown. Every solution should be able to answer the risk of corona. It must go beyond the current epidemic in laying out plans for facing similar risks. Work will be doubled up for analysis of probable crisis situations in addition to a problem addressed by the companies. Company staff should not use corona for hiding work defects or personal failures. To some, corona is no less than escape from responsibility. It is time to take more responsibility than ever. Companies should allow customers to pay for the delivered outputs in a more flexible manner after evaluation of end users' acceptance, experience and feedback. It requires the readiness of the company to work without advance or free on some portion of output. Work for customers, don't work for money. This is a way to manage the corona crisis. It does not mean that companies should go on experimenting with no value projects only to keep them alive in crisis. The time should be diverted to customers to understand what they want for the future in the products and solution outputs. Let customers rip your past work, understand their concerns. Be ready to handle critical analysis of your present deliverables in future. Start working with new future initiatives right now to avoid unnecessary last minute issues with customers.

Encourage the companies to work from two different perspectives, first thing is coronavirus and the other is lockdown as its effect, leading to more side effects, which could last longer than expected. The virus and its health impact can not be overcome without humongous efforts laid over a long time but firms must come out with new solutions for resistant material, clinical treated items, medical stuff, or other things to keep off the virus. The plastic, cardboard, metal, synthetic and other types of material hold the virus active for short duration of intervals typically 1-48 hours. Human skin needs to be washed to get rid of the virus before it is in our system. Gloves or face masks have to be disposed of after single use. Customers should ask companies to make synthetic that won't let the virus throb on it. Or certain solutions should be discovered to get an auto sterilization effect on gloves for recurring use or on things that can not be washed. The lockdown is holding us from going out of the homes but not from doing our best work at home. Companies have to derive ways of reviewing and improving work outputs from remote management to maintain the quality promised to customers.
Enjoy the opportunity to work with companies in voluntary and paid surveys not more for earning but voicing your concerns, experience, views or complaints on corona lockdown,

government schemes (standing in queues could be better replaced by drone dropping or home delivery, expenditures have to be incurred on hiring exotic gadgets and men, and these can bring more good than hassle, for even future times). We have to be free in expression of all our feelings, fears, anger, questions, issues, appreciations, satisfaction, expectations or doubts in the government and industrial practices so this can further help improve their operations without repeating inconveniences.

Bond with the family to make better demands, decisions, and choices of products, based on prices or interpretation of even more intriguing information or by intricate participation in the future digital open houses conducted by management boards (Companies like Reliance, JPMorgan and others are holding online AGMs). The companies will come up with the virtual meeting ideas more than any personal meeting venues in future where all stakeholders along with the family members can be part of discussion on how to extract more work from machines. Onus is on the family and customer to get together and understand the more important priorities in the changing lifestyle, or work style, to suit the combined living environment that used to be more of the bird nest type with the birds returning to homes at the end of day or their work. Today the family is a unit when so far a child used to go out for the movie with her friends, mom would party with the other homemakers of the city and dad used to go on official trips all of the family members gathering on the weekend or on the vacation trip. The next set of ideas would change with the change in the living environment that is to encompass the working day or study day where all participants are in heterogeneous groups unlike homogeneous groups till corona lockdown. The students are not in schools with other classmates but at home, the level of thinking and output is different when with family and other students. Same thing applies to workers and employed people. The output quality may be better under no peer presence, pressure or performance may fall due to lack of handling or guidance by bosses because bosses are under household chore pressures of their spouses or kids. Jokes unintended. The customer in the post lockdown period, is everyone from the kids on the house to the parents and grandparents. The joint responsibility in adaptation of the environment that promotes skills of all members is that of the family members, digital technology companies and other counterparts with or under whom we are training, working, studying, teaching or collaborating on the task, assignment, project, programs or initiative. The challenge is how best we can adapt the environments on provision of the best technology, skills and tools to facilitate customer goals in their location or homes. One exclusive way of differentiating your company from competition in crisis is to give away the impossible to a customer. Forget the profit and promise more output in less time, better quality in less price, now instead of a sunny future, don't wait for things to improve because everyone is doing that, we would be in chaos then, get more machines than men because machines won't be killed by coronavirus. Build machines that can run themselves without waiting for manual intervention. It's not late. The impact of corona is going to stay for at least 2 more years for which we have to prepare 5-year plans to assess the business impact of corona on all initiatives, old and upcoming. It is not going to take less than that to recover the lockdown losses because the additional costs are debilitating, new revenue is no easy, margin won't be fat. Even the Big 5, top consulting firms all without exception would see steep falls in their income - from KPMG, BCG, E&Y, Capgemini, McKinsey to Bain, BAH, ATKearney and other companies in similar growth trajectory. Nobody can give a sure shot solution to overcome corona effects and get more business, even this book is an exploratory analysis (causes, effects, problems, solutions) of the situation. We have to take each and every side effect of the corona lockdown and address it at every possible level, take the food scarcity and supply free food wherever possible and here's where government is of help because no individual can resolve it to complete satisfaction, although organizations like Akshay Patra try to ensure maximum coverage, there are individuals who distribute water bottles on roads, yet there are many who go hungry and thirsty because our robust technologies cannot help with basic solutions but branded solutions for few top notch business leaders. This is a major disconnect between the customers and companies because we don't offer them what they need.

Agricultural Economy

"...there's always going to be someone...to point out your mistakes..." - Jessica Heren

World is predominantly rooted in agriculture as the foundation for economic development, followed by industry as the backbone (by technological, financial and macroeconomic policies) and services as differentiating (by cultural factors and innovation) the growth of nations. More than 60% of the global economy is agricultural and development cannot be studied without including farmers, food processing companies, agri finance institutions, government agents and other participants in the sector. Of the population of over 7billion people, more than half belong to agricultural families or are farmers themselves. Today, farmers are preparing children to work for corporates instead of cultivating family-owned lands or serving as slaves under loan pressures of rich landlords (less than 5% of the farmers own large pieces of lands, as per the results of a survey conducted by Tietoz in 2014 and conditions have clearly not improved significantly). All others are into prosperous business except the farmers who in most nations are subject to exploitation and penury. The wastage of farm produce is not a small number even for advanced economies, with more than 30% produce going waste every year. In emerging economies, wastage is an additional issue beyond threatening farmers' sustenance. The countries like Israel and Japan are working towards complete technologisation of farming, digitisation of farm produce sales and distribution, automation of inventory management (storage, measurement and disbursals) and point-to-point logistics to avoid wastages. We have to take our lessons as relevant to our nation, from nations successful in growing agricultural economies.

Financing and funding of agricultural activities could be meaningful if shifted from corporates to farmers directly. Today most agricultural companies avail of government schemes and rich farmers succeed in getting approvals on the farming aid that is otherwise intended for the needy farmers. More than 80% farmers are impoverished and depend on small pieces of land for earning livelihood out of farming as occupation, profession or business. Digital mandis end up buying from such farmers at pennies and sell to us for pounds after passing the produce through multiple intermediaries without adding much value, otherwise sold at hundred of times margins if the produce gets processed in factories using artificial ingredients like chemicals or preservatives. Packaging and storage activities form at least 20% of the entire cost of products and solutions. The tinned foods or frozen vegetables though not replenished with the nutrients are in demand by the smart world of professionals to meet their food hygiene needs, partly because we do not have access to the fresh produce.

A new model for the post pandemic agricultural development could focus completely on individual farmers by changing the supply chain modalities completely. Government or private company leaders can take it as a responsibility for the sake of facilitating for their future generations, sufficient stocks, availability and access of fresh agricultural products. We need to follow the hub and spokes method to locate our agricultural distributors at every short distance near the farmer groups for collecting their produce at no less than 90% of our price. If a household pays $1 for a watermelon then the farmer growing it must get 90 cents. The profits of other channel participants should be subsidized by government funds or wait for scales to gain margins over volumes growing in the future. Lot of unemployed folks loitering in the cities for petty jobs daily on the streets of Mumbai or New York could be thankful to governments for giving them a permanent job. If they are not fitting the role, technology could help by launching drones at every village and the metal devices would do it for free over the life of 10-20 years of operational warranty. Everyday fresh orders can be packaged and delivered straight from the farmers' place to the nearest urban localities for enabling the residents to enjoy the health from consuming freshly grown tomatoes or spinach. Earlier times used to see fairs when farmers used to sell that day's produce in the nearby urban markets by spreading the heaps of vegetables or fruits on streets. Today the mid-segment or big farmers are not allowing the small farmers do the free business without paying heavy street dues or selling at miniscule prices.

The selling and distribution model in advanced economies is developing good earnings for farmers who are able to sell harvests to companies for reasonable margins.

In developing nations, we neither let the farmers earn, nor let the population get the fresh produce nor manage to route the goods without wasting.

The online grocery and supermarkets are tied with few major farmers because of the high costs involved in collecting stuff from multiple small farmers, even if they do so they would not forgo the profits for a social service kind of farming support. Farmers should be encouraged to create their own apps for selling products, they should get packaging material and shipping facilities free of charge initially, and then a small percentage of sales revenue could pay for supply chain functions facilitated by others. In the USA and Canada, landlords pick up online orders, pack themselves and deliver to local buyers because the numbers are small. One way is to enrol as sellers with players selling online or doing it on small scale entrepreneurship. Micro loans and small sized investments should be funded by government vehicles to pick up stakes or profits in the farmers' business as it grows well. Innovation is essential for providing skills (automated pesticide sprinklers, water drones, robotic irrigators and tillers, harvesting drones) but technology funding must be made accessible to small farmers so that they buy advanced machinery and equipment for mechanising irrigation and farming methods. It would then increase yields, reduce weeds or pests, develop soils for better cultivation and improve the quality of harvest.

Small farmers can enter into group initiatives for encouraging the nearby urban families to enter into monthly subscriptions according to which the products like fruits and vegetables or staples could be seasonally supplied to the consumer doorstep every day or bi-weekly for continuous availability of grocery to homes and demand to farmers. Awareness programs have to be launched by locals in educating farmers of growing organic vegetables, grains and fruits without much use of harmful chemicals or too much of hybrid seeds losing some essential nutrients. The impact of Covid-19 cannot be denied on the farming sector because of locust attacks or isolation leading to less field activity. The farmers stopped the street selling or reduced the number of orders from local buyers because of restrictions on delivery to homes. Panic piling in coronavirus - backed recession has been witnessed in most nations. Safety and hygiene protocols have grown the sector into more organized from the unorganized of the past, with most purchases of agri-food products happening online today. Options of crisis gardening and terrace gardening have also been adopted by households to reduce risk of covid-19. Agri trade activities have reduced due to the impact of corona on the exim segment. We have to use the covid-19 crisis as an opportunity for boosting the agricultural sector within the globe.

Effort in the agricultural sector has to be serious and strong for the economy to show real sustainable growth otherwise it would be vulnerable to crisis failures and recessions.

Post Pandemic Growth of Services Sector

"...it does not matter ...if a car has a dent... but the price reduces by a few thousands of dollars... better than buying a new car...when I can save more than ...a new car than a used one as good as a new…" - Warren Buffett, answering a question on why he bought a used car with a dent.

Covid-19 pandemic has slowed down the progress in the global services sector due to sliding overseas demand and dwindling new business activity. Massive job cuts have to be evaded by the monetary and economic policy changes. Small businesses in the service sector are hit harder than big ones due to the prohibitions and pressures dragging down Asia's growth by more than expected. As the pandemic paralyzes economies all over the world, the services sector is taking maximum impact because of its non-essential nature of business. The skills and knowledge must be updated by the professionals sitting at homes in order to provide value addition (by innovation or change of job or change of profession) by the time revival starts afresh. Developed nations have shifted to digitization of services where certified professionals are training the customers in hourly paid sessions of self-service due to social isolation. A more complicated task may not be done without the help of professionals but simple tasks are becoming 'guided DIY' in the isolation era. Personal guidance is still available but not personal meetings or visits or presence.

Future innovation may be for the service providers to develop and sell easy DIY kits with simple 3-4 step guides to simplify the tasks otherwise requiring expert intervention for customers. Reduction in business activity could motivate service workers to invest time and resources in collaborating with small business groups to bring out handy self-service products or gadgets. It would create a new small sub segment of market for consumers in the service industry where buyers would get to buy the ways and tools of completing service needs on a small scale without depending on the group of experts utilised by the large populations for meeting service needs at individual levels, for which the providers invest heavily keeping in mind the long term demands of large number of customers and repeat business. Now the customers would share the investment in preparing themselves to be personal service providers for the possible set of tasks and activities (e.g. personal fitness, doorstep spa or beauty or grooming, chef cooking, personal coaching, etc.). Some services like courier and food delivery could not be done away with except for taking precaution while serving the customers. The risk is as much for the customers as for the service providers, so innovation would be needed to either digitize the functions or remain without availing of the services involving human interactions. Public emergency services must be automated soon to avoid negligence in future because human intervention may limit the attention and mishaps may rise in number.

Services like law and healthcare are yet to take digital shape. Law professionals are adept at getting the paperwork done online. But the real advancement would be when technology could be used to create virtual courts or digital hearing of cases by video-conferencing lawyers, defendants, complainants, judges, defaulters, victims, criminals, police, staff and other officials to quick conclusions of pending cases. The increasing number of issues to be resolved in public courts could cause havoc if not addressed soon. Vain should be replaced by work. Covid-19 havoc is more dangerous than any other existing economic or political havoc. If we can handle Covid-19, we can handle any other tough task as well. Public servants must take inspiration and opportunity from Covid-19 situation and use it to bring to resolution any of the existing blockades in the economy. Nations like India should utilise the time for digitising operations in law and public services. We can hope to resolve faster by involving experts and knowledge sources, online, than by continuous advancements of hearing dates and pushing final sentences or decisions to endless time extensions. The key advantage of digital court hearings is low risk of threat to the concerned people by the defaulters, or reduced blackmailing for verdicts. The judges and lawyers can understand the case parties in detail by taking sufficient time before proceeding to the next stage. Officials have to follow proper checks to avoid punishing innocent or letting criminals free, (type 1/ 2 error, when things are right we feel they are not, when we feel things are right, they may be actually wrong; applies to people also).

Healthcare professionals are increasingly adopting technological diagnostics through online body scanners and robotic nurses to take care of patients admitted in hospitals. Future technological innovation may be to equip smartphones or Smart TVs with special cameras to enable doctors perform digital consulting with patients, some advanced features like X-rays or medical scanning can be enabled from distance, so that the prescription of tests or medicines could be made possible online. Blood tests and few other minor tests could be performed by robots, to leave the major tests, surgeries and interactions for expert doctors to handle in person. Depending on the condition and type of ailment, dentists or cardiac experts or dermatologists or neurologists or clinical psychiatrists could use a combination of digital, personal or telephonic interactions for treatment and reviews. Medical professionals are in full active involvement even in covid-19 by taking some precautions and the sector has not seen any slowdown but further growth in the crisis situations. Even if economic recessions do not involve pandemics on health disorders, people face health problems in periods of turmoil and crisis due to tension, stress and pressure from all interconnected segments of society dependent on industries impacted by the downturn.

Modern Education

"Don't sweat with the haters...because the haters are going to hate..." - Melanie Whelan

Post pandemic education activity may resume normalcy but lessons have to be implemented for future readiness. Universal distance education may be the norm of tomorrow with students and teachers communicating on smart devices, virtual classrooms and online tests. Digital surveillance and technological security along with verification and authentication have to be attained by advanced infrastructural innovation by national governments. The same would facilitate the next step of accreditation online colleges with recognisable degrees in graduation and post graduation. The confinement environment is demanding that we allow people to complete their education from homes. Further education could see entrance exams to be taken from home laptops under highly controlled and digitally inspected conditions for avoiding cases of cheating or misrepresentation or wrong identities. Teachers and students have to be provided with the necessary skills and tools for online education that is a recommended mode of learning even after the end of the pandemic era. According to the International Labor Organization (ILO), more than 1.5 billion students are affected by lockdowns. Primary, secondary, vocational training, higher education and professional education teachers, besides the research camaraderie are highly affected by the closure of educational institutions. Future crisis preparation today can help build confidence for the continued activity of education and economic development. Video-conferencing, school-based intranet messaging, emails, college portals for sharing assignments, internal communication and telephonic conversations are some options in countries having infrastructure to support the technologies required for digital education. Affordability and access to technology can increase disparities between the already unequal segments of societies. Appropriate cross border aid and collaboration could help resolve the problems of low-literacy in many nations. Countries signing bilateral nuclear deals and cross-border trade or technology collaboration deals should come forward to sign basic education deals to support the other country's literacy drives in attaining global mileage. NGOs anyway are not able to eliminate illiteracy, poverty or crime in spite of investing tremendous effort and huge investments. Now NGOs must join the technology drive so that everybody is equipped with the basic technology to learn, work and communicate with the needy. Online programs must be subsidized for the low-income sections of the society and free for the highly impoverished. Online Books and other accessories would not increase costs because a single book can be shared by millions online. Internet speeds and server capacities have to be of top quality so that unhindered education is possible in any place of the world. Though government schemes like food-in-school or socialisation programmes cannot be digitally executed, we could still have drones dropping food supplies in students' homes, or online student cultural meets to have students perform from their homes. There is a risk of increase in child labor in the post crisis time due to rise in unemployment and school dropout rates now. Poor parents can employ their kids for additional family income. Digital education can solve problems of child labor thereby preparing the citizens better for the next crisis. Free online accredited education programs can award degrees based on performance in exams conducted online or hygienic protected centres. More students are likely to enrol and fulfil the dreams of education through free recognised digital colleges even though they may work in the daytime. Such students are sure to study in free time or even without sleeping because the genuine interest in children can make them study well despite unfavorable conditions. Self-directed learning, without the help of teachers, is possible in digital education. Teachers have a vital role that can be made voluntary, and paid services can be utilised for training more teachers for personal digital coaching for preparation of curriculum, setting and evaluating assignments and exam papers, most of which can be entrusted to technology but for the sake of retaining human interaction with the kids, we could have online meetings with teachers. Alternative job options could be provided for teachers or further training of teachers for change of profession, should be facilitated. Free internet connections, phone facility and health check privilege for ensuring socio-emotional and mental health should be made available to teachers, students and other staff involved in the education sector. Free child care could help workers give better quality output in the workplace once the pandemic is over. Playful means of educating small kids at child care centers would grow the mental faculties to prepare for schooling early.

Education is essential for economic development to take place in any nation. Government must take steps to bring reforms in the sector that is not working with reasonable terms of employment as of now. Teachers are losing jobs and facing salary cuts in the lockdown environment, the situation is true for multiple nations, where education sector laws are not friendly to staff. Amendments are required though digitisation of education would eliminate some of the risks like losing a job due to personal absence (because even a sick teacher can manage to teach online classes, to think of extremes). Digitisation would make it easier for extra classes, night tuitions or even overtime in work. Terms of employment must be in favor of employed whether as worker, daily wage earner, teacher, or corporate or other professional. Modifications are necessary to accommodate extraordinary circumstances in the teaching laws.

How should digitised schools offset the rising importance or overestimated use of technology to imprint the essential social ethics within students? Schools teach several subjects like English, Mathematics, Science, Arts and other subjects. Science and technology are becoming more essential to modern society, but schools should devote equal time to teaching technological sciences as well as social sciences like humanities. Schools can play an important role in not letting the social sciences lose their grip in the globalized technological world. The importance of one cannot be overemphasized nor that of the other underplayed. Role of Technological Sciences is visible in our Life. Modern society has been gaining out of the rapid technological advancement. Modern machines and gadgets have made life more comfortable than earlier. For example, Airplanes have made travel faster and easier. TV provides entertainment as well as information of the happenings in the rest of the world. The washing machines help save effort and time in washing clothes. Refrigerators store food keeping it fresh, air conditioner helps in staying cool in summer and warm in winter. Advent of the Internet has reduced the distances within the world. There is instant communication with email, mobile phones and fax machines.

Role of Social Sciences is key in our Life. Learning social science is as important as science & technology. At the same time, society still needs to know the civilization of its people and management by studying social sciences. For example, History could teach us about the civilization and evolution of the nation's identity. Science and Technology do not eliminate the need for knowing our country's demographics. Geography gives information on population, the country's resources - rivers, forests, land, minerals, metals etc. Other subjects in arts and humanities can inform us of the various regulatory bodies in the countries, the role of different institutions - courts, municipalities etc. and foremost, we can learn about our role and duty towards the society.

The role of schools is to teach balance between the Technological & Social Sciences. Can teaching social sciences substitute for the continued daily use of technologies at home without breaking the norms of social isolation? The importance of none of these can be underrated under the pretext of increasing importance of science and technology. Hence virtual schools should balance the time devoted to teaching subjects in sciences. In fact knowing all these would facilitate optimum use of science and technology in the best interest of the society. For example, knowledge of India's culture would help developing scientific and technological innovations suitable and acceptable in that country. Similarly, knowledge of management tactics in Japan would help encourage innovation capable and preferable in that country. Better designs of products emerge, suitable to the people's needs and culture with better management of sciences (logical or social or neural sciences!). Thus, schools should devote equal time to teaching of technological sciences as well as social sciences. Students will then appreciate the advent of technology in the presence of societal needs better. They won't be left behind as geeks who do not understand the importance of management and softer skills like teamwork. Society needs the knowledge of social sciences also. It is as essential as science and technology in the modern society.

Curriculum transition

Educational programs need some reforms, for the graduates to be valuable to different types of corporations.it applies to all streams, engineering, arts, humanities, sciences, technology or others.

First, the curricula itself needs to undergo some changes to enable students integrate their learning and apply multiple disciplines on the job as required by the situation at hand.

Second, students must also display interest in choosing courses outside the traditional curriculum. A student group may voice their interest in Six-Sigma certification while pursuing MBA.

Thirdly, schools must create a differentiation by offering tailored courses to the graduates to pursue investment banking or consulting or engineering careers. To wait for 2 years and then join a company is not the path to building passion in an area. An upfront introductory 2-3 week course can make the students familiar with the career paths so that the pursued course is aligned with career goals.

Fourthly, theories of economics, measurement, governance, psychology, human behavior and leadership help students go beyond case studies and handle new situations other than the existing types spontaneously with better solutions. A nuance of research theories in any course as rainbow can work wonders to extracting innovative ideas from students.

Fifthly, more courses in such behavioral aspects prepare the students with skills in effectively managing people and team-driven organizations.

Finally, courses should aim at providing basic skills and tools needed in problem solving. On-job work involves problem-solving rather than application of tools and formula (for which various software are lying out there!). Cases or real time scenarios micro-cased into specific situations can train students with conflict resolution, negotiations, or profit, loss, growth or other related problem solving skills.

How many schools teach us problem-solving?

Digital degrees are providing students with specialised skills without going much into the general book stuff. Such courses are supplemented by real projects in companies to work as apprentices for six months to one year. It gives immense opportunity to the students to see hands-on approach for solving company problems at various levels of organization. Students walk out with degrees after participating in the routines, processes and operations right from the bottom through the top management decision making activities. Though at perfunctory levels such graduates are better equipped to be inducted into the workforces than fresh MBA batches from top colleges.

Modern education should teach us to perform our duties and shoulder our responsibilities without much deliberation and force. A lot of convincing power can be saved for better things if all of us learn to act responsibly.

Changing employment contractual models

As mentioned by the successful Infosys head Mr Narayana Murthy, the bosses should not concern themselves with how many hours the employees are spending but the fact that those who concentrate on work during the designated hours and finish the task are more efficient than those spending more than half of the day at office (by staying in through midnight toils proving the inefficiency of not able to finish the task in the given official work hours, but by wasting much of time in tea-breaks, lunch-break, chitchatting or other such distracting activities). Can digital employment models check for such disengagement caveats in the employee work habits? Or are the migrant workers better at handling such ethics in committing themselves and families to day long work continuously working more to finish the manual tasks either due to lack of technology application or personal skill deficiencies or other reasons? The wage earners are still human and need our attention with cooperation in improving lifestyles of the temporary labor class.

The advantages of digital trends are increasing literacy rates with more white collared employment and decrease in the child labor or exploitation, also due to concerns on migrant workers, rising indoor employment (home and factory instead of street and adhoc labor). Future laws could facilitate better protection of migrants in not letting the workforce on lower task segments and avoid getting stuck with the biased labor agreements tending to bounded labor or temporary low pay high intensity jobs like real-estate, factory machine operations and repair or other man-mechanical imbalances at workplaces. More projects and new businesses could be a savior for future provision of work to the local labourers to prevent from moving to far off locations in search of daily wages or nomadic sustenance of families depending on menial jobs in different parts of the country or globe. The immigrant or migrant groups of workers have to be provided with friendly labor laws, family sustenance job packages and alternative work options based terms of disengagement or labor clause for ending the work contracts. Work quality and money including medicines, clothes, children education and other related survival support must be given to such labor segments without which the industries cannot execute the related tasks of short term and manual nature because the group cannot voice for rights and cannot claim what is due to the workers.society, government and companies have to step into the addressing of the problems of the large segment of unorganized labor that cannot be ignored if national progress has to be wholesome. A known trend is the still operative movement of even educated folks from east and down south to the middle east and Saudi parts of the globe where we have seen multiple cases of labor exploitation including that of women, children and men in deploying on less eligible tasks like tailoring, cleaning, personal slacery or bonded labor, often the official work rules used to 'abdicate' the laborers and students under the pretext of serving the masters or employers with unrelated (to education) rough works otherwise not suiting the local citizens, who would not return the passport or allow movement back to native nations to tie the workers to the destitute employment unknown to the outside world. The recent trend has only extended the brand of earning more in exploiting the currency rate between the countries by draining educated brains to the same countries on a ostentatiously better levels of work tasks like technology development or financial consulting that could otherwise be achieved even in the native countries if only we develop a little compassion for our fellow citizens exploited in other nations and a bit resentment attitude to convey to the exploiters that we do not support such treatment of out brethren or sisters. The current crisis should guide and enable us to encourage the path of educating and employing the local citizens to the benefit of national growth instead of contributing to other foreign countries' development. Unless we develop our nation we cannot claim that our citizens are helping other nations with international progress or growth because the work starts from home and then goes outside. Friendly agreements and laws have to be made to motivate collaborative cross border rules for healthy employment generation. How many middle east or european uneduacated youth are exploited by the Asian employers in the name of slavery and job provision? The answer is not to do otherwise but to carry the same employment culture for those getting exploited in the different states or countries by replicating better terms of employment in vocational activities if not high paying jobs requiring branded school degrees. Otherwise the crisis will continue beyond the crisis even after the end of the pandemic. Contract employment and home office business implementation models are on a rise, a slight fall in salaries is also inevitable as more companies are seen to be moving towards machination while others could be preferring more staff size at low cost payroll and high cost technology support with provision to mitigate risk of lapses in communication, lack of success in home office output, switching options for multiple employment options for workers responsible for quality deliverables to multiple tasks executed for more than one employer located in different parts of the world. The easy employment hiring, firing and resignation terms could see more employees exercising the skill preference options than money need compulsion. The same employees could make more money from multiple employers located in different timezones with separate terms of contract and variations in expectations from employees. Competition laws need a revision to enable integrity of the workforce operating with rivals offering varying terms and pay on the same products or output. Can digital social surveillance help bond the employees better with employers without compromising on the end user goals and data?

Data protection is thus a key concern of future business 'disengagement' models that would see more and more employees working from remote locations delivering individual output more than team interaction based cascading cycle product or service pies. Will a single home machine provide a space slot to each employer, task or teamwork? Would each employee work with personalised devices or machines provided by each business competitor employing the person for a specific time period or particular task completion or a combination thereof? Is a collaboration possible between such rivals reaping results out of personnel working with niche skills? Would such employment disengagement models change the course of competition and emergence or evolution of cartels or oligarchic societies becoming more and more focused on personal goals, health and familial achievements growing the horizontal communities instead of the vertical leadership patterns enriching the single industry or company with the technology or solution goals satisfying a limited group of stakeholders? In the latter case technology would become a driver and determinant of economic success because the first case accounts for total societal development by allowing every family and its members to accumulate the root-level national growth at the unit level of citizens to the macro level of regions and nations. Again technology is the enabler in both cases except for the significance attributed to humanity in the former. The dignity of labor is restored in such cases as advocated by the past socialists and economists thereby giving the best of both worlds to the employees and employers, not to deny that the second seems to be faster, and more exhaustive than the first but only to reveal disparities between the rich and poor, educated and illiterates, strugglers and lucky ones as is witnessed today. Today the picture seems rosy if we do not go into the details of the maximum size of population lying in the middle class bracket who cannot depend on the recommendation, family lineage or 'say' in the 'going ahead' ventures of work and life. The digital employment could create disengagement harmonies and parities of skill-knowledge-capability advantages provided the online verifiers do not discriminate between the families of Buffets or Tom-Dick-Harrys with the first question of eligibility as "Do you belong to a family of knowns or unknowns?"

Our Responsibilities

We have to give before we take from others. We have to ask ourselves, 'what have we done for the country or the government?' Before we ask, ' what has the government done for us?' Are we preparing the right kind of citizens for tomorrow by bringing up our children in the proper manner? Each of us is bound by the duty of nurturing today's kids with values and care. There are some basic essential duties from our side before demanding for things that need to be done for us. We must ensure that we are taking care of ourselves, others and our duties as best as we can. Some of the key responsibilities are highlighted below-

1. File taxes on time. Take the help of online tax filing resources to file taxes in the country you are working. You could heave a sigh of relief if you are in tax-free countries of the Middle-East. It's our responsibility because public welfare schemes are run using taxpayer funds. If we err on tax payments then we are not paying for our own welfare in the society.
2. Inform social networks about our feedback on products and services. Voice your rights, comments, experiences, appreciation and feelings instead of hiding praise or waiting for others to go through your plight. Social media are powerful means of influencing the

governments and people. Responsible usage can direct in the right way with invaluable benefits to the society otherwise it may lead to unpalatable results. Cybercrime must be reported without fail as part of citizen duty. Or voice for your right to food, health, safety, education and other deprived rights or those of others.

3. Use online or institutional learning sources to achieve education for competing in the corporate world. Take initiative to educate yourself, Jack Ma and Elon Musk are self-educated, they are now leaders and teachers of business to the world. Enrol yourself in online courses or classroom education because everybody cannot rake up the issues and still solve without having the educational authority to do so. Not many can be like business leaders to deal with the existing risk in the economy, to bring success without any formal degrees or education.

4. Co-operate in the resolution of environmental issues. Accept as your responsibility that you have to stop use of plastics, consumption of unhealthy stuff and cutting trees. If you can't be healthy you cannot help others. If nature is not healthy, nature cannot help us. Health of the environment is as important as that of ours. Use electric vehicles as compared to the fuel vehicles with carbon emissions.

5. Adopt bio-friendly products and solutions. Encourage companies to work for biodegradable solutions that we can use to preserve our natural resources. Nexgen citizens should not write books on how their ancestors enjoyed leaving all the problems to them for solution.

6. Be safe and indoors. In the current pandemic of covid-19, we have to cooperate by not becoming victims to spread the disease further. We should take all precautions and still strive to make the world a better place to live.

7. Use digital resources as much as possible and avoid human interaction except online. Without forgetting the importance of human values and social interaction, we have to train ourselves in protecting ourselves and others by distancing physically. After the end of the chaotic era, we may still continue to follow the precautionary steps in reduced intensity, we can meet people but not hug or touch. Social value comes from true intentions and compassion that may be conveyed even without physical human touch. Digitisation would solve most of the existing problems in the society aggravated by human biases or irrationalities. As human beings we must vow to be humane so that we don't allow machinist tendencies to take over our human traits.

8. Cut down personal luxury wishlist and go by essentials. Empathy during crisis is understanding the plight of others in worse conditions than we, they cannot even get daily needs met when we curse Covid-19 to deprive us of our weekend dinners, lavish birthday parties or comfortable vacation plans to a hill station. Either help others get the essentials or show solidarity by cutting down personal requirements in luxury items like fruit juices, soft drinks, chocolates, sweets, pastries, AC rooms, etc. Self accountability is all we need to have and not ostentatious declarations on social media channels saying we are sacrificing this or that to show our compassion with the less privileged.

9. Use wisdom and not comparison with others. Please do not adopt unfavorable habits because others are doing that. Do not skip taxes because some defaulters are. Most societies are in race for social-esteem with people doing everything to match some activity of neighbour or colleague or friend or somebody else. We have to start living for ourselves, families, nations and the economy in order to develop qualities to be one of the possible contributors of economic growth.

10. Adopt a simple lifestyle and contribute as much as possible by work, knowledge, donations or other feasible means. Sponsor food, education or health of other kids, sick, poor, disabled, underprivileged and needy. Adopt villages for development and provision of electricity, food, water, internet or medicines. Start by improving your life, then help your family grow after which work for the local regions and country in possible ways to

make a mark in the non-monetary methods of helping others because money was not there when man was born, it came in the middle and it should be shared with others to make its existence relevant.

How to and what to or not

There are several ways that public movements would spring up in the post covid world. Our economic development depends on what we do outside of our professions as a civic activity or championing cause of public pain. As individuals, we often act in different capacities to contribute our own bit to society. A lot of us don't find avenues to give that bit. It's not always the rights that we should yearn for, but for duties too at times. We should share at least one of our services or belongings with others in the community. Each one of us is capable of giving back to the society in one way or the other.

  Take inspiration from leaders like Mother Teresa. If Mother Teresa had not volunteered to nurture street-children and serve the dying, we wouldn't have known the meaning of true service.

  Participate in important events like Earth Day, Women's Day, Hygiene Day, Independence Day or some World Pretext Day.

  We are all busy with our work and goals in life. Weekends are still available for us to spare one or two every quarter.

  Donate money, clothes or articles to NGOs. Sponsor a child or two or adopt a village in India or South Africa or China or Russia or Cuba.

  Plant trees and help fight pollution. Our future generations need trees to get oxygen, food and wood.

  Participate in blood donation camps. Blood banks can gain a lot in continuing their generous service if we extend our voluntary support.

  Volunteer to create awareness campaigns about elections. A lot of us still don't vote all over the world.

  Participate in collection drives, marathons and public speeches. Collect and give to the needy.

  Refer a stray puppy to a NGO for animals or call up Red Cross for volunteering on an education drive for poor students or adult education or a city cleaning drive.

  Make personal resolutions for giving up use of polythene bags (save nature), meat (save the food chain) or drugs (save yourself).

Support a public cause and sign up a public petition or invest in a public cause or provide need-based employment rather than education-based employment.

Volunteering need not always be in kind but can be for a service. There is no dearth of benefactors and beneficiaries across the globe.

Don't volunteer for unnecessary tasks like strikes, burning effigies, protesting or hampering activities (White, 2013-14).

A small public movement may seem harmless but it would have long lasting spiralling effects on the growth of the economy and would hinder root level development because our technology could take off but the masses are seen struggling for literacy, which is quite happening in today's world. To tackle from the other side, economic development has to involve every citizen in nations to avoid unfavorable involvement in other non productive activities. A nation not working for economic growth would waste valuable resources in non value adding activities (local protests, drug trafficking, smuggling, global chaos) or time movements to show presence on the international map.

Seniors - our last but most important responsibility

The societal shift from nuclear to joint families could bring back the importance and better participation of senior citizens mostly ignored by us in the name of privacy, modernity, generation gap and individualism. However these are considered to be foolishness by ethics, trust, socialisation, heritage and evolution.

If juniors are our future, seniors are our foundation! Senior citizens are the stores of wisdom, knowledge and values that can save marriages, promote our careers, guide our education and/or provide monetary help. Usually, we recognize seniors for the last help but not others. They are the experienced people who have emerged successful in life after time-tested times. Our minimum gift to them is to respect all seniors and to carry forth their ideals.

Governments ensure their well-being by pensions, insurance and life-long old-age welfare schemes. However, they miss family life to a great extent. Senior citizens are neglected in families to the extent they lose interest in life. In families, we have senior citizens in the form of grandmothers or grandfathers.

Life is not possible without the support of all family members. The marriage of Queen Elizabeth and King Philip is a very good example. Usually a king's palace does not consist of just the family but hundreds of other members. This includes grandparents, in-laws, brothers, sisters, their families, distant relatives, visiting relatives, other kith and kin, servants, their families and working staff members. Both the king and queen go by family values more than any other value.

First they keep their families intact and then they rule the people of their states. Queen Elizabeth has inherited and maintained throughout the times that a strong family is the first need of their life. She has always insisted on certain family values that her sons, daughters-in-law, daughters, sons-in-law, grand-children and other members in the family must follow. She has followed the system of joint family throughout the times. Her love for family has won her a lot of respect inside and outside the palace.

Governments in different nations have to develop more employment schemes for seniors. Though they retire, they prefer to work on their convenience. More options of online consultancies for senior citizens can help them find easy jobs in old age. It not only helps them financially but also emotionally. They get ways of spending time productively. Or companies and NGOs can seek seniors on their boards so that they get good points of advice for growth. Seniors know the best practices from the past and the lacunae in present systems of society and industry. They can help us guide with future requirements to some extent.

Seniors need to be made aware that the world cares for them, whether they live with us or not (in fact, we live with our elders because we are dependent on them in one way or the other, they are better off without us), to make it a better society.

Government

As we are aware of children's curiosity leading to creativity, Akio Morita also said that curiosity was the key to creativity.

Government will play a key role in developing the post corona world. One way can be to make a global improvement council GIC, by including the national and financial heads of every country so that responsibility will follow accountability for wholesome protection from life to business without losing ground with environmental, legal and public issues. One nation may focus on global warming, another country can re- channelize its capability in restoration of international health care and reform and like this we have a great global economy boost happening from all corners of the globe. It is not a cakewalk but might demand total universal health care synchronization or financial regulation transformation or uniform global law or single international code of conduct. We will provide an accurate and efficient future business to the next generation of leaders if we start working with macroeconomic reforms instead of creating a new forest of blind win, blame game or other means of monopolistic victory in the mean savagery of corona.

1. The irreversible damage to the life of men and psyches can be justified by building a new educated and protected society flourishing with health and employment because the current impact of virus is best diminished if everyone is involved in a healthy lifestyle by pursuing a good work lifestyle for deviation of mind to productivity from fear.

2. Clearly cleaner environment can thwart the virus of any type, working with the global grass in safeguarding the world through more forest areas, makes the most sense to keep the grasshoppers away from the glass by giving them more green otherwise they will continue to use our food landscape. Governments have to devise ways to encourage people to plant trees. Today if we plant or provide donations to the green champions to help them grow trees, it will not be late. By 2050, in a span of thirty years, the world will be happy to witness a greater chance of being healthy in green cities by more than 7 billion trees, some of which come from their own grandparents. Such global contributions may be rewarded with a special name tag or a special vacation package in the hills or education guarantees to children or job opportunities to families. The government will have to provide the fertile free lands for the citizens to plant seeds or bushes on certain occasions like the birthday, global environment day or public holiday.

Either rains or drones can help them grow into forests. The more we delay the more expensive we will find future life to prosper on the planet. Otherwise businesses will take a back seat in front of health issues in the coming times.

3. Make sure that everyone is able to get clean water, milk, food, besides hand wash and sanitizer. The requirements are a global level and not regional. But the government in every nation should be leading the states towards the provision of medicine, food, housing and other such basic amenities in every city and village of the globe.

4. Free housing and shelter (by converting spacious unused public buildings, libraries, stadiums, museums, etc. into living spaces) should be provided by the government agencies to reduce the cost of living in the open area.

5. The public events like exhibitions, fairs or others can be digitized thereby saving hugely on the cost of organizing. It increases the reach and participation to remote places even on an international scale. The themes if wisely selected can be useful in penetrating global change for more cultural harmony and economic growth with the regional collaboration using the diversely distributed resources across the world. The opportunity is given by corona lockdown as we should motivate ourselves in the unproductive time. Agricultural events gathering farmers across the world could be conducted by the national governments. Farm products, seeds, funding options, irrigation methods, price strategy, technologies and logistics can be illustrated, demonstrated or shared among international communities. It is bound to go a long way in improving work methods, working conditions, farmers prospect, wastage reduction, online knowledge repository and hence better utilisation of the global produce. The same can be made applicable to other sectors largely human centric, labor intensive, demand oriented and interaction generating segments.

6. Open the new special economic zones to reduce commercialization and increase private sector pure players. Priority sectors are on hygiene, personal fitness, real estate, food, textiles and online work - education. Digital payment and transaction capabilities have to be built in-house by each national government to avoid security issues arising out of the systems procured from MNC firms outside the country. Even if they come and work from native land safety and defense capabilities have to be our own because we can not depend on others for protection from 'others'. Defense capabilities have to be built by us not as

national safeguards alone but now for fighting against the corona virus and the after effects.

7. Reduce the direct and indirect tax rates for inspiring people to work more to earn more and spend more money besides saving and buying insurance or other investments. Governments should frame more labor friendly policies and allow the earning from multiple jobs, entrepreneurial incentives and online work.

8. Take preemptive measures to manage fire outbreaks, gas leaks (Visakhapatnam in India faced life and financial loss due to leakage of poisonous gas in the factory). It should have been controlled or predicted (more important and needed like weather forecasts on cyclones that we are not failing but managing better to save life than costs, globally) as general safeguarding by adoption of the latest advanced system dynamic technology for event simulation, trended modeling and forecast based on the past similar risks faced by Haldiram when it closed down the Nagpur factory in 2019 following the leakage of harmful chemicals. It applies to the governments of all nations to take precautions against locating the chemical industries in the residential areas. Beirut Lebanon has faced havoc in the process of storage of chemicals in the warehouse near the populated areas of the city, when the ammonium nitrate (other ports and cities storing harmful substances should monitor the situation and take prevention steps) leaked out causing a deadly explosion. Appropriate remediation measures have to be taken in compensating the victims and their families in the affected cities. The long-term effects on global economy should be studied, though isolated incidents in different nations, people can't live in such affected areas, nor can industries conduct business in office with employees breathing the infected air in and around the disaster region, nor can we consume the produce coming from the polluted regions: thus the local development is slowed down, water pollution should be checked and treated to prevent more harm and, animals and plants should be provided protection along with the people. It is not a small task to get life back to normal and restore the environment to health. Still, the rest of the citizens have to shoulder responsibility for the re-establishment of cities by providing the necessary help to the concerned victims.

9. Governments of all countries have to be extra careful in monitoring corona aftermath by using the best decision science system technology because the global economy is a bit in state of shock, though the announcement of

employment rise, growth numbers and other positive results in the crisis world are not free of sugar coats. Less than 5% of the global workforces earn salaries to lead a comfortable life. Less than 2% get hefty salaries for a more luxurious life as per WEF data. Employment of all people in the working age bracket is no new achievement unless the working lot is paid satisfactorily. Online work portals must be introduced that would allow the capable and skilled persons to enrol and complete tasks for getting paid immediately without waiting for the end of month.
10. Governments in all countries must restore the confidence of the middle class economy by balancing interest rates, inflation, tax rates, price changes and other welfare measures.

Facilitation is not the only role of government as seen in most of the nations where governments either open up or close down the windows for investments, foreign collaborators or private players to start businesses and solve the national problems but consumer or economic development are not the responsibility of private companies alone rather government should become a role model in solving the national issues that others can emulate in normal times because fact remains that trust levels deteriorate in times of crisis and citizens should not be forced to wish for another government when trouble occurs. Though cumbersome for companies or individuals or governments to shoulder the responsibility for an entire society we have to start implementing action plans from all corners of administration and sustenance mechanisms. Systems and procedures are not needed for recording the achievements, only solutions are needed for meeting the goals of zero hungry, zero homeless and zero people losses. Since we know that the expenses would be enormous we have to work without counting (money but not on government). Simple solution is to create provisions to fund the institutions and instruct them to achieve the people's goals because the government can readily provide finances but not restructure its systems to generate new business models or supply chains or logistics, upfront. It should pick up immediately in matching with the private players completing their initiatives successfully either in meeting transportation needs or hygiene needs of the public in every state. The third step is to prepare for the future in government making itself ready for the post- crisis world by creating secure channels of digital payments, or allowing alternative medicines for ensuring health of citizens in future or generating insurance and funding schemes, or better traffic management systems or transparent defense force mechanisms. One thing should be met by all governments, in not getting bogged down or not engaging in unnecessary cross border activity creating stress for the world because any petty deviation from collaboration is not required as the priority is well-known to us -to revive the global economy.

Industry

According to philosopher and artist Antoine de Saint-Exupery, we have to teach men to yearn for vast and endless ocean, instead of delegation of work, if we want to build a ship.

Company culture has to provide competent and customer friendly services, not protecting the company profit goals but the consumer beliefs. The first company that will bear the loss of the corona cost is bound to be the best leader in the future industry.

1. Associate with the concern of buyers, teams and communities instead of selling the corona options.
2. Don't quit your business ideas and be ready for shockprone years for at least a year despite your great success trail with the market and clients.
3. Don't forget that we have a corporate onus in amendment that dictates us to support the customer before we proceed with our sales goals. It is highly possible that companies are shown back door or closure opportunities by the disillusioned buyers who have been in the pursuit of selling their fears in return for buying the best product that can take care of their families.
4. Insurance will be a good next sector to undergo rapid innovation in growth - risks - recovery procedures. More products are predicted in the direction of investment rather than management of disaster. A disease will find free schemes for testing, treatment and recovery instead of creating a funding plan for the surviving family of the victims.
5. Data is an important thing to be recognised by all companies to be recorded in future market research and recognised in information analysis on the annual reports, technology changes and more modern media management services.
6. Media has been a major significant single source of information about our industry, politics, technology and other trends pertaining to the corona era of November 2019 to June 2020, which is the first peak of pandemic, afterwards July to December 2020 can be labeled as the 'wary peak' when we are observing the descaling of virus, development of medical vaccine or drug through the therapy (is likely to remain as general as possible).
7. The goal of business is to bear losses in the corona crisis and not to make profits from customer agony. If consumers take the loss then, they will not, even cannot, sometimes, pay for the service or product but if companies are willing to become

loss leaders then the markets will send an assurance signal that a better larger entity can bear losses on behalf of the buyers.

8. Industry curves will be dangling to reflect corona failure, supply and demand will vary independent of the price changes punching holes in the elasticity thereby losing correlation unless healthy economy measures like supply incentive to companies and spending opportunities to customers are created in the post lockdown period by the appropriate strategic agencies globally. The failures of corona, though not to be blamed on any other cause than men because the origin followed by initial spread alone is to be considered as out of our control. The next interstate and cross border pandemic losses should be controlled or no forces can stop the relapse of corona leading to doubling of loss in industrial productivity by erosion of confidence, haphazard swings in market sentiments and irrational market movement. The trends would lead to illogical financial decisions because of weak customer assumptions, illogical investor behavior, awry machine quotients, failing or falling expectations and other such unheard of effects of corona on the value generation factors of all countries. The industry has to function continuously in order to get new social changes at all times whether favorable or no, and we have to, in fact we are revisiting the theory times as it seems that the intellectual visionaries like Adam Smith, Frederick Taylor, et al are staring in our face. By default we would be following the footsteps of all great advocates of economic growth because the grandma tips never fail in the healthy growth of babies with ailment that our national economies are right now. All ancient economists said the same and we have to get out of the economic rut by the constant slow performance in the slow down unless the need to shutdown is absolute. The industry has to produce goods and we have to get new services models suiting our global market transition. The class disparities might emerge again but not last longer if managed by careful monitoring of bureaucratic intervention, labor friendly policies and informed synchronization with community preferences. The reversals of hierarchy repeatedly, would show group highlights in our global growth change. The importance of line workers will be overemphasized despite line automation and some worker groups will argue that their role is more important than that of the minority creamy white collar groups and they will not be wrong. The trend may change with the increase in the numbers at the top headcount and with the compulsion of work responsibility to

flow from line activities because then only decisions can be made correctly at the top by the top level management. Soon we can have the top managers working for double the hours and with the different line functions moving up the chain every single day to justify their fat takeaway packages from the company or we have to see open labour unrest, top level retrenchment, production stoppage or industry lockdown.

Corona lockdown as it ends could end up in sub lockdown in industry, company or other institution level for more intermittent periods to smoothen the performance curves balancing the output, yield, price and demand slopes.

Strategy will not depend on anything because it will be standalone, strong one for saving the life of a consumer towards the end of stress and risk of corona -

1. Structure because of the high level corona cost of universal risk of uncertainty, no structural transformation is helpful unless the strategy is to help customers out of the corona pandemonium, and the goal is to save lives, not money.
2. Success of business in the past will be irrelevant unless you strategize the exclusion of your customers from getting victimized by the pandemic.
3. People will not decide what strategy you want to make because you have the right business goal for saving your customers best.
4. Technology will help only if it follows the same strategy of business alignment to save the lives, monies and other costs of people associated or not with the corona crisis because all are equal in the eyes of the corona crisis.
5. Solution is to provide the best amenities, reduce crime and increase the future preparation of facing similar issues but first adherence to the 'save all' strategy is needed.

Companies need not aim at increasing the riches of their consumers by merely slashing the prices by a point or two as the task is not worth the end of making the consumers happy or at least trying to save their happiness. It is seen that after using certain products the inherent happiness of consumers is replaced by undue concern and discontent. Industries can aim to become more self responsible instead of commercially responsible. Dealing with the environmental issues is better than coming out with a new pesky plastic bag for impressing the customers. The industry downturn is not unimaginable, it is going through hard times every now and then. Science diplomacy or strategic collaboration should be attested by trust of people to win across the tide of crisis in jointly marching towards a healthy economic growth of over 10% for all nations by 2030. Industry growth has to be taken to the range of 20-30% by 2030 in all the countries because we should start looking at producing what can be made out of the resources available in a given region. We should start avoiding the cross border transportation thereby building huge transaction and agency costs in making the same products. Exim laws should encourage global trade across countries so that a nation may import what it cannot make. The cost of import may be less than the local costs adding up the extra processing costs after the transportation of raw material and other skills or technologies. Patriotic business does not mean that a nation has to produce what other nations are producing even at high costs. Patriotism and indigineous business mean that the nations respect each other's boundaries and citizens, without imposing superiority nor inflicting losses on each other; and that the nation produces everything 'possible' at low costs for finally facilitating low-priced supplies to the end users or consumers; while importing any required goods or services or technologies or information or solutions to solve the problems of consumers in the native nation. Collaborative arrangements get the imports at low cost and negotiations on friendly terms. Formal trade agreements can only get the stuff but not establish long term trustworthy bilateral relations between the importer and exporter nations. Relaxing trade laws and encouraging foreign trade just for the sake of improving bilateral relations do not really achieve the objective because the consumers of both nations are under strain where such economies would both struggle to flourish on enforced mutual trust or fake mutual relations.

Sport & Fitness industry - Health is wealth

The covid-19 tyranny is stirring our souls in growing us from the inside out. Swami Vivekananda emphasized that nobody can teach us or make us spiritual except our own souls.

Sports is an affected sector in the corona times, with many of the professionals staying in the homes and training themselves on their own. This will result in withdrawal from the professional sponsorship to some extent. Schools and other institutions are not allowed to function during the lockdown due to which they are not able to help grow their sports events. Therefore personal, cultural, group and commercial events that used to promote sports and leisure are not taking place anymore. The $756 billion sports industry needs support from united nations and who to spread the positive attitude and virtual sports opportunities, in radio and television programmes to encourage physical activities in the houses. According to the UN report, sports revenues have been falling in all the four sources, professional, retail, food and beverages, and clubs or gyms. Millions of jobs are at risk even in the related industries of events, tourism, travel, transportation , catering, media and infrastructure. Young people are the key influencers for the sport sector and the relevant steps to motivate them in the post covid times will help bring back sustainability along with recovery and reorientation of the sports sector strengthening the role of sports to achieve economic development. Government and other stakeholders will have to provide competent resources to further the initiatives in research and education sectors to make sports indispensable with the aim of developing global awareness.

Fitness and leisure centres have to be established in the residential vicinity to encourage people with families individual sports for both normal and special people in the cities of each country. Global peace and growth will be the result of a healthy sports industry.

Guidance will help foster mental well-being and safety in the household activities like yoga, dance, meditation, swimming and other minor sports.

Even if the economy opens up it may take a while to get the sports sector back into work. Tokyo Olympics slated for July - August has been postponed to 2021 by the International Olympics committee (earlier also leap year Olympics did not get finished without problems as revealed by Tokyo scientists). New Zealand is trying to boost its sports industry by taking government aid of $157m over the next four years as tremendous pressure on sports organizations put them in tight financial conditions with the competitions canceled and community sports reeling under the lock down. The Indian premier league cricket match slated for March has been postponed earlier this year by the International Cricket Council. As of August 2020, IPL will be conducted from September in UAE, exactly when the second wave of COVID-19 is supposed to occur as per the BBC news report. 60% stadium capacity is the best expected in the infected season. It may not be possible but digital audiences will be the next solution in case of any continued crisis lockdown with the players in action after wearing masks and further precautions. The match telecast can be subscribed for nominal charges to make up for the lost revenue from the stadium tickets. Auctions and broadcasting rights will be able to help grow their sports revenues. China is making their professional teams play in front of cardboard spectators to make it look good on the screen. Only few cities have a better chance to host the games with the travel restrictions on the athletes. Accommodation facilities for the sport professionals may be constructed within the stadium to avoid unnecessary commute (thereby creating a bio bubble) and restricted access to the premises may be granted to authorized people. Fair decision can be taken by using AI decision services by the local umpires and coaches.

People know that a healthy body can allow for a healthy mind and vice versa. Similarly the economy is like a mind for a nation whose body is formed of its citizens. Without economic health, the physical health of citizens will not be certain and vice versa. Cross border sporting events should be replaced by more national events and local individual sporting events like paragliding or swimming or trekking or other sorts to entertain individual participation with the appropriate preventive and hygiene law. This will add to the activity as well as revenue streams of the sports sector because equipment, clothing, training and health measures all need to be taken care of by the experts for the people or their families finding a getaway in their vicinity. Open day sports should be encouraged more than the night indoor games to avoid spread of infections and allow for more ventilation in spaces under sun. Charges need to be reasonable and not hefty to maintain healthy demand from the otherwise homesick people. Multiple sporting points must be operative to avoid crowding at spots. This is a chance for the trained experts to display their skills in front of the masses of the middle class and earn a brand recognition that would carry forward in the later years after full recovery from the corona crisis. What loss is the sports industry at, if we train some children and adults from the bottom of the pyramid for free? We may be able to develop some athletes for future gaming events of the international level. Professional groups must take government aid (for which schemes need to fund hidden poor athletes' development and sponsorship) for identification, nurturing, nourishment and nutrition, equipping, teaching or recommendation for global events based on merit and training but first provide them food, accessories, shelter and tricks of the trade with all honesty to prepare for the future events instead of languishing in the sorrow of Corona crisis. Some day, the crisis is going to end and that should be the driver of all industries suffering in today's lockdown.

The corona and post lockdown periods will win market share for nutritionists, food experts, physical training groups and wellness professionals, who are our responsible mentors constantly giving personalized recommendations for suiting our family and environmental demand. Gyms will catch upon resumption of activities because we are totally confined to household environments on account of lockdown. Online subscription base is increasing for seminars, yoga workshops, fitness coaching, wellness professional certification and other guided meditation group platforms. A rise of over 30% has been confirmed by the food delivery apps in organic and wholesome meal segments. Women prefer to order nutritious food for the lockdown inflicted family members who would otherwise eat in the canteen or outside. Worldwide fitness sector is predicted to grow by over $50b in the post lockdown period (62% rise). The rise will come from digital and group membership schemes. Corporate and non working people both come with the need for stress buster, mind booster, body wellness and lifestyle guidance.

Life coaching is expected to gain more audience. Both working and non working class people are on their toes, globally, to get new advice for matters related to office, and home. Personal and professional issues are being discussed because of the rise in the number of experts and nuclear families. The case is true for the entire world in getting confused with individuality as not depending on family but outsider. We can afford to waste money and time discussing our life with certified professional teams creating our life history, even telling us what to do. Nothing wrong. We can do it in dire times when we are alone on the planet but we are on the verge of modernization by isolation and exclusion. The corona lockdown has taught us the same tact that we are better off in the company of our family members at our homes. We have known one another for decades to solve the mutual problems without waiting for the weekly sessions or counseling appointment. Utilize the family more than the professional help. As a life coach I prefer to refer my subjects to a close friend or parents or grandparents for counseling about any aspects of life unless they really need 'educated' advice on a topic. Preparation of entrance exams, settlement abroad or tuition on technology are things to be guided by professional teams. Only your family and friends can guide you on how to get out of the loneliness or headache of overspending a salary, or how to even talk to them without ruining the relationships formed by birth or any other conundrums faced by us in our day to day activities.

Fitness from the point of physical training, mental wellness and other modes of active involvement in life, has been controlled by happiness and has been taken care of by us in our daily activities so far. Today companies teach us on how to be happy. We are not enjoying ourselves because we have to achieve so many things like success, promotion, wealth, professional degrees, property, and even family. We continuously evaluate aims, gains and losses in our way of life thereby losing satisfaction and happiness besides increasing tension for the family members. The best book on personal development can also not stop the next generation falling for more professional help. Companies will continue to make money and we are going to continue to visit the life coaches because of the hype, freedom, esteem and other reasons linked to a more certified professional working quality hours on your life. We feel as if our burden moves onto someone else once our money moves onto their bank account. We can pay but not lead our life and solve the problems related to ourselves. The weaknesses have been brought to the forefront by the corona lockdown in giving personal time to be with ourselves. We can find ways to overcome them without any professional help but it is a possibility that more and more people are going to visit the wellness professionals once the lockdown period is over. Till then online registrations for virtual wellness seminars are getting filled up by the students and working professionals besides the non working others in our global communities. Discounts are being offered by the experts to attract masses to attend workshops on themes related to life, technology, sports, arts and many more fields. Children can learn from such online sessions without any hassle of going out in the risky environment. Adults can multitask and complete household or other works while being part of online conferences. It is no complete solution but we have to get things done somehow in the crisis affected times. Fitness sector is promising as experts offer customized services for each subscriber and her family members to chalk out healthy routines in food, exercise, work, play and prayer. Laughter clubs and group meditation forums are functioning online. Brazil government is funding its citizens to get bicycles for more secure transportation means in the post lockdown world. The issues of pollution, isolation, fitness and cost including accidents are resolved to a good extent. The government of India is providing free food rations till November 2020 to get the poor fit by food. Prague government is organizing free public fairs after 20 days of corona free test results. The citizens are allowed to mingle outside strolling across parks, food stalls, water parks, museums and malls. Fitness begins right now to be able to get the virus away from us while remaining healthy. Companies training groups in yoga should devise breathing exercises to keep off the disease and should suggest good health food options that can help build a sturdy immune system. We don't need to worry much about isolation because by now, the technology has let us be independent of all people- based facets of life, anyway and in many ways we are used to leading virtual life whether by virtual interactions or audiovisual or telephony methods. The best solution for the corona problem addressed by the fitness companies lies not in making healthy independent individuals but making them realize the importance of family members. The two industries of sports and fitness have hence been grouped into the same theme because they are not separate. Sportsmen need to be fit and sports do provide fitness to the players but when the sectors are not functioning due to the lockdowns, fitness has to get the upper slot. Whether sports events are held or not, fitness regimes have to be followed and enforced on the citizens to keep the world healthy by the time economic development picks up. Infected people are largely depending on natural remedies like turmeric, ginger, or yoga and meditation. Wait for a concrete result from medical experts. Till then stay isolated, try some prescribed medication and wait for testing negative with positive thinking. Hospitalisation brings the risk of congestion and contact with other patients. Governments must remember that they should expedite the task of economic recovery and revival so that individuals find their motivation in a pink economic health.

Global apparel and textiles

JQ Adams, former US President remarked that we can consider ourselves to be leaders if our actions inspire others to dream more, learn more, do more and become more...

The fall is more than 50% compared to the pre-COVID 19 growth in sales for the apparel sector globally. Emergence of the D2C business model is on rise with the increasing use of online shopping apps by buyers. More informal transactional model is being seen in India where manufacturers are directly pitching to end-users of clothing in readymade and fabric textile segments. The payments are secure using Paypal, Paytm, UPI and other bank transfer mechanisms thereby making Indian textiles sector an interesting case study for the global markets. Promising sellers are ready to supply globally without charging for courier or packaging as extra. The model is helpful for both resellers and end customers. Retailers and wholesalers are seen collaborating with the buyers in all segments of the pyramid - lower middle class, upper middle class and rich. Even the poor segment has got the option to choose from surplus material often with minor damages or sparsely used clothes. The low cost surpluses are collected by the sellers from all over the world as revealed in a survey by our in-house consultant teams. The margins are low but not lower than 50% when compared to the over 100% margins in clothing sold in malls and branded stores. Prices start from as low as $2 and can go upto $100 depending on the requirement for clothing. Manufacturers store inventories in more than 6000 square feet offices, where they employ hundreds of tailors to meet the rising demand of customers. The unorganised sector has seen more than 20% rise in sales in the covid era. New sourcing options and supply chain financing are the key challenges to the companies in the post crisis global apparel industry that have taken the harsh winds of covid19 by seeing a more than 30% fall in demand globally. Matching supply and demand remains to be fixed from the pre-covid industry times because most of the inventories get piled up in anticipation of getting sold but orders get cancelled leading to loss of billions of dollars, wastage of the clothing, leading to pest attacks (insects, rodents etc) or wear and tears in the godowns. The $2.5 trillion industry requires global innovation in working with fast on-demand models to eliminate inventories, fabric waste and warehousing. This reduces costs, losses, upfront cash need and inventory while increasing customer retention and sales. Customers won't buy what they cannot sell and manufacturers won't produce unless orders are placed by buyers. On-demand manufacturing will be transformative to the industry and requires more patience for global acceptance than investment in equipment and labor. Players can choose to copy the business model of Amazon by locating their facilities at multiple points to be based near the customers so that quick manufacturing and deliveries are possible to ease the cluttering logistics and burdensome peak season volumes as and when customers place orders from across the world. The existing global value chain model has left the players high and dry due to Covid lockdown effects of laying off workers, closures of factories and / or delays in international shipping. Local production and inventory warehousing were expected to come to rescue but the sellers faced large scale cancellations. The costs are not really low as expected due to expectations on quality, risk management needs, time value changes, shipping needs and fashion demands. A balance is required in supporting local skills, craft, designs, arts, embroideries, prints, colors or patterns while adapting to global conditions using traditional method of 2-20-day cycles (order to manufacture to shipping) or robotic wholesale management of orders where some companies in India (Kolkata) are directly working with enterprise technologies in informing the robotic tailors about the order as soon as it is placed. The material fabric is packaged and despatched immediately after completing the inspection and quality checks. The dress is stitched by the next line robotic tailor according to the requested measurements and customization preferences. It is packed according to the shipping location and destination of the buyer. The whole process is more efficient than the manual execution of orders and takes a few hours or a day at the most before the shipment reaches the logistics points of delivery. Otherwise the traditional cycles are volatile with repeated changes and interactions between buyer and seller, taking days to finalise the output before leaving it in mass cargo shipments for more days. The industry will do better by foregoing the seasonality blues by offering short term catalogues to customers who can choose to skip an order in waiting for a new catalogue of designs each time. Fashion brands can find better acceptance this way than offering a limited heap of designs endlessly to wait for inventories to be exhausted as waste or orders. Digital clothing needs to find a greater space since the transactions are physical store-based to the tune of 80%, since e-store gives opportunity for buyers to try the clothes virtually or order at home and then decide on what to buy. The close interaction between fashion brands and customers sometimes allows the buyers to negotiate prices on the apps. Multi brand retailers should understand the trends and preferences of customers, before justifying their point of difference by price, curation or location. The demand in rental clothing is on a rise when it comes to sustainable and vintage clothing because consumers don't want seasonal purchases that are less eco-friendly. Companies have to shun excess production and take advantage of the opportunity of purpose-driven sustainable fashion clothing thrown by the covid chaos. Waste producing business models are no longer encouraged by markets. The textiles industry is facing an existential crisis due to reduced trade flows, and increasing shift to buy essentials and medicines, during the corona lockdown, by the customers across the globe. Companies are selling more comfort items that consumers require more while staying at homes. Discounts are mounting up to accrue incomes for the seller segment without depending on advertising but using social media to promote products.

Environmental pressures in terms of reducing carbon emissions are creating social responsibility issues for apparel manufacturers and sellers. Right from raw material to shipping carton or plastic materials everything needs to be eco friendly in the future if players want to promote sustainability. Online training lessons, without any fees, to buyers of fabric, is another possible opportunity for apparel and accessories players in yarn, thread, recyclers of extra cloth or thread or unsold clothing, cutting or stitching equipment manufacturers. Buyers can learn from the expert tailors and branded designers to enable them design and stitch clothing as per personal preferences or conveniences. Future customization needs can be directly handled by customers to a great extent leaving the time and resources of companies to be invested in innovating the business models or developing new technologies related to the sector. Fashion brands can be in the name of customers, when the real personalisation or customization is enabled by the companies to give more confidence and trust to the buyer, it would lead to an increase in the sales of fabric because of lower costs than readymade clothing; next it would increase demand for the tailoring equipment because of one-time investment. D2C sales of accessories can find better margin avenues for the related industries that sell to wholesalers and retailers at a thin price margin.

Shift in Global transportation industry

Charles Darwin proposed in the theory of evolution that the most responsive ones to change, survive, neither the strongest ones nor the most intelligent species.

Growth is bound to occur within the post covid global transportation sector in preferring individual rides, to avoid unnecessary risk arising from group rides whether in public transportation means or private vehicles. The preference for driverless vehicles would increase by more than 50% in 2022 from the present market of less than $24b for land, $1336b for total air, over $767b for total water transportation and hence development of innovative vehicles would increase in the post crisis world. Innovative solar vehicles, battery cars, electric vehicles would strive to build larger vehicles like buses, trains, trams, trucks, and even unmanned aircraft with no driver but individual partitions for passengers to avoid interaction based infections. Water based transportation would innovate similar automatic cruise, boat, ship or submarine. Technology will be at its functional best if aimed at protection of the planet by reducing pollution and saving the natural resources. Drone based transportation would soon find ways to passenger movement against low pressure, dynamic track hyperloop and drones can be attached to cars, trains, or other vehicles on easy conversion of land to air to water mode in any sequence. AI with electronic technology and electric system inclusion will be in the mainstream of all industries of the future and transportation is no exception. The robotics would be a crowning achievement for humanity in reduction of accidents and extension of spacecraft capabilities. We may colonise another planet in the next three decades traveling to Mars for the space scientists conference and living in the new architecture housing with new modes of transportation there. Drones may be able to travel from one planet to the other without loss due to environmental changes. All navigation and location related worries, issues or aspects can be better handled by robots. A robot team as traffic guide or route advisor can safely drop a lost kid from the highway to home. Transportation would be improved to manage the health needs more than a first aid, to perform on- the- spot surgery or treatment related to accidents or personal emergencies to avoid losses due to time delays. Future transportation in post lockdown period would not encourage group travels with unknown people but at the same time planning is needed for more than safety precautions and travel facilities of including hygiene measures, clean water and food availability, citizen-non-citizen separation of compartments, coaches or seats to avoid transmission of disease to and from foreigners traveling by buses, trains, planes or other means of transportation. Automatic sterilization sprays should be installed in all the modes of transport. As much as possible travel with strangers must not be encouraged to eliminate the possible contacting of disease and pathogens.

A healthy way of looking at the lockdown stalking the process of continued transportation, is to appreciate the falling pollution levels across the globe in the span of 6-12 months. The global temperature has been rising due to the heat released by the moving vehicles constantly emitting gases based on compounds of carbon, sulphur, nitrogen and other non healthy elements. Now with the advent of rules on reduced traffic operations and limited transportation due to corona lockdown the global temperature has fallen more than 5degrees Celsius according to WEF. Robustness, reliability and automation make sense if means of transportation are equipped with state of art water filters to supply drinking water to passengers to cut down the spread of waterborne diseases. Infection due to sneezing or crowding or air borne diseases should be minimized by medicinal sprays emanating from the aerosols continuously in the vehicles. Reverse osmosis and block chain techniques are on the new acceptance in many countries like India, Mexico, Singapore and Dubai to facilitate provision of food and water to every passenger. The modes of transport can be manufactured using the material alloys resistant to pathogens so as not to breed diseases. Automatic dispensers for masks, gloves, sanitizer and hand wash must be installed in the traveling or ticket booking points. Doctor help should be accessible to all passengers in the way or vehicles. Next, digitally literate passengers can take a higher advantage of travel technology than if we don't make efforts on educating the world on the new development of technology. Teach them to create awareness of the technology assistance, facilities and equipment present in the different modes of travel. A coach should show out the cradle or other accessories when babies are on board. Mechanical aid should be able to help special passengers in entering into and exiting from the vehicles. Patients should be provided separate stretchers and beds on travel. It's not specific to corona but the crisis is reminding us of many forgotten aspects of travel. It may be a better idea to allow passengers to bring home cooked food because hygiene does not recommend outside food, rules can be made to allow vegan or vegetarian food because meats carry pathogens. Pilots, drivers and crews on board must be given full support and facilities to help them conduct healthy travel without need for frequent communication with ground or interdepartmental staff as otherwise there would be risk of wastage of time, resources or output in complying by unnecessary processes or bureaucracy norms. Innovation is required in making the passenger spaces more natural and friendly by allowing sunlight even in AC seats, arrangements of plants and floral pots except for allergic travellers, open air spaces for free ventilation and healthy maintenance of journey. Short travel must be encouraged so that passengers are not exposed to risks faced during the journey. Bicycles, marked walking tracks, and solo car rides must be preferred for short distances. Slow moving trams could allow passengers to hop in and out at the required spots as against the fast sliding tubes for quick travel. The number of vehicles and frequency of transportation need to increase in avoiding too many people in a coach at one time. The key trends to change global transportation are reduced spans of travel, more frequency, and more spacious movement in a more hygienic environment assisted by doctor consultation and technology to give home atmosphere to the local or foreign passengers at nominal price. Health is more of a criterion than price for the post lockdown passengers. Government exchequers and treasuries should be exploited in full restoration of public health and convenience along with safety in the global means of transportation. The stations and airports must be well equipped with free clean drinking water (hot and cold), as the first priority in transportation reforms. Space should be increased in the restrooms and lounges to avoid cluttering and crowding. Medical support counters with the diagnostics, doctors, medicines and aid-staff (beyond first aid in helping patients in staff or passengers or visitors) must be located at multiple points of waiting stations, pick-up, check-in, boarding or drop-off, departures and arrivals to facilitate travellers of all modes- private taxis, buses, trains, planes and even ships to cover it better. Pollution control norms should be reframed to follow practices in order not to increase the pollution of the already treated or cleaned environments owing to the lockdown effects. Let us ensure that we stay the same as far as hygiene and green are concerned, otherwise we can resume our activity in the post covid world to proceed with a continued goal of global economic sustenance followed by growth and development.

Entertainment & Media

Napoleon insisted that a leader was a dealer in hope.

There could be no other industry with more hope in a downturn than media and entertainment. The top industry growth is expected to be in media and entertainment when we are on our own because we have to get enjoyment, even though we are confined indoors. The content is taking a more digital shape and shared across the top channels of entertainment like Amazon Prime Video, YouTube, MXplayer, hotstar or online entertainment portals of TV networks (Star, Sony, Zee, etc.) in national, international and regional versions. The mobile services providers are not far behind in offering packages from the entertainment channels to the customers on paid or complementary schemes. The trends -reduction of visits to cinema halls, rise in number of hours of on-mobile screens, more volumes of download (video, picture, audio clips).

Entertainment and Media is a leader indeed because people can live without food for a day but not a single hour without news or information updates. News channels are on the top charts because everyone including business groups, families, employees, students, stock market participants and other people are closely watching the turns of all countries in our world of corona lockdown. As if the world is possessed by corona the news items are not on any other topic to get 90% news on corona and related briefs. Less than 10% discussion is on other topics such as sports, entertainment or space. We can not deny the importance of news so we can not demand for more. The information to get tested, new developments in our global economy, advancements in medical research, expert advice and much more is conveyed so much so that we are getting movies made on the corona virus and lockdown. Children are on the receiving end to the extent of getting bored by the excess on corona. We as adults can be curious and tolerate the endless streaming news on the epidemic but kids need more entertaining stuff. Future content is expected to be in the animations, cartoons and songs in kids category because we tend to take the focus to corona in every genre of horror, action, comedy or drama. Entertaining stuff is readily available on virus obliteration prayers sounding like movie songs. But movies on adapting the characters to include our viewers in the scenes either as silent or talking participants, is something that is in the next generation output in the goals of some companies. A kid watching the movie or cartoon film on Snowhite can see herself on the screen conversing with the dwarfs. We can welcome with cheer and enthusiasm, such innovative ideas in the next generation entertainment. Another innovative development is a personalized movie whether animated or human character based, scripted by the end-viewer herself. The present technology supports the story writing software for book creation. We can feed the names for characters, story themes and broad ideas running around the story. The book is written by the software in a matter of hours and a lot of us read such books online. The software in extension to audiovisual mode can offer a ready instant movie made by the family members to watch at home. The royalty will be made payable to the actors for using their digital characters including voice and personal features. The payment will vary for cartoon images used in personalized movies.

The sector seems to be on steroids with minimal time off to those working in the media and entertainment. You can see it in action anytime. The responsibility factor for the media sector is on rise because more eyes are on it for informational purposes. All other sectors from food to payment to transportation to technology and most of the industry seem to be suppliers for the media players. Corporations of every sector count the success on the responsibility towards social fabric. Social networks themselves face the daunting task of showing responsibility in facilitating the flow of information by combining authenticity and systems within the scope of public cause without reclining towards a particular view or group of people. In one sentence, all corporates must be responsible to society. Incredible global transformation has occurred in the industry growing from mute moving videography to a more dynamic digital entertainment without any tradeoffs in depicting viewer preference, conveying real-time news, or relaying on the spot incidents in risky environments. Celebrities don't hesitate in putting the personal comfort at stake in order to complete the entertainment with action and thrill. Media and entertainment faces risk of a radical distortion in perception vs reality because they have to do what they don't want to do. The news reporters go to areas not free of disease but we may not see any periods of non activity in newspaper, TV, or other such sub sectors like hollywood, bollywood, etc. Corona lockdown period has been growing at a controlled rate of less than normal time with new content taking a digital form. The advantage of direct to consumer business model inherent in the entertainment industry promises better growth than any other industry because of absence of middle men or stakeholder pressures except for managing the end consumer expectations (viewers are the users or direct consumers in the business of media). Technology advancements have led to a boost of edutainment by providing educational entertainment with the help of reality quiz shows, online seminars or other learning programs. More innovation is needed for furtherance of general awareness and education on public causes through media so that the society problems, industry solutions and economic trends can be reviewed more closely with the objective of aligning global health with local national growth goals. According to studies conducted by our consultant group across the six continents (not required in Antarctica), the corona crisis may bring a 80% reduction of global workforce in direct employment in the coming decades, the seed of which is sown by coronavirus but we are not witnessing a direct downsizing wave. As CXOs have admitted themselves they don't want to create a shockwave by firing employees immediately but we can not escape it altogether. It may become an integral part of future hiring policy for companies to increase the ratio of remote : full time office based employees. Media does not really face the risk because it requires more people day by day because we can not bear machines reading out news or analysing public reactions or acting out a heroine role. And the workers from top to bottom have 20-80% resources working in remote locations depending on the requirement at all times. D2C strategy innovation is no less than necessary thing in the coming times because we need more productive involvement in terms of enabling on the spot decision making or political agility inspired by public response relayed on media, economic changes based on information restored in the sector because it's the more direct and complete source of information (primary, quantitative and qualitative) than any other sector. We can think of globalisation in the sector in terms of following uniform standards because we are in need of authentic data whether Europe or Asia. Collaboration with analytic and advertising sectors can give better insight and impact from and to people (as viewers, critics, data collectors, analysts, reviewers, regulators, approvers, sponsors et al). It is also the need of other sectors to collaborate for reaping the gains of cross-industry initiatives through the increasing TRPs collected on media channels. Further the responsibility increases for the workers in entertainment and media to be more accountable, transparent and open about conveying the facts fearlessly. There is no other input or data source except the journalists in the post-covid or during the lockdowns. Everybody cannot collate the information on social networks or conduct digital surveys to know the public views. The said sector can do it more efficiently than the rest of us. It is a risky job and we must reward them with trust, warmth, affection, confidence and gratitude more than laurels or money (though the last two are also important for survival and encouragement of those working as professionals).

Information technology

Albert Schweitzer said that example... was the only thing in influencing others.

Software companies in the post crisis world of corona and previous such threatening conditions with the need for more than innovative business solutions demanded from the business leaders, face the tough challenge of working for result orientated changes at playing the role of change agent themselves. The task is no easy one when we have to get the multiple problems of customers and users addressed by single or multiple solutions, then it has to be unique solution for each customer to nurture sustainable competency in the markets, while giving maximum opportunity to the users become part of our business execution process in the solution life cycle. We have to be more than multi taskers to lead in a crisis affected world because the information flows are not without biases where multiple people are involved, so common owners for multiple solutions are required. Change leaders who would have capabilities to change sponsors to managers to customers to end users, aptly, are on the top hire section of competition in a healthy attempt to get new results in better response to the situation. IT is like a destitute industry in crisis since the best response becomes a vague attempt to get magic effects out of the failure but we have to understand what the real problems in the present world are. The products and services going out of our global bag of solutions for the customers are not required anymore. What's the use of the luxury cruise when the waters are struggling against tempest? That does not mean that we have to do away with new innovation or regular solutions. The best way forward is to simplify the new solution to suit the changing needs of users. At present and even for the coming five year term, (not election) the top priorities are on the side effects of the corona virus and not as much on the market penetration, or size increase by leadership in sales or other usual business goals. The goals lie in providing a simple day to day solution to help users perform their activities well. It is a more useful app or simplified process or other 'do it yourself' solution that should be in the answer. Sounds a lot easier than any of the proposed complex solutions in a stead to impress the customers who are on the other side of the business table as buyer and we as sellers become more excited without waiting for the customers rise to an equal participation level, when instead, we have to be capable of coming down to match the customer understanding or way of business. The new problems are how best to face the change in reduction of side effects of the corona lockdown followed by the conquest of viruses (not computer but human virus), can software companies develop programs to invade or cleanse the human systems free of virus? One way is to constantly create awareness and remind of all dos' and don'ts' of anti-corona requirement, in the end user instruction of our solutions but to begin with new digital progress has to be nurtured in enabling secure remote working from homes because the office operations have been hampered by the lockdown. The scope of all problems, processes and solutions need to be reviewed, discussed and confirmed by the solution mongers. The customers might work for more crisis specific problems relevant to the coming times. The priority may shift from exotic products to more of creating a support environment that focuses on user assistance and security in daily operations, banking customers have suspended sophisticated solutions, they have been looking at better customer understanding or safe plain investment products to park their funds without any losses due to corona.

The nexgen software solution will have more to do with new recruitment software for hiring without any personal meeting between management and candidate at all levels. The solution will then focus on remote working system technology without any chance for customer questions on security, quality or interaction, by taking help of virtual reality imagery to have office at home. The users at the new end of business can only get better interaction with the employees and not get into long irrelevant group discussion as a formality of the office era. The office era has more than shifted to the work era where all that matters is the output and the location of employees is not important. The core customer solution for the new growth in software services and information technology would not be in a more reduction of costs, or exponential surge of sales or completion of strict compliance, it is a step into automation at making machines more reliable than or on par with men, so as to reduce dependence of business on remote employees. The working norms of the future will be in favor of employees who would be free to quit in a day's notice or without any notice at all. The new software will ensure replacement of men by machines or technology to perform until the new resources resume the tasks of old employees. Software will be in a more critical role of employees for intermittent gaps created between attrition and rehiring. The change is a major one and new labour rules have to be formed by treating machines as employees. The benefits can be briefly mentioned as hassle free implementation because man is the boss and machines can't argue about salary or timeline or holiday or personal limitations. The demerits are loss of human interaction or other communication delimiters because the customer has to accept what the machines give. The new innovative patents can find a way in software with emotional intelligence more than logical implementation skills. Customers would then ask for a solution to connect machines with men or users at making business experience enriching at the end of users. Occasionally community fairs, user gathering, feedback meetings with founder or group user outings may be arranged by companies to bring together the employees, customers and user communities. Some robotic employees may be in a get together or two.

The IT sector is up for a fall in growth with the revenues taking a hit due to the probable quality fall of deliverables in the work from home scenario reducing the personal interactions between clients and employees owing to the international travel restrictions. It would result in the software cycle disruption by increasing the frequency of scope checks, defect correction (on the user end) and delays in final output. However if strong management teams can keep these aspects in check and reduce the risk of project holds by using robust IT governance models then the sector might emerge more adept at handling challenges in the post covid world, even gaining some market valuations both for clients and vendors. However the investments are expected to fall in the sector because companies are reluctant to spend much on outsourcing, they want to expand in-house IT capabilities existing but ignored by and large till now due to time bound software requirements better addressed by the external experts. Now is the time to train internal teams and get going with the development of software essential for business thereby saving costs or building up strengths to become future vendors for other firms in case the employees are able to garner specialised skills of the market. Blockchain, SAP modules, AI, blue prism, AA, UI path, AWS, full-stack programming, BI, reporting, python, devops, Java, selenium, dotnet, ASP, PMP, DBA, digital marketing, ruby and php networks are some of the popular software mechanisms, programming languages, tools and methods for the modern world to be equipped with the capabilities of coding and developing packages for business process implementation and business unit growth by uptodate automation.

State of Energy sector

World War II army general George Patton suggested that if we tell people what to do instead of how, we would be surprised with their results.

Pressures on energy transition are building as usage in the volumes of fuel goes up in industry, individual lifestyle and recycling or regeneration activities. The high costs of generation, storage, reuse, disposal and recycling are the next goals of research to understand what needs to be done to improve consumer journey through energy transition. Energy usage, billing mechanism and accessibility are points for continued exercise of optimization. Right from the morning coffee preparation to reaching office to a resting sleep overnight, energy is utilized in different modes round the clock by every citizen of the world. No activities can be completed without any application of energy as electricity, fuel, gas, power or otherwise. We replicate natural energy when we are using fans to generate wind energy by applying electricity into the devices. Technology adoption to support multiple conversion of energy without wasting its sources is a need of the hour. Energy consumption in the corona world is on a rise at homes, hospitals and public venues. Post-corona world is going to see more demand for energy in offices, isolated transportation or extra sterilization of resources as preventive measures.

Future energy sector is banking upon the use of renewable resources along with new uses of recycled waste. Corona aftermath includes destruction of Amazon forests that have been adversely affected by the virus according to WEF, in terms of vastly spreading forest fire (whether by virus or changing climate, it's not less than a threat to environment). The black sludge emitted from forest fire, recently in Arizona, is poisoning the environment, and measures are needed to divert the flow to uninhabited areas. It poses threat to the fertility of soil, existence of insects, survival of animals, birds and humans and growth of meadows in the nearby locations. It has further increased the frequency of forest fires and depletion has reduced the natural resources to add to the woes of increasing carbon dioxide emissions. Electric vehicles can reduce CO_2 footprint. Carbon residues are exciting companies like Lafarge, Dalmia, GFG, in aluminum, chemical, steel and cement industries while exploring options for building alternate energy sources. Financial and regulatory arrangements are needed for investing in the new low carbon economy. Technology collaboration besides that between interrelated industries can enable build a collective vision in energy transition of achieving gains in agility and scale. Carbon emissions range from the tune of 30 to 36 giga tonnes globally. Net zero emission scenario is no easy transition objective but we have to aim at heating the policy acceleration by tax mechanics to travel in the direction of reduction in direct and indirect emissions. Greenhouse gas emissions if not managed will heat up the planet before long. Decarbonization journey is led by industry leaders as a challenge without disturbing the integrated value chains while implementation of strategy at company level. Petrochemical internal combustion using raw material should be replaced by green energy or other technology allowing neutral carbon footprint. Process improvement with new technology is a need to recapture carbon or electricity reuse to compress carbon. Power sourcing and recycling are studied to improve the quality of carbon. Steel is working on the issue of rising global energy consumption by measures in recycling, managing use of hydrogen, renewable resources and cutting costs of global usages. Fossil fuel solutions in carbon capture, storage and use by incentivising technology transition are motivating industry collaboration. Demand has to be built within the value chain by working on public procurement, carbon pricing and decision making activities. Carbon usage in oil and gas, geological storage (needs social acceptance), demineralization, cement and other industries requires more collaboration in collective R&D for analysing the global potential. Licenses have to be built across the industry before entering into partnership or joint initiatives.

Storage is a concern of the future and we want to move beyond lithium ions that can not store for longer than a few hours. Solar and wind energy sources have to be stored to convert to electricity. Alternatives are studied for low cost options. Manufacturing techniques and economies of scale have brought down the price. Competition depends on flow batteries with reduced risks of leakage of power thus increasing capacity. Zinc bromine storage is gaining demand. ESS is providing low cost technology to energy companies across the globe. Some companies are looking at pumped hydro technology using huge volumes of water but it comes with disruption of the environment. Hundreds of megawatts of capacity is added by this method (96% use is met). Other companies are on storage of solar and wind energy to be converted to electricity later when needed. Hydrostor converts excess electricity into compressed air for use in future. Phenomenal investments are required in the areas of geothermal and biomass to 'combine-innovate' the two for radical generation of energy.

Seawater desalination (more than 350 billion billion gallons) is expected to solve the water crisis in the world. Removing salt by thermal (boiling and converting steam to fresh water) desalination or reverse osmosis could provide drinkable safe water. Huge energy investment makes it costly to build infrastructure to break up the salts and water. Plants have started inviting private capital in the USA. Reverse osmosis produces 50% freshwater and rest is brine that can cause havoc to sea plants. Brine disposal is still an issue. Repeated desalination is a future option but then we have to think of disposal of salt dunes building as residues. It is a tool to solve the water crisis. Simultaneously we should reduce water wastage and find ways to recycle water with more efficient use (10 times more water can be recovered than desalination). Climate change should evolve new ways to solve water scarcity. Medical research should additionally come up with disinfectants to purify water making it free of disease causing pathogens.

Innovation is possible in the generation of power by combination of iron and salt water, using the electricity later for more productive purposes of desalination itself or purification of recycled water. A lot of work is needed before it is accepted as a healthy green solution for the world of post corona crisis. Clean and green is a more than profitable global philosophy to get cheaper sources of energy but a lot of support is needed for long term investment from developing countries. Developed countries have to share the costs in higher ratios. Policy makers should embed the costs in the initial process to avoid pressure on supply and demand.

Nuclear power can be encouraged to be another source of energy generation but we have to study the complete environmental impact. Nuclear power in future clean energy space is expected to be accepted more for fusion (energy is released when hydrogen combines to form helium like in the sun and other stars) and fission (energy is released by the splitting of atoms but not that preferred by scientists) options though quite expensive. This is to fill the gap when the sun is set or wind is not blowing. Business and economy can look at fusion as a viable electricity generation alternative to attract profitable investment. Compressors of high quality will be required by nuclear power plants to pulse the steam and liquid ions on and on. Trillion dollar energy market has players like General Fusion, Lebarge, Lawrence Livermore, Lockheed Martin, deploying huge plants equal to the size of a hundred thousand homes. They are expected to be breaking even and self sustaining not before 20-30 years of research experiments.

The future of healthy energy lies in solar power utilization. Let's have a look at a brief case study to understand the (im)practicalities.

Solar Energy - A Case for Household or Small Business

Solar energy is a renewable energy and is a potential source of energy for future home and office power requirements. However, you have to be aware of some problems with solar panels (White, 2013-14).

We installed solar panels for energy in the kitchen, backyard and bathrooms. The panels are fixed in open spaces where there is a lot of sunlight during the day.

1. The first major problem starts here in the rainy season. On the days when it rains, the panels don't work well as solar energy is not stored properly; rather, some of the existing amount is released into the thin air as vapor. Our panels got installed on the terrace and garden. The panels capture solar energy and convert it in times of need or when we switch on the solar inverter. The connection can be automated for use in times of power-cuts so that the solar energy powers the bulbs and fans in some rooms of the house.

2. The resale value of a house reduces and the mortgaging problems may arise due to the rashes on roof slopes. A lot of house-buyers skip houses with solar panels because they don't want roofs in ugly condition. The panels do get overloaded on the roof-tops and leave damages for sure while installing. Rain water may even seep through the roof tops.

3. Install solar panels with a lot of patience. The return on investment is low. You need to invest more than $15000 and you get about $1000 return in the form of savings on electricity bill and for leasing solar power to state enterprises to some extent. It takes 15-20 years to recover the gains.

4. There are legal commitments about installing panels, maintenance of solar panels, leasing terms and home owners must consider long-term implications after consulting their legal advisors. Buy from branded sellers with substantial warranty (25 years), authentic certification like TUV IEC 61215 and make sure that you get efficient inverters to avoid energy wastage.

Get planning permissions and building regulation certificates in place. Don't take much heat!

Analysis of costs, benefits, equipment maintenance, space or installation requirements, constraints and other aspects involved in the industrial and household use of applying various forms of energy, could help us unearth alternative applications or productive uses thereon.

It depends on us how we could combine the different forms of energy sources for restoring economic health in industries and societies.

Electronic future

Bard of Avon, Shakespeare implied in a verse that we feel ourselves to be cursed that we are responsible to set it right when time is out of joint.

Electronic industries are in a debilitating phase and in need of a chance. Innovation might be of help.

Innovative multimedia equipment should be made available to support multi dimensional views at home. We should be able to watch a 3-D movie at home instead of going to a theatre. The current technology does not enable total adaptability to 3D movies even after wearing the earphones or eyesets. Google launched simple 3D real time graphics during the corona lockdown period, whereby kids can also click a snap with the shark at home. Alexa mini pods could be improved on inclusion of 3D techniques for enhanced user experience.

Multimedia devices are smartphones but today's palm sized phones may be in more than TV sized fixed devices at home and office to go back in time when we are on terms with miniaturization after fighting against the issues of space, portability and complexity in large devices. Still big Washing machines exist for the clothes and dishes, large stoves can't be done away with if we want to cook for groups and large devices for men will become no less than common soon. The portability and mobility would persist in the form of all accessories like a more than handy headset or invisible audio filters to allow the hearing of conversation by the recipient of the call and not anybody else except for the caller. The Herculean task can be achieved with radical innovation by extending biometric techniques to eye, ear and voice recognition, only my voice will be conveyed to a caller, data will be shown to my eyes only (by retina or iris or other unique identification), information will be made audible only to my ears (by association with ear drums or other receptors in ears) and system will be able to derive instant factors of differentiation among human beings. The inputs typed by me alone would be accepted in documents, not by whoever logs into the system. These and more changes are expected to arrive in electronic equipment of post crisis tomorrow not due to corona but due to a massive wave of change asking us to be prepared to work from anywhere, live without giving up the technological luxury and without touching much of the devices (how many times would we remember to wash hands?), so better leave everything at one place like home or office and move with a wrist band or other unique identifier like a code or password to be allowed to use a system. The home music system technology is a recipient of commands of family members by voice recognition or another friend who would have to say a pass code and start playing songs. Another key change in using a healthy coating of virus preventing chemicals on the holding areas of all electronic equipment is a welcome thing. Systems generating auto warning of user health failure, initial virus symptoms and risk of falling sick would be sought after changes to have in the electronics industry of tomorrow. The new feature will be more from the side of the devices without any request or initiatives from the user, or other family members can ask for the complete information about wherever the user goes, including data on the topics unknown to the users, the family members might not know what to ask about the mode of transportation because they don't know that the city has only bicycles to ride. The electronic system on the bicycle will connect with the home system to inform family and the user that it may affect the new cardiac surgery performed on the user.

The trend of miniaturization is thus taking a different direction. The cars can't be shrunken but their electronic technology can be. The new developments in the future electronics industry can convert a single car into a house, office, or hospital with all amenities. You can make a call without having a separate device. You can cook food in the inbuilt microwave. You can complete the office work by logging via secure remote working protocols. If you fall sick, immediate assistance can be provided in first aid or minor surgery might be performed on you by the robotic doctor system built within the car. We have to be more than independent in the technology and daily use of electronic equipment, in the wake of isolation or quarantine lessons learnt in the corona lockdown. It is a more distant route but not as difficult as it sounds. Multi utility electronic technology is a healthy innovative business goal of tomorrow. Drones are catching on manufacturing volumes but not on application. We have to know how best to use the new electronic devices, here more than 50% global gadgets users don't know how to use their device beyond a limited set of requirements or other such uses discovered in serendipity. We have to demonstrate the entire set of capabilities by preparing entertaining movies on the extraction of all functions from the devices and some things possible in future. User manual is meant to be thrown in a bin but not a movie. Drones can be used in express delivery of parcels, advanced high speed drones can be flown for cross border delivery, under surveillance and regulations. As we have extended the capabilities of smartphone to camera, similar fate is assigned to drones that are used for shooting videos. Some countries like Israel and Canada are using drones for irrigation purposes by sprinkling pesticides, water, monitoring plant growth but not as plucking agents for fruits or harvesting agents for grains that we are dependent on for manual intervention. As ad hoc measure drones can be in a more than assigned job of driving away the pests or insects ruining the crop. It is a mandatory thing or rather should be, for companies to spend an equal participation time as users in analysis of all possible uses of discovered technologies. We can have an overflow of innovative gadgets if we are unable to put them to use in various activities of our life. It's upon us to explore and exploit the vastly innovative business of the electronics industry. Growth is a must in terms of user feedback, because we are on the new peaks of sales every time to saturate volume growth by users who are all willing to spend money on procuring new devices on the shelves. Government schemes in promoting industry by incentives for starting new plants and factories in economically backward areas can revive the sector in the post lockdown operations, if companies are wise enough today in preparing themselves with innovative product ideas for tomorrow, thereby increasing employment in both skilled and unskilled labor. Green innovation should be the goal of companies to reduce emissions and chemical wastes from the electronics plant facilities.

Electronics industry is a supplier to automotive, personal electronics, communications equipment, industrial electronics, enterprise systems, semiconductors and memory storage. The allied sectors have fallen victim to falling sales except communications (Fig 2).

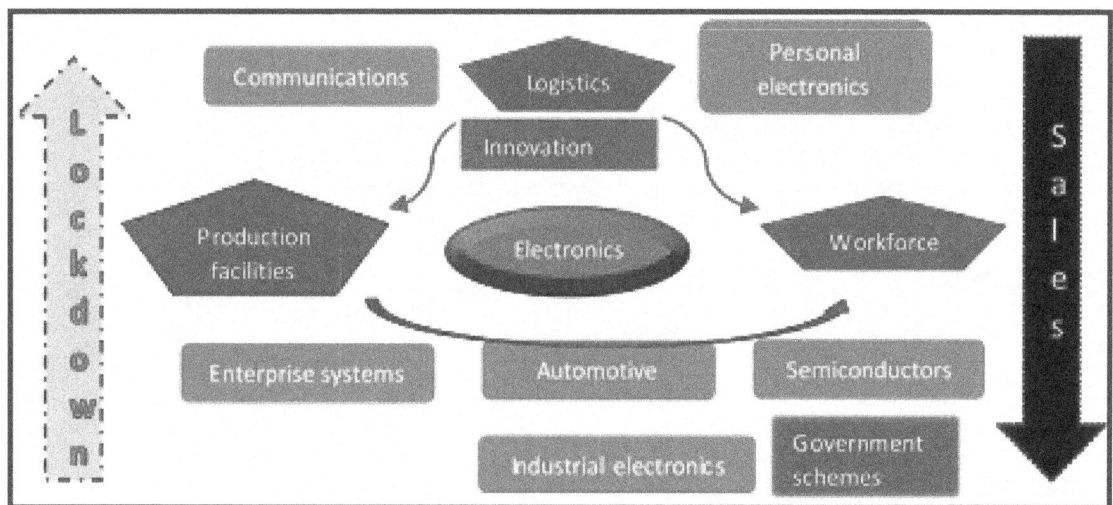

Fig 2: Electronics industry

The communications segment is on a slight increase of 5% in the beginning of the corona crisis and during the intermittent lifting of lockdown, due to increased activity in the media. Personal electronics is the most affected segment of corona crisis times. Being a non essential category the sales are falling sharply (more than 20%) in Italy, France, Russia, Spain, USA, India, Germany and Canada due to closure of shops and markets during the lockdown. Trade deficits may be contributed by the sector in post covid countries. Foreign trade has seen a steep fall in the covid times. Cross border tensions will impact trade with countries like USA and India cutting down imports from China in the covid era. Post corona situation might also not work in favor of foreign trade because countries have not yet finalised the penalty and mainly reduced the exim volumes. Production facilities have been shut down, labor is not available, logistics have slowed down and new product launches are suspended. Leaders like Apple, Samsung, Sony, Toshiba and Canon have been affected by the crisis so there is little doubt that small companies are preparing to either shut down, or collaborate with larger players or enter into acquisitions in the post covid period of business revival.

Semiconductors and memory storage

Fitzgerald had expressed that the fallout from the Asian currency crisis would lead to steep cuts in capital spending by leaders in Japanese, Korean and Taiwanese industries.

The Corona crisis does not come for rubbles though it has hounded the economy to rouble making all the nations bite dust of time. It is expected to cost the economy more than $45-65 trillion globally (or at least $20b by the most conservative estimates) by the end of year 2020, as estimated from the UN calculated number that reached $7.8 trillion at the end of April 2020, given that the global economic loss was $40b after the 2001 SARS where Covid made its first appearance in the 21st century. Industry growth overall, is expected to fall below 2% for 2020 and the $500b semiconductor sector has been slowing less than the industry average. It has slowed down from 2018 owing to rising costs of procurement of raw material, infrastructural capabilities, laboratory tests and regulatory pressures.

The memory storage is a key subsector totally dependent on innovation or it gets outdated faster than any other product. Global demand for the industry output comes from all electronic devices companies (laptops, vehicles, smartphones, watches, wifi, telecomm, etal) and met by the likes of Broadcom, Qualcomm, Toshiba, Texas Instruments, Samsung, Intel, Micron, AMD and many others. The fall in pricing and more competitive supply in a struggling global economy might work against the new growth goals of the sector.

A more than miniaturization drive is no new thing in the sector with the nexgen memory storage fighting space in cached and primary memories. RAM and DRAM form crucial part of the industry sales. ROM is in need for dynamic digital innovation to short term memory enhancement. Password security is expected to be replaced by biometric in the future but it is going to take some time.

Though optimistic in projection at more than 10% by the Semiconductor Industry Association (SIA), industry growth is no misnomer due to Covid-19 impact of increasing gaming, ecommerce, virtual learning and work from home activities followed by strong demand from data centers, cloud centers, servers and computing segments. Another sector is media and entertainment that we expect to grow by the crisis more than in normal time. New business models after the corona lockdown period may emphasize that we centralize the technology. Though seen as black swan event, the short term challenge in the corona crisis still poses a risk to the long term growth prospect of leaders due to emerging small players supplying low cost output to customers. In the post corona world, a lot of foundries may have to shut down the operations in the wake of disrupted supply chain activities. Innovation in power, functionality and experience might demand larger reinvestment of revenues into R&D (more than 25%) by the companies in the USA, Japan, South Korea, China, et al for maximizing productivity, or improving time-to-market.

Innovation (maybe consolidation too in this case) is a healthy driver of the industry and more is needed in the space of Dram, motherboard chip circuit, embedded microprocessors, network interface controllers, ICs (design & validation), solid state drives, flash memory, optical sensors, Enterprise software, controllers, graphics cards, 6G and beyond the boundaries of semiconductor technology. Innovative means of disposal of wastes from heavy metals, alkalis, acids, toxic and hazardous organic and inorganic chemicals used in the semiconductor companies pose environmental problems. Acceptance is needed, to reuse ultrapure deionized water, acids and recovered chemicals with the help of biofilters and biotrickling filters, coagulation, biosorption, bioremediation, and phytoremediation techniques, as possible methods for disposal of toxic sludge. Environmental issues can not be ignored and alternative efficiency solutions (e.g. using sulphur trioxide, photonic crystal, vapor deposition) have to be proposed. Global warming potential is high for the industry and collaboration between governments and companies is needed for diminishing the side effects of emissions, implementation of waste directives, process optimization, alternative chemistries, point of operation cleaning, recycling and abatement. Future could witness green advancements (to reduce engineering costs and improve performance) in equipment, new materials, microoptics, nanotechnology, micro fabrication, modeling and design techniques, new process node adoption, genetic algorithm optimization, polarization devices, wafer handling, carrier handling, wafer processing, vacuum application, metallic impurities absorption methods in the frontend, and sealing from contamination in the back end. Majority of the market opportunities for semiconductor technology lie in the acceleration of the AI, machine learning and Internet of things (IoT) domain in the new smart cities and devices, smart medicine, autonomous vehicles and smart everything world. We have to accept that the manufacturing processes or protocols are complex or siloed but the capital expenditure requirement for increasing existing capacity is much less than that required in building new capacity. Omnipotent efforts are needed for facing the post corona challenge of capacity increase, yield improvement, tool performance, complete supply chain innovation, reliability, sophisticated integration flows, better contamination control, product roadmap tracking, top quality standards, etc towards showing differentiation and social responsibility.

Competition strategy in supporting customers to solve business challenges, leverage data analytics, change management, workflow management, strategic business alignment or digital transformation strategy, can only help create new technology leaders by customer retention, revenue boosts, brand bolstering in the semiconductor segment of future decades.

Corona aftermath is no less than a storm and might include insufficient documentation, inconsistent data, unskilled or outdated employees, disconnected value chain participants, compliance complications, eroded brand reputation or quality issues. This is applicable for all industries and not semiconductor companies only.

Build a healthy culture of quality enthusiasts and work with strategic partners to build appropriate technology infrastructure (along disruptive processes, trained people, skilled persons, data intelligence, positive brand recognition, sound business decisions, and people commitment).

Semiconductor industry is no less than a pathfinder given the expansion of digitization all across the world. Increasing application in solar industries can propel more reliable miniaturized solutions in aggressive chemical environments. It is a leading supplier for players in big data and machine learning. More dynamic attention by pulling tactics in agility is needed in embedded vision, life cycle support for the product ecosystem, process migration, or else ROI can fall drastically. The non-memory market is expected to follow a slower growth trajectory than the memory segment. The new threat lies in disconnected supplier networks. Security is both a challenge and opportunity, companies should look for sustainability hence before monetizing silicon and services. Mergers and acquisitions could drive revenue growth in the near term but eroding ASPs pose unsuspecting risk to companies that are looking at PaaS (Platform as a Service) to offer customers an easy, remote and secure way of working with applications without investing in complex infrastructure.

A more open and collaborative role is envisaged for the future to grow the semiconductor industry by proactive interaction with customers.

Insurance

Kempthorne argued that the government alone could not solve our problems with correctional facilities, treatment centres, homeless shelters and crisis centres, we would need our faith based and community partners.

In future, the insurance industry has to restructure itself to be more responsive to the global health turmoil because corona did not wait for government policy reform. The disease took away the financial muscle of the world so who would expect individuals to be any different? Many lives that were lost due to the corona disease could not get insurance benefit because organizations would not make gains. Now new insurance schemes are flying out with the greed of turning around profit. Governments have to instruct insurance players to be more 'humanistic' than materialistic. Feedback from USA to Indonesia to Africa to Greece, all indicate that every insurance company levies a whole lot of hell-revoking complex paperwork, proof circus and bribe hegemony when it comes to the question of paying back to people for suffering the loss. Simple logic says that a loss is no gain if done deliberately or beyond the rules of the book. The real thieves escape anyway thereby paving way to large scale economic blackouts and genuine defaulters will have to be punished without a thought. The humming of Acts does not help a common man , maybe the insurance company official can rant knowledgeably in front of the celebrities or well-to-do intellectuals , when they come to claim. In the first place they don't need insurance because they have more money to take precautions, second thing is that they know how to protect their hard earned or easy inherited money. If the government faces the constant risk of being cheated by the public, the public is equally vulnerable to the private players in the insurance industry. Agreed that everyone thrives in risk, now is the time to pay for any and every risk arising from national pandemic that brings to knees mobility, employment, health and education. The pandemic has relocated millions, housing insurance needs to be provided in the world governments taking a lead to ensure that each and every person whether local or foreigner has a shelter. If not, give them insurance, a house, a job, maybe as an insurance agent to pay for the favor. It's better if insurance agents are trained to be more interactive and visit the insurance buyers enquiring about the well-being, understanding their limitations while observing untoward situation propping up, this offers a two way operational flexibility, one is to identify and prevent loss by knowledge based warning, an official agent could control fire damage by asking the housewife to shift her car from parking under an electric pole to a safe place. Any deliberate cheating attempt could also be punished. The second thing is to assist the loss bearer in recording, claiming and recovering the damage because we would not be normal and free of tension when something goes wrong or when our insured car gets stolen. The claim conversion and recovery rate will have to be 100% when the global average is much less than 50%. The man is born free so let him act free without waiting for the damage or restricting his happiness under the fear of damage because we are not new to the risk or danger inherent in the disease and other warnings of universal nature (we know how to walk in the traffic ridden road). Don't ignore the numbers but from the global citizen point of view, not from the global CEO point of view. As an MBA I want to get bonuses by cutting down the global company expenses and not paying back to insurance buyers is no less than saving cost. But the chaos and stress built by the disease could also lead to avoidance of insurance industry by the buyer for saving face, time, personal costs, transactional hassles or disappointment. Some countries claim that their insurance system is foolproof and their companies assure that buyers have everything to gain but things take u- turn after a loss is claimed.

Corona tests should be jointly sponsored by government and insurance companies, diagnosed patients should be the responsibility of insurance companies until the patients are completely cured because they would not be interested in getting infected with the disease to take advantage of insurance nor enjoy the hospitality of the hospitals. Another way is to auto-insure citizens of all countries as a preemptive measure to provide assurance in the global corona mess. The sense of belonging that comes to the world population can only promote economic revival by boosting the governmental morale. It encourages not only the government to act with vigor but also the other groups across the world to cooperate with solidarity in tandem with the individual and industry goal of restoring things to normalcy.

Insurance industry, believe me, we are not for extras, should be able to provide food insurance to jobless, salary or wage insurance to farmers with field loss, job insurance to the school dropouts, life insurance to the diseased as not to be deceased, with or without corona. As a life coach, I want to accept that not every citizen wants to be illiterate, unemployed, sick or loser, those who are, would not disappoint you if you lend a helping hand otherwise they would not escape self ruin even if you provide facilities of the world. As a business group you can only promote profitable firms by cultivation of trust, innovative flexible premium products, post insurance premium products (provide low interest loan insurance to the students and they'd not default on the payments after getting a job earned from the graduating college). It may be a better idea for companies to issue catastrophe bonds (like corona bonds) with a slightly higher premium partly funded by the local government to enable a lump sum to the customers after a defined duration or occurrence of calamity or loss of the life whichever is earlier.

New ideas can be elicited from the smart insurance professionals community for development of the insurance sector because this is the most crucial industry in the post lockdown/corona revival of global industry. The first thing that applies to the corona lockdown or any crisis is insurance whether individual (in a health crisis) or economic (in lockdown or business crisis slowdown). Hence the next to next leap would be to support the start-up insurance to help them grow after a slowdown in the absence of which the companies would have grown their employee size to increase the business of insurance!

Banking

Henry Ford said that winning the trust of customers was like winning the hearts of customers, and that he would make affordable cars to be in every common man's assets.

Trust is the most important factor to build the entire cycle of banking operations hit by the catastrophe whether commercial or capital markets.

Holding onto technology and not judging anymore will work to be in favor of banking though the basics are questioned in terms of borrowing and lending. Supply chain and demand factors on the customer end make a huge difference to the banks. Business is trying to get going into the future post corona era. Law and order, taxation regime and policy have to be revisited for more flawless implementation because profit and money making are not the criteria of institutions anymore, at least 2-5 years will be the time to restore the industry growth after the massive corona crisis. Evaluation of business takes backseat and rebuilding of client relationships is on the placards floating in front of small businesses and large institutional clients alike. The customers have to restore their sales strategy in boosting the revenue in the post lockdown period. The time is worst for the banking sector as pointed out by analysts, despite the government stimulus, because penetration is no easy one. Execution and communication in the digital world are keys to facilitate our global banking health that so far has been growing around technology initiatives though not without adherence to compliance.

Innovation in future would have to bring out new alternative modes of payment beyond cash and bitcoins. Something in between will work well in the next era banking. Opportunities will find collaboration with customers if we can provide security and liquidity with the single right product that will withstand the changes and pressures of crisis. Information and data related infrastructure are needed more than any other things to smoothen the nexgen banking curves. Digital infrastructure is no less than restructuring given limitations of paperwork, concerns of customers and high costs that can not be passed onto the customers. Investment levels may also thus need a healthy rise in conjunction with green banking initiatives.

It is important for the banking sector to take a lead in helping create a healthy credit flow in the economy and the financial markets. The economic situation is not uncorrelated when it comes to Banking, MSMEs, Farming, Telecom and other related dependent industries. One can not be prescriptive but only look for signals. Global ratings won't make much difference to the post lockdown world. Long term patience (not patients) is a must in the banking sector to be able to make sound profitable investments. Banking personnel should suggest more acquisition strategies than starting new business by the customers because then they don't need to fund out of the pockets but find funding sources for structured deals where banks can make their margin. Partner trouble, diversification objectives, cash flow issues or other personal reasons can get good businesses sold so that you can bring improvements to the bought business by using established business practices or strategies. It is also projected that companies in the post corona world will aim at 8-10% growth for covering the crisis losses and that banks will enter into creation of more structured finance for the deals arising out of decisions and measures related to cutting high operating leverage, large institutions can survive better though the basic activities can pick up soon. More than 10% of the economy will be left non functional in the post corona times and is in need of revival. The woes of all the other sectors in the economy could flow down to banking with the cost of funding coming down as well. Uncertainty in global regulations and decision making can tell the strong companies to stay overweight in the best interest of the banking sector.

Nothing can be truer than truth. Developed and developing countries are not different anymore in the post Anthropause era because both categories of nations have to work on creative structuring with new ways of financing, negotiating and profit making. The banking sector is resting on the principle of nurturing a financial capability that we can think of as the backbone of all economic growth. Companies should cooperate in terms of controlled expenditures, healthy debt equity ratios and other relevant financials. Instead of depending on banks for the last minute bankruptcy solutions, industries can be better off in following financial checks without challenging whole market action and waiting for the punitive effects on the economy.

With low growth, debt to GDP rate will rise in most of the nations unless de- risking and refueling of the economy (though the US Fed's act of pumping money into the economy does not seem to help much) come to the rescue in the wake of a failing forecast of demand. Base the price on tradable commodities like oil to get clarity in the post crisis banking world. Doubtless to assume that we are up for billions of dollars of losses, extra costs and high risk capital loss, followed by NPA rises that have to be aided by payroll funding, food provision to labor and lower taxes in future. Corporates, governments and banks have to come together if we want to get new solutions for supporting the failing companies in the economies. Though not logical but a coincidence in NBFCs omitting the current mistake scenario, banks can escape big shock of post corona economic failure by bonding with the bond markets that we can see sending positive signals (not much liquidity loss) though asset class quality will have to be reviewed. The more modern effects of corona lockdown can be seen in banking swings towards microfinance that is a reversal of the normal time trend, rise in securitization deal and PTC deals assisted partly by regulatory measures. Yield compression will continue though banks are quality cautious before considering NBFCs (some could raise debt and equity capital during the corona lockdown) to be the clientele. The reasons could lie in the small to medium to large size or fear of apocalypse like a double edged sword with corona following the collapse of DHFL to threaten the banking sector with similar financial failure (AA companies are also able to access the markets).

Real estate parody

Judy Smith, like John F Kennedy, believed that there was always an opportunity with a crisis, to force a company to re-examine its policies and practices and to force an individual to look inside himself.

A lot of momentum is present in the housing market more than the stock market but we carry forecasts from the latter. Housing markets have very high traction and transaction cost, little research or data collection is no easy, price indexes get little relevant information, behavior of repeat sales index is not monitored as it is not available. Enormous swings with irrational movement is expected in the real estate prices, demand and supply in the post Covid industry. There is no opportunity for smart money in the form of shorting houses nor futures in the real estate market. Quality of houses may rise without any capital gains and this is no surprise because the case has been the same across the globe for decades. People would want more housing because migrants are going back. Single family homes might come to futures markets or trade in price index markets but we need more liquidity that need more trading again.

Home price hedging and risk management tactics are bound to emerge in home price fluctuations to manage crises in future. Home equity insurance beyond fire bases home value protection against neighborhood price changes and awareness needs to be spread among people to be concerned more about home price than fire damage. Negative net worth can then be avoided provided trading takes off by institutional and other investors.

Post lockdown period demand, supply and price trends in the real estate market would be more volatile than the stock market. Trend reverting is expected to object constant price changes in one direction because property price fall or rise alone contains risk of market prediction. The real estate sector is as vulnerable to pandemic as other sectors facing risks. Prices are expected to decline due to changes in the prices of raw materials (better alternatives like fibre at cheap costs), changing technologies (easy availability reducing manual labor costs) used in the construction and change in customers' demand patterns in the post pandemic season.

Innovation in smart homes , energy efficient kitchens and rooms, and low carbon emissions may give better deals in the post crisis world to customers who are expected to increase demand for housing for future security of their families, still the global prices are expected to fall about 10% due to the covid19 effect on the real estate sector. Digital virtual 3D housing demos and online interactions would replace the personal rental agent interactions or the owner visits for intermittent inspection. More purchases would be made by depending on online data and less frequent visits by buyer, so far buyers used to have a personal visit to their plot sites at least 3 times and a house at least 5 times before making the final deal after which the customers visit the construction site as many times needed for customization of the house based on their preferences for room alterations or other house modifications, the latter part would be replaced by virtual monitoring until the final occupancy is granted when the relocation would take place in person. Paper work would be replaced completely by the online deal registration and digital payment mechanisms. Demonetisation, RERA and GST changes have been squashing the sector for the last five years with the developers facing a total of 19-24% fall in prices in India from the past decade. The real estate developers are required to drop their prices especially if they have taken loans for financing ventures. US norms have eased the borrowing for house buyers in the wake of the Corona crisis. The interest rates are expected to see a slight fall in the post covid era. Stoppage of production in allied industries like iron and steel is slowing down the real estate sector a bit more. Commercial property may see a continued investment with a fall in the volume or amount of investment in the latter years. Russia is heading for a slump due to the oil spill. Italy is into recession and so is Europe. Shattered conditions of Spain and Canada don't offer bright growth to real estate. Residential property segment is expected to see a rise in the future because you need to have homes to remain indoors under crisis lockdowns. Unemployment is on the rise in the real estate sector all over the world according to an Economic Times report. Raw material prices, approval conundrums, labor costs and technological inclusions in real estate form a set of parameters majorly dependent on economic development because we don't want to resend the economy into a mortgage led crisis or recession again though the effect of double recession is seen on each and every nation of the globe, in fact trickling triple effect of tricking recession from 2001 SARS Covid economy failure to 2008 mortgage based slowdown to 2020 Covid19 economic lockdown is hard to forget and resolve but nations have to go on saving their economies from sinking down because global economic development is not one country's growth nor dependent on USA alone, it a cumulative result of over 170 nations' effort and collaboration alone can get back economy on tracks. Before the end of two decades, we have seen at least three major depression events on the global economy, which wont mistake our rational expectations carried forward from the 1997 Asian financial flu that sent the tremors to the developed economies. The country risk premium has been rising for nations that are direct victims or originators of any particular pandemic, like the post first world war spanish flu that killed more than 40 million people in 1918-19 worldwide. Post COVID economy is ready to accommodate a forward looking intertemporal behavior of economists as well as consumers who are seeking relief from the epidemic while preparing themselves to save the economy in their own ways.

Government has to form innovative joint ventures with the top real estate players to avoid the unruly or undue emergence or monopoly led by the unorganised sector because today buyers are willing to deal with the seller directly or a single estate agent instead of going through the branded agents or sellers taking a whole lot of time consuming process and prices. If the seller has clear documentation the buyer won't mind closing the deal without waiting for the frills offered by the real estate barons. Buyers want to purchase a house by making the first instalment and loaning the remaining so that they get a ready occupation in the Corona affected world. This is not without the risk of price bubbles due to demand generation for short term cycles of sporadic activity in the sector.

Innovation in the sector includes use of aluminium and other metal support structures filled with concrete so that the robustness remains same as that of traditional pillar erection in deep ground. The advantages lie in saving time without waiting for weather conditions, and removing the uneven brick outlays to be set right by spreading extra concrete. Earlier pillars could not be erected if soils were not favorable in the rainy season or otherwise. Metal and scrap waste can be processed and put into use by construction companies thereby reducing the resource inefficiency. Such walls are easy to maintain and don't crack or leak like traditional brick cement walls. With the use of robotics as constructors, houses could be built within days instead of months, reducing the time to few hours in future assignments. The quality is quite good as tried in some countries but the capacity to withstand natural disasters must be tested, robotics has to ensure that the house or office built by automatic machines would not collapse in rain, hurricane, earthquakes or calamities. Such victory of transferring human work to robotics would not bring tears of employers losing jobs because of the high quality output generated by machines; and skilled employers can be taught machine learning or other things useful in making progress along innovative projects besides analyzing data for bringing improvements in future.

Kids industry segments

A radical crisis challenges the old ways of being in the world, of interacting with one another as well as the realm of nature, to threaten survival by insurmountable problems. Like Darwin,

Eckhart stated that Life forms would either become extinct or rise above the limitations of their condition through an evolutionary leap.

Physical distancing and not social distancing is the proposed solution for corona pandemonium. Kids are becoming increasingly outrageous for having to give up the company of children and to bear the constant watch of elders in homes. Online workshops in coding and robotics are not able to fill in the fears and time of children in the pandemonium. According to our research data (conducted by the Consultant team of Tietoz), growth in the kids sector is expected to be more than 4% in 2020. Post corona lockdown should be seen as an opportunity for addressing the problems of kids in terms of additional initiatives to give education and entertainment in equal measure. One thing essential for children growing in dire poverty is the provision of food, followed by emotional support and other things needed for full fledged healthy living otherwise brain development could be adversely affected. Kids become smarter than earlier generations and we need to get initiatives in cognitive development besides giving nutritional value to balance the future capabilities of kids so that they become responsible in handling their strengths and weaknesses. We have a great responsibility for working with character strengthening in the children as global citizens of tomorrow. Children have to feel better and not blinded by the systems teaching them how to live. They have to learn to give besides making money. Training methods are mostly adopted from the eastern cultures to understand attention and concentration aspects. What is needed in the post corona world is working with the dynamic of emotion. Tomorrow the economy can grow if today children learn the power of relationship. Social and emotional learning should become part of the study curriculum for furthest personality development right from childhood. Skill deficit should not be exploited by pharmaceutical companies in prescribing drugs to children who have acceptability to several other alternative solutions like emotional support, group or team activity, cultural intelligence and gameplay involvement. Circumstances reveal the state of mind to the fullest extent and global data suggests that the kids are doing well and fast. They have a capacity to see what's right and not what's wrong. They are more caring than believed to be, motivating people to stay indoors and not risk their lives by going out, as observed in the viral videos of corona lockdown.

In fact children teach us to calm down and manage our world better. Games, toys, entertainment, clothing, confectionery, food, and other intermingling industries levy a chance to give more importance to kids' segments than adults'. From both hygiene and medical perspectives we have to grow our economy by resolution of ALL problems of children before moving on with that of industries. Nutrition, mortality, clothing, schooling, entertainment, housing, healthcare and urban facilities have to be made accessible to all the children under teens across the globe if you have a genuine interest in global economic development. I would personally prefer to consider the 50% or more population under 25 to be children but for feasibility sake we can afford to ignore even the teens and aim at energizing the bud stage of children in newborns, infants and kids under 13. Formative years have a social responsibility for us to get kids growing up well. It's quite relevant for all parts of the world, east side needs more physical nutrition, west side needs more emotional nutrition for children of the global economy. Corona lockdown teaches us to feed the children with milk and other things boosting the immune system but who's taking the responsibility of the destitute community? Companies will not lose anything if all children stop consuming candy, coke and cake. Children will lose everything if they're deprived of basic amenities. Should Kraft turn into a child NGO? True in any sense. Anthropause should not be exploited to stop child development at restarting economic development. It's not possible to get children to grow up in a debilitating economy, likewise, it's not possible to grow our economy without ensuring complete growth of children. As any other parents, you might be feeding your kids well, keeping up with hygiene requirements, treating any ill health, teaching them to pray and play, and monitoring their progress in life and school. Gender discrimination and child labour ought to be prohibited by law or the national governments should prepare for the economic wreck. Corona has given us time to rethink and reimagine the future of children, globally. Let's do our best. Companies should start growing children to help grow industries and further it to economic development. It may sound weird and different but it sure is going to find full acceptability of parents because nobody is insensitive to children's needs. It's especially important for the lower middle class and poor segment of children in getting the best food, medicine and education besides play, friends, shelter and clothing. Companies should adopt villages and towns of kids in providing them with the needful. The next consensus should show fall in child mortality, rise in health statistics, fall in drop-outs and rise in quality children prepared by every nation. Quality children means healthy, growing children ready for going to the next step in education equipping them to be good citizens of tomorrow.

The Internet is getting flooded with videos, messages or articles on parents pleading for the cause of their children suffering from premature birth or family problems or health issues and waiting for a chance to change their fate. Whether you donate or not, governments all over the world must appoint agencies to study and take up such cases for taking care of children in need. Children growing up in corona times should not get the impression that their needs are ignored to give the economy a chance to grow. This is true for any crisis situations and slow down though it seems like children are too small to stop economic development.

Government/ NGO vehicles must pick up the kids on streets and drop them at public orphanage homes or kid shelter homes, not to leave a single kid to perish. Complete infrastructure must be procured in the shelters to feed, treat, educate and inspire the children, preparing future generations for the continued process of development. It is not possible that economic development can take place without child development. At the same time, any growth in the economy ought to aim at reinvesting and reinforcing trends to support child development using the gains in economic development. Every nation should take the lead, in governments providing parents a fixed amount of money to facilitate the growth and development of all children right from the time of their birth. The amount may be in the name of children and allowed for use in feeding, schooling, health improvement and other activities pertaining to a specific child alone. Exploitation and misuse of such funds could be further avoided by appointing child inspectors to periodically check progress of children by meeting parents or guardians.

Data analytics

Magic Johnson advised that we should know who our true friends are, when we face a crisis.

Big and small data cultures are getting replaced by pertinent data because we know that we can increase or decrease the parameters as we want but we cannot play with the dynamics of the interpretations and underlying drivers of data retrieved from various sources. It all matters that all correlates with the customer perceptions and nothing else is needed as data. Rest is junk or waste. Information is made, born and stored for further processing in terms of understanding alone and not changing the context of data otherwise the markets can never be managed by the company strategies and our economy will go to ground zero each time a customer changes her demand pattern. Companies have tried to do that in the beginning of the decade when data analytics systems were seen as some magic churning software but miserably failed when reality did not meet their expectations. Daewoo's shutdown due to uncontrollable defect graphs in its vehicles cannot be forgotten by the market players. The top management tried to use every bit of data in a bid to exploit profits and opportunities. They ended up working on unnecessary silos of data and ignored the quality of the product. Analysis could not decide what to have and what not. They could not leave the minor things and had to forgo the major things like sales, customer loyalty and finally their operations.

The scenario of the existing corona crisis is like a chaotic turmoil where companies would feel like collecting and analysing data more than required however the time demands only a limited amount of information pertaining to the consumer psyche and required products for safe conduct of life. There is no need, now, maybe later, to know what additional things to offer to the customer to make their life comfortable or luxurious. In abnormal times we don't run behind the comforts of life but life itself. Industries are limping and the economy has to be put back on its toes otherwise we cannot hope for a normal life even for the next generations. How will they feel if they have to wear masks for every outing or office day waiting to be fired because of lack of business? The covid crisis serves a notice to both the health and wealth aspects of the economy at global level, not at the level of select nations or regions. According to Business Line, the $130b+ market sector is fragmented and largely dependent on business in North America with most of its applications in the smart cities of the future. A major change in the present crisis should be on working with the sector as a niche and core industry not treating it as a technology tool or subsector of other industries. Unless companies let competition thrive in it by letting a separate industry operate on its own rules like the information technology (so far it is treated like a branch of IT and this limits the innovation in the data analytics sector). Microsoft or Dell cannot deviate from their core business to concentrate completely on data analytics but new companies can and must focus on analytics as a new industry on its own. The future economic development lies in the heart of data analytics per se. The surveillance, impact and public response could be well managed on systems but it is not taking a shape anywhere in the world except usa. We are waiting for the markets to be normal and running to use data analytics for other industries only to make profits and huge pays. Both industries and employees are wrong in getting that on the goalsheet. Pharma companies should be using data analytics for tracking their research progress and commercial lab reporting but as revealed in a digital survey the heads have all voraciously opposed the use of analytics 'now' and first want to bring out a medicine by traditional means of trial and error development and testing. Why can't we accept and dare to allow usage of technology in really helping mankind cope with diseases instead of a dire set of complex calculations? India could have decreased the impact of corona if the government and industry had taken the help of data analytics in their local state hospitals and research labs. Now it's not too late, we need to imbibe the importance of reactionary approach for revival of an already shattered economy, here we cannot afford to be proactive by saying that we would wait for normalcy to dawn before preparing ourselves for the next crisis. The companies must use the data lessons from other nations or states globally in managing the crisis well, on both economic and individual health accounts, without waiting for the virus to recede on the pretext of waiting for a vaccine.

Agricultural technology could find better applications with the help of perfect logistics streamlining technologies in corporate farming thereby minimising farmer losses or wastages to near zero levels. Data analytics is not just about R-Programmers or data scientists aiming to give profit maximising suggestions (thus resulting in layoffs). It is about sharing the right data for improving the customer experience or removing seller woes within the entire journey of business- making value chain. Analytics is for business - making and not profit - making because data does not exist without the input of consumers in any industry. Even updating the models is not a tough job if the right inputs are treated to the changing environment, new questions, differing customer behavior from the past and the changing demands. Analytics will make more sense after we retrain the models and recast the customer segments to suit the present. Companies falter when wanting to do something drastically different to counter the crisis situation. Top managers instruct the teams to get different sources, new attributes and features for business decisions, analysis and generation of colorful bar charts to be incorporated in flashy presentations. You know that nothing is going to change because sources are the same, still holy customers, attributes and parameters cannot change unless the product is completely reshuffled with a new one or innovative one. What will change and be different is the customer input, feedback, perceptions, perspective and expectations in terms of , 'earlier a mother wanted milk for her teenager, and now a mother wants unadulterated milk to avoid the spread of infections, so she prefers to go to get milk from a nearby cattle owner (with high quality cows), she heats it to bring a boil and cools it further to store in the refrigerator, reheats the milk before serving to her child, heaving a sigh of relief that the immune system is unaffected if not strengthened'. This is a real-time data gathered and interpreted from real mothers across the world, literate and illiterate, and the data analytics systems were used wisely so as not to disturb the human factors of concern and safety that are brought out again by the human analysts.

Adaptability and agility will drive analytics into AI space in order to serve the companies better by enabling them to understand customer directions, company capabilities and market conditions in alignment with the economic needs of a nation or a group of nations.

Case Example - Data Intelligence and Accessibility by One Mall Card

The shopping malls in the USA are undoubtedly large in number. Different cities have different malls with different types of functioning. A mall in New York is different from a mall in Dallas. The malls consist of several types of chains, stores, restaurants, etc. A customer has different store cards for Costco, Amazon and WalMart with different websites to view items on each of these stores. A better idea would be to centralize the information through one mall card with all stores as members in it. One website that provides information on all the stores located within a mall and its branches elsewhere will help the customer in searching for items as well as in deciding which mall to go instead of visiting innumerable individual websites.

Use- Data intelligence and accessibility can be increased. One card for all malls will give the customer more accessibility to the mall information. This is better intelligent use of data that is otherwise fragmented. Even the malls themselves can use the results to interpret the efficient stores, revenue-generating business, customer preferences and future likely trends.

Gains- It benefits the mall owners and customers the most. New product lines can be easily introduced without the risk of loss. The cost of market testing can also be reduced. The cost of advertising is also reduced. Results for one mall may be generalized or specialized for a product or other malls. Mall owners thus can account for their profits/ losses better than earlier. Deals, coupons, rebates, offers can be placed and updated online. Similarly customers can get a better deal on each of their requirements. Availability of combined data will reduce dependency on just one mall or result in better planning based on distances and location of stores in the malls. Not the least, it will also reduce the incidents of fraud. Using and securing one card is easier than maintaining multiple store cards for each buyer. At large, the state and the nation benefits (White, 2013-14).

Steps-

Initial steps would be to invite the malls to use a common access through one card and one log-in.

A common website needs to be designed covering all the malls and the stores within the malls.

Customers should be able to search for an item and compare prices across stores and across malls.

For this all data would need to be integrated.

Finally the measure is easy. The number of customers logging into the website is a measure of success. The number of malls covered in the task will also be a measure of success. If the customer spend increases then it is a measure of success of ease of shopping on a single card and access.

GDP (Genetics, Diagnostic and Pharmaceutical)

"Don't think 'why-me' when you face a problem, everybody has their share of trouble." - Chinna Jeeyar Swamiji

Learning from SARS corona of 2001: It may take decades to get the best results in the fields of medicine or genetic engineering not due to lack of experts but because of the long time required in research, development, testing, approval, distribution and other such measures of regulatory nature.

Everybody is not well versed to even understand what can be expected but we're surrounded by negatives except covid-19 that is positive, so now we have to dream big.

In July 2020, Corosure (made by IIT Delhi's NewTech Medical Devices) was approved by the Indian medical council and Drug control General of India as the most effective low cost testing kit for the world. It's pretty cheap at less than$6 for commercial use.

Some common suggestions are -

Make general medication that if consumed after lunch, dinner or snacks can obliterate the harmful bacteria, virus and other organisms in the body. Panaceas of the sort are a big magic, not bitter truth. The next generation of medical research could take the plunge in this direction. Post disease treatment is so far a common practice, vaccination to prevent some disease is no news, but sterilization of the body by removing the risk posing elements from blood, stomach, waters and other possible storage areas of the human body would be the next challenge for the professionals. It is tough though it sounds better to prevent the sources of disease than the disease itself. Today we are at the third level for trying to cure patients after coronavirus manifests itself as a disease. The only known ways of avoiding the sources of all forms of sicknesses are to get hygienic, cleanliness, consumption of fresh hot food, isolation and doctor consultation.

Make genetic advances to modify human genes towards showing immunity against the harmful organisms. Animals are not totally immune but their genes can be studied to understand the best physical defense to be able to get medical solutions for human health. Doctor community has been reiterating that it is no easy task to prepare vaccines for corona. We may not even get one in the present decade. Some animals like tortoises are known to live beyond a century without any major ailments. Have you heard of a vet treating turtles like dogs, horses, cats, cows or pigs? There can be more such healthy species that we have to understand in the genetic build, to be able to recommend genetic mutation in the human body from a medical point of view alone. Other wise new healthy species can be cloned to satisfy the planet with the presence of all-healthy species! Economy can be in the best times of growth if medical research is successful in removing the worry of good health, but right now we have a more than important job of treatment of patients infected with coronavirus. We can say that a winning organism against the corona virus should be infused into the receptors but had it been so easy, why would the world be in lockdown? More studies ought to be, as some are being conducted over the extraction of elements from the space by analysing the material falling from the space to understand what different medicinal benefits reside in them so as to get new ways to protect our health by preparing medicine out of such raw material. Gold particles are used in preparation of certain medicines because of the health benefits in them. Human body also appreciates the intake of precious metal and is found to respond better to the treatment with the use of gold dust 'in edible form'. The end product would come in the list of "price-intact items" because of the high cost of production vs utility for end-users. The medicinal utility can't be sold if companies levy the price with cost and profit, to give high priced medicine, does not make sense to users unless the price is kept intact at affordable rate for buyers to give it a try but in the long term, the subsidized investment can be recovered with margins from the loyalty volumes or patent royalties to be earned from the foreign collaboration or exports to foreign governments. The price-intact items follow different pricing on getting priced by affordability (one cannot add margins to cost or with the intent of breaking even after a certain time) of buyers at the lowest level in the pyramid (who deserve effective expensive treatment, as much as the rich patients).

Medical technology is a healthy growing global market of more than $380b. Machine innovation is a requirement and machines have to be made in enablement of better technology assistance while the diagnostic process is on. The person often has to go through a very unpleasant experience in the series of tests through painful procedures. Diagnosis must be conducted by advanced technology to get the best overview of all diseases, anything and everything that is going wrong in our bodies, not revealing just one ailment in one test.

Zydus, Pfizer, BioNTech and other companies are on the testing trials for the vaccines. China, India, USA and other countries are at it trying to get new vaccines for fighting the threat of corona virus but constant research in the direction of finding cure for more pathogens by prediction of their possible birth in future, is needed. Will future doctors be equipped with new technology to predict, avoid, diagnose and cure the advent of unknown health disturbances due to new pathogens? We may not get time long enough to address the risks posed by the outbreak as witnessed by the Corona crisis. Victims are not getting a sure shot solution with some succumbing to the symptoms and some living by luck. What was stopping the pharma companies from making the vaccine till now when we saw the virus traces at least a decade and half ago? We don't know how the doctor community has been unsuccessful in finding a cure for coronavirus when it showed impact as early as 2001 in the form of SARS. Will it be added to the list of unconquered diseases cancer and aids? Not if we are indomitable and determined in medical research and development. Till then it is in our best interest to be wary and take precautions for avoiding the risk followed by the disease itself. The resumption of development is three times tougher than prevention of the disease in the absence of which the regular growth will be somewhat slower both for individuals and markets. If technology strides can invent medicinal wavelengths like lasers or other that can destroy the harmful organisms by sending rays in our body, then real innovation is happening. But teams are working still on knowing about viruses and their counter organisms. The scope is immense and we are counting on the global collaboration of infrastructure, information, research and resources for making the medicine. The field of medicine is no less than a miracle and a doctor is equal to God though she may depend on God for restoration of health and life to patients after doing the best in treatment. Governments across the globe must ensure availability of complete infrastructure (food, water, restroom hygiene, systems) and staffing of hospitals with doctors, nurses and medicines (pay higher salaries without any doubt). In this context, it is a laudable step by global companies like Wipro when vacant office spaces have been converted into fully equipped healthcare units for treatment of corona patients.

Total transformation in FMCG

Michelle Rosenthal disclosed that the power discovered inside ourselves as we would survive a life-threatening condition could be utilised equally well outside of crisis too... In all such times, we would be capable of mustering strengths to survive again or tapping strengths in other good, productive, healthy ways...

The recruitment and all center operations are expected to rise in the post crisis world. FMCG is commuting to a solution-trend model which is helping trends to predict solutions. It is not new for lockdown to increase purchase of consumer durable goods like security systems, washing machines, music systems, home theatre, dishwashers or robotic moppers when servants or maids or watchmen can't make it to your house and you have to arrange for more entertainment at home. The time spent and the number of family members is all at home. There is no time and space to call for change in products, though the case is different for services going into complete personalisation as per situation of user and market, backed by slight increase on price front. Still corona has come with a new sense that provokes urgency, quality consciousness, total adaptability and fast track product modifications without waiting for bureaucracy adherents but for providing a more fulfilling experience to the buyers. FMCG companies at lockdown juncture are producing most user friendly and automatic products for home use by kids, women, grandparents and family members rather than servants who are not without their limitations while operating, voice commanding or verifying (biometric or credential) with multiple equipment at different households. A family that used to stream movies on personal smartphone in BC era (before corona) is now buying a 65" Hidef smart TV for the entire family to watch a movie instead of going to a movie screening theatre, a different thing is that digital entertainment will slow down the progress of conventional movie making business.

Food stores, departmental stores, supermarkets and kirana stores are replaced by one single digital store via ecommerce. In the covid lockdown, people are not going to kirana stores as expected in the beginning but relying on them for less than 10% needs, that too only in emergencies when the online orders get delayed in the hectic times. Not for no reason did Alibaba invest more than $50m in Bigbasket only to meet the increasing net traffic and voluminous online grocery orders during the lockdown in India. Case is not different for americas and europe or australia and rest of asia where more and more orders are placed online. Earlier orders by phone were executed by known sellers in the unorganised fmcg. Today all that works is the Covid - proof seller with the fullest range of hygiene measures for the commodity storage, washing before packing, packaging itself, logistics, isolation of delivery crew that is following the masking methods to avoid any risks. As expected flying drones for mass deliveries is not seen but could be adopted in future because that would save the crew from tireless traveling and their risk is higher than that of the customers, if we can assuage our fears before thinking of others. The intelligent step of suspending all luxury items orders and taking only those for essentials has globally helped ecommerce companies like amazon, Walmart, Flipkart and other local service providers in meeting the needs of all customers at least 2 out of 5 times. In a research conducted by outside 3rd party consultants it is revealed that not 100% orders were executed in the corona lockdown period. Globally buyers had to face rejections of 3 out of 5 orders of essentials. This of course works in favor of equitable distribution so that few regions do not panic order and stock excesses at homes or other places. Online food delivery also saw some initial cancellation of orders to manage the rising traffic of buyers. Some seller discrepancies like raising prices unduly over 100% or wholesaling millions of handwashes to sell at higher prices online, were punished by the ecommerce companies by blocking those sellers or slashing the prices to less than half matching the regular prices. A crisis should not try to exploit people's fears because the economy cannot grow out of cringing or scared people under strain. Globally billions of square feet of retail spaces are turned redundant due to covid crisis. They could be converted into healthcare and testing facilities to cut down on the impacts of the virus infection from spreading to masses. Companies should themselves top up their stocks by procuring more fresh food than packaged or frozen pre-processed foods in the health interests of people. Demand for footwear has fallen by more than 80% for lockdown reasons globally and started becoming a discretionary item. Consumption of cold items like ice creams has fallen by more than 50% (Jan-Jun 2020 study by Tietoz) globally, because of warnings from the healthcare professionals that ice breeds germs. Supply chain breakdowns, stockpiling, stockouts and temporary bans (alcohol, tobacco, luxury items) are common trends in the corona crisis. Governments all over the world can be wiser in using this crisis as a pretext of preparing their citizens into leading healthy lifestyles because no economic growth is led by citizens not healthy due to bad habits of drinking or smoking. It is undeniable that crisis generates an atmosphere of stress and doubt where people succumb to vices but it is upto the digital media to feed us with healthy clips or ads instilling optimism and determination in us to face the crisis and come out of it in full or better health than earlier. The same cannot be said of economy but of people because Youtube surveys say that people did take up healthy and productive activities online like learning new language, practising yoga or new form of martial arts, learning new skill like painting or coding, doing the chores of cooking and cleaning themselves, teaching students online or stitching, weaving or even preparing for online exams (like entrance tests and admissions to some of the top colleges like IIMs, Harvard etc. happened after online interviews) at homes. FMCG or fast moving consumer goods can be renamed to IMCG or DMCG for instant or digital movement of goods and services though it has been found by Tietoz in a global online study conducted in July 2020 that more than 94% of the consumers are reluctant to buy local or new brands and prefer ordering the branded products for health and reliability reasons because they cannot trust others with the health of their family members unless recommended by known local sellers.

Patanjali - a case study

"... what is in a name ... rose is a rose..." - William Shakespeare

The 45000+ million rupees company from India, is all about the development of healthy organics in products like toothpaste, shampoos, herbal soap, biscuits, jam, instant noodles, sweets, fruit cakes, atta, Ayurveda medicinal stuff, oils and other consumables. It has recently claimed the development of corona medication that if effective will revolutionize world medical research. Protests against Patanjali led to filing of FIR against the vaccine/ medicine. All necessary licences, medical regulations, consumer safety standards have to be verified by the competent authorities. The medicine has to be completely analysed for benefits related to its ayurvedic, allopathy, homeopath or generic properties. It has to be thoroughly tested on corona patients and other groups across the world before acceptance and adaptation to global health care requirements. The company is witnessing more than 8000% increase in stock price of its subsidiary (Ruchi Soya) during the lockdown period Jan-Jun 2020. It is clear that market sentiments and buyer preference are running in the direction of traditional formula, ancient remedies and saints Baba Ramdev and Swami Balakrishna Acharya. In future the company is all set to take the space of healthcare, hygiene, food, snacks by sticking to the medicinal benefits in products but post lockdown period demands products with sure shot immunity against any external viruses or bacteria or protozoa etc. The company has been spruiking its sugar free diabetics friendly atta flour that if consumed by diabetes patients should cure them. It is one too many claims as advertising gimmicks strategized by other companies. A case is different or difficult once it becomes the question of health and disease for consumers of medicine. Medication that 'proscribes' the role of deadly virus like corona, is but a new reality and is no less than welcome provided it is no placebo wasting time, money and resources. The present world is seriously struggling to bring out new medication from research initiated in the first half of the decade of 2000. As a company Patanjali has been growing most rapidly to become a full fledged conglomerate competing with the best in the league, Dabur, Unilever, Parle, Britannia, Pepsi, Amul and Nescafe, but not Johnson, Novartis, cipla, Glaxo SmithKline Beecham or their merged subsidiaries. Still Ayurveda medication is a welcome change in the present world of corona. Not all working employees are saints like the founders of the company to overcome the stress of corona so their medical research inputs can be shadowed by some extra prejudices or hopes or other subjectivity that may creep into the output thereby paving possibility for undue hype faith leading to the medical negligence or the bright side could be a pocket friendly dose to cure and prevent corona because when nothing works, God's messengers work. The aim is not to demean the best intention or efforts of those working for the corona medicine. The medication should be made accessible across the entire world in the best suitable allergy free, side effect free and reaction free form that can be also considered as preventive medicine like a pill or digestive tablet that can be consumed in limited numbers by any and many people. Tonic is a more preferred intake to help kids and old. We have to look for motivation in the slowdown and Patanjali can not be ignored in the post lockdown world.

The onus that Patanjali has shouldered in toiling for the medical solution during the corona lockdown period is no less than exemplary production and other countries or companies should admire the work at emulation of similar work ethics to contribute to their share in productivity. The best sterilization and hygiene measures have been followed in Patanjali workspaces without compromising on the health of staff or quality of the products. The future plans also include more mechanisation, automation and innovative business operations in the plants, and factories to support continued supply in the wake of panic buying situations. Hereby the company can also think of having its own logistics fixations to bring independence of the supply chain management or deploy independent kiosks dispensing products in return for card swipes or cash payments, with robots guarding the stocks. The post lockdown period has to see Patanjali as a new leader in championing the cause of environmental health. The buyer can be promised that for every product purchased, a new tree would be planted and grown by the company staff. New staff have to be hired or tie ups with farmers can help. The land has to be acquired for meeting the larger goal in the post lockdown period. Who would be able to stop the next generation from following the best ideals of such altruistic company? Who can stop such a company from going global for becoming a dream stock pick on NASDAQ? More companies are foraging to find food for thought in the corona lockdown. They have to take cues from Patanjali in maintaining a productivity streak in crisis by working on something related to the crisis itself. Instead of working on irrelevant outputs one might stay relevant by generating corona specific solutions for easy acceptance and supply would have even global expectations in such cases. Another idea for more fruitful operations is a local or international or government joint venture for combining the best efforts of all players from all sides. It lends more accountability because you don't wish to be taken for a ride by your partner. Also better mutual quality checks are possible when better minds get to work for the products and services pertaining to community welfare. The next set of products could be Ayurveda mixtures to fight against the virus in Toto. The concoction should be medicinal in nature as well as consumption friendly. Kids may get to eat in the form of biscuits (like threptin biscuits) or as small candy. It should be able to be prescribed for patients of hypertension, cholesterol, diabetes and other ailments without posing any risk for them. Lot of progress needs to be made in the post lockdown period whether by the world industry or a single company anywhere as it is throwing high frequency chaos with possibility for multiple relapses and the risk runs through all countries without exception.

Global Payments industry

"... if you have studied engineering ... and know how to design things,... it is easy to create a company... you just need to have a prototype ...have to get like-minded people ..." - Elon Musk

The financial payment which has been going digital for quite some time now can be found as stuck in the corona lockdown due to the intersection with one or more of the above mentioned sectors crudely affected by the COVID-19. Travel, retail and other spends have been going on the downward trend besides manufacturing and hospitality. The negative impact is flowing to the digital payments industry though it seems to be stable and innovative. Volumes of digital payment have been declining except for health insurance and other medical care services, but we're going through fall in airlines, restaurants, e-commerce non essential groups, entertainment, tourism, hotels and hospitality. International remittances and cross border payments have already been declining more rapidly owing to restricted foreign transactions. The negative influence of digital payment has gone positive in online shopping for groceries, recharges, bill payment, educational technology and media. The positive climbs on digital payment volumes in digital transfer of funds to bank accounts of the poor by governments should prepare for a reboot of the global economy. Germany, India, Brazil and other countries are doing digital payments to meet one or needs of citizens during the lockdown. Digital payments for convenience vs necessity, contact vs contactless and risk vs refund are doing rounds of questions for counting the effects of pandemic on our industry. Disruption of supply chains, demand and logistics for payments by individuals and businesses, is facing headwinds due to unusual fall in transaction volumes. The negative financial impact of corona is shown as below-

Forced lockdown- ..Shutdown in business activities-... Loss of business-... Loss of digital payments

NPAs are expected to rise in capital loan and small and medium businesses due to impact on repayments. Temporary shutdown will reduce the working capital. Default risk is on rise to the global traders struggling with shipping facilities, supply uncertainty and other trade barriers. Foreign workers might not be able to avoid a fall in salaries.

Credit and debit cards are expected to get fee cuts with the e-commerce or mobile shops at fee hikes. Physical currency exchange has fallen in frequency because people don't want to transmit viruses. Telecommunications industry would get an upsurge in digital payments due to increased transaction volumes for online recharge, internet services, online coaching, online school fees, online certification, game apps and virtual work conference calls with foreign clients. Insurance renewal and fresh subscription payments are moving to digital mode. New home buyers and existing instalment payers would adopt mode of digital payments for the handling fees, and upfront payments at replacing cash with Googlepay or Amazon pay or other e-pay apps. The positive side is that the sectors will gain efficiency with the adoption of digital modes of payment. Security and privacy have to be ensured by the service and solutions provider for both buyer and seller sides. Online sellers should prepare for scaling up with the increasing volumes of orders executed in essential items. The digital payments are increasing for online donations to help corona victims. The local vendors and maids by monthly cash payments are shifting to IMPS bank transfer or digital payment or QR code based payment or P2P or P2M or SMS link based payments or PIN based or non PIN face recognition based payment due to covid-19 battle.

The digital payments ecosystem has to understand the changes to behaviour and expectations of customers, along with those of business enterprises, in providing the best form of economic development for the long term by giving short term fee waiver, moratorium, financial assistance, EMI facilities, free fraud coverage and prevention, process simplifications or online Bitcoin wallet. The efforts have to be more in customer education, quality, infrastructure and capacity building with Omni channel capabilities. Digital payments would not stop without facilitating the process simplifications in the Settlements segment in future. The financial mechanisms and agreements will go forward with online real-time closures instead of T+n routes. The digital payments would thus reduce the spreads and risks a bit in return for quick and safe transaction completion. Confirmation and other messages could be real-time, SMS and email combination. If accepted by the global community, we would soon have a digital global stock exchange that is operating round the clock without any opening or closing costs. Post COVID-19 innovation in the digital payments and settlement space would determine the best future strategy for growth.

Governments and central banks must support settlement and resettlement needs of industries to provide competent motivation for the healthy growth in post covid times. Debt settlement can be handled better by reducing costs of litigation or processing and interest rates, extending the one time settlement dates , releasing the blocked investments and assets to be put into productive use thereby reducing the pressure of lock down on the revival of our industrial economies.

For individuals, market values have been falling in the stock or property liquidation, capital assets and other mortgages. Laws have to be modified and communication modes have to be made in favor of the deserving. Insurance providers will have to provide quicker redemption for health care bill payments.

Case study: Trusted Digital technology after lockdown

The world of future technology would have participants adapting to one another without having to adapt them.

Global business would have to decide what to do now, sooner and later.

The social media is using participants while users feel that they are the only ones using social media.

New business model in real estate is about turning thoughts and dreams into true projects.

Modern business is not about mining data, or reading research reports or narrating business cases of failure and success, or advertising endlessly, or pressuring investors to invest in ecommerce or dotcoms. Set of innovative Discoveries include use of digital exhausts or digital footprints; digital exhaust is like a carbon footprint leaving data logs of users as surplus data to be used later for fine grained trend generations turning into money making extra behavioral data. Companies can increase revenues by thousands of times if they can master the use of digital footprints. These data have to utilise AI for convincing the markets about its predictive value. During the Covid trouble, in July 2020, business men like Bill Gates, Elon Musk and a few others promised investors on social media networks that they would double or send more money (sent as cryptocurrency or bitcoins) for the window of 30 minutes. It was again data collection though it entailed generosity of the leaders in giving out free monies. it could be about understanding social media trends in real time because an extraordinary amount of information could be used in micro behavioral targeting for future product innovations instead of wasting effort in vague advertising. machine intelligence capabilities and data science skills could alter the data application methodologies by risking data privacy if protection is not prioritised.

Technology has got a place in our lives because we gave it but not because the industry has earned goodwill. we feel that technology makes our life better.

Machine learning has the ability for manipulation like in elections or public polls. scientists have to ensure that algorithms are used wisely without creating rifts between interests and values of people in the society. Wrong data can mislead customers into buying products, but even if one company selling products could make millions of dollars a car manufacturer could drag 1 million followers from other auto players and even if half of them believe the false ads or fake data claims, to buy the vehicles giving a profit of $1000 each, it is a neat profit of half a million dollars. Google, Facebook, Amazon, Comcast, AT&T, Huawei, Alibaba are companies in risk of developing conflicts with rivals who aim once-in-a-lifetime opportunity to steal the customer segments in getting a lump sum one time profit if not able to stay in the market for long. The market cap of the firms could fizzle out if not properly managed on data privacy issues. negotiations would fail when partners lose trust. The public should have confidence in the products as run by responsible companies and regulators otherwise even the trusted pharma sector would lose its relevance in the future. However healthcare has pervaded so many layers of our consumers that the apprehensions are low for failures. social institutions have hidden a lot of analyses because we feel like having no accountability at seeing so much data in automated machines making decisions, showing skills, telling stories and having no charge with us or themselves.

Social stability wont come without the government using AI for scanning the country for knowing the opportunities for economic development. The most advanced artificial intelligence should be used to use real time data for determining action, facial recognition technology should analyse people walking in public venues to identify who each person is in order to build surveillance nations. It could be useful in avoiding riots or protests or public sabotage activities or terrorism. Human rights can be managed better by such technological utilization. Monitoring behavior can help decide how to re-educate people in the society for encouraging normal life. The kind of airport checks are extended to a universal level in all parts of our life. Argentina, Africa, USA, India, Singapore, Pakistan, Venezuela, Sudan, China can find multiple uses of such technological initiatives.

Spending and investment in massive infrastructure projects to build observation type surveillance technologies with alarm and action triggers can effectively achieve the process of social reform by averting incidents of unpalatable nerve. It would be more of a global tech sector instead of a national tech competence when we can arrest a terrorist or employee in China by monitoring activities in the USA and sending the signals or modus operandi in India. It will be a multinational decentralised bureau of investigation under a centralised AI globally; transparency would increase in companies and countries following such responsive systems. Bad companies can be easily blacklisted because everybody knows the response. The authoritarian grips would loosen in wake of policing technologies making the world more democratic than autocratic. Control would've to be taken by technologies to wipe out the biases and emotions interrupting the correct decisions and timely actions.

Trade war and distrust would be replaced by healthy competition, confidence and convergence in politics, economics and trade. The whole model of cross country engagement would change to alignment from questioning with a completely different framework. The new reality is emerging in the age of AI with so much intellectual power, accumulated investment and customer curiosity, science and finance would step into a new world of success and warmth flourishing in environmental good. An age of enlightenment in not having to do routine jobs but to be taught what it is to be human by AI, is not far off. Social control would use AI for the good of society by limiting ourselves from encroaching on individuals' privacy and right. We would like the government to use AI in favor of our rights, discipline and concentration on public causes for beneficial results on society. We need a careful strategy to harness the skill and power of social tools, to enhance collective wisdom and resolve our concerns to play with endless possibilities to get pride in our solutions of the future. The ecosystem design and personal biases all will change in favor of larger development driven by personal growth thereby attaining total social development and global economic leaps in short spans of time. Digital currency is not distant, but a dream come true sooner than later. All that needs to be addressed are financial inclusion for the lowering costs of transactions, credit schemes for micropayments by broadening access, and reducing illicit finance routed through digital modes. Cryptocurrency can be part of public policy for reducing corruption in the cash economy. Visible and invisible routing should be monitored to avert mishaps online. Ethical ecosystems by setting principles can get international participation and cooperation.

Cryptocurrency is redefining how to do business. Innovation by using stable coins as digital tokens stored or against collaterals or digital assets on gold, real estate or commodities to be stored as software packs. Digital currency does not like blockchain alone but electronic transfers work on different interfaces not always involving another agency. the horserace of different initiatives may cause inefficiency in the cross border payments.

advanced economies and emerging economies are putting strong focus on retail digital currency payments with more than 80%-90% willing to move to digital payments in central banks according to WEF. cross border payments can be cheaper. central banks issue digital currencies with the aim of letting business focus on products by solving the efficiency problem of payments and serving consumers. fuel the growth of economies by using hybrid models like enabling banks or wallets to have digital currency facilities with the ability of tracking. The whole world has attention on the digital currency because collaboration would gain easy acceptance by more than 1.2 b people who don't have bank accounts for money as a public option. It has been over six decades since we have started using various technologies in public applications but new acceptance is yet to be seen after solving shortcomings, by initiatives as to the value of transactions. Unauthorised needs, fast cheap cross border deals carry huge risk of system corruption in the Europe zone. International pace has to pick up on scale and the banking system has to update itself to address demand in faster and cheaper ways. Tax evasion, data protection and consumer protection have to be resolved by having risk management, legal systems and rule based systems. Technology stacks, use cases, platforms have yet to be decided because the concept is in a nascent stage. Interoperability and intercommunication with value addition in wallets along core networks could stop you from paying outside wallet, some allow flexible payments, so technology solutions by networks and assets have to be worked upon to come up ahead with standards to move digital currency, people could stand by the currency. Competition is good because of technological change coming from the sector dealing with money, flaws have to be removed to care about system and financial stability in real-time processes. Payment solutions offer a lot of room for innovation. Money laundering and theft have to be handled by regulatory infrastructure for public faith by open interoperable systems and intraoperative systems within national stacks. Realms and constructs have to encourage more innovation to see retail confidence and risk is much more than in a banking system. Option for restoring to the original state has to be evaluated after dollarisation. It may entail difficulties for countries and banks. Innovation must not be crowded out. Financial system must not snuff off innovation but may make it sound by allowing smart contracts, automatic insurance contracts in natural disasters, and public - private sectors can jointly collaborate for developing innovative solutions.

E-Dollar and E-Yen should be handled equally efficiently in all countries. Forex rates should be correspondingly updated by the regulators for e-currency swaps or e-deals. Data warehousing has to be ready for a big reset so as not to push the balance because we are re-handling the systems in a different context. Different vehicles must be devised for managing different purposes of traders to grow trust without letting stress hover the investors. Energy and money should not go waste so the efforts have to be professed in the right direction. Digital engineering should create the right kind of ecosystem for facilitating digital currency transactions without any loss of peace. It should not create stress and not cut down the relaxation levels of users, so engineering would have to ensure secure deals without letting fake dealers enter the system. We have to create chemistry between the systems and people so that technology becomes an inner tool in people's homes and not a system connection at a distant e-stock house or e-bank. Money is not all, nor more of power or work. The process of convenience accumulation has changed the face of the planet beyond recognition, deserving and desire. Joy of using technology must not get reduced or lost but reality is seeing the same happening now.

Technology should not be a source of misery but ecstasy for customers. Regulators must ensure that it does not happen 100% in the way of technology nor customers. We have to manage money, objectives and resources by engineering the natural ways of application, utilisation and default handling for avoiding panic and for not losing the control of our systems. It does not matter how capable businesses are otherwise. We must intellectually dissect the very fundamentals of engineering and technology for better remodeling of systems in better use of digital currency.Law makers have to set rules to gain trust in systems, to overcome self doubt, not to be feeling stuck and be able to work with surprising new goals each time. We should not walk away from technology without really assessing the looks and health of the innovation in digital currency space.

Excellent decisions about implementation of development policies can be in favor of credit settlement terms or else conditions for digital NPA would be rampant. Makeshift and temporary finance will not allow for the healthy growth of our business economy but a good systematic investment guarantee can provide confidence to our SMB customers to equip them with the best skill and expertise in making quality output. Monetary recovery is possible but not without further economic recovery, and the relevant steps to motivate the industry have to be taken by the investors. Industry has to take safety steps to motivate consumers to spend more. Again the result is contingent on the revival of our global economy.

Markets

Dante's warning, that the darkest place in hell would be reserved for those who would be neutral in times of moral crisis: the idea would shake and wake us to responsive behaviour in crisis. We must take a stand.

Markets have to be respected and as efficient markets would not let us believe people we have to go by security and stock prices to understand the change in true value of underlying assets though corona lockdown period has seen swing on prices (today's fall is followed by tomorrow's rise, don't trade when we have a crisis, secrets are anyway leaked), whether weak or semi strong or strong companies. Price is a form of expected value of dividends that reflect the true value of the stocks. Though all theories seem to apply or no theory seems to work during the crisis, corona collapse sends the public information to the difficult capital market when cynicism leads to erratic investment patterns, unusual investor community behavior and misleading signals. Investors buy more stocks because of low price-earnings ratio but at the same time skeptical about the performance of the company in future. What's the scenario if there does not exist any dividend, why would anybody buy such a share under zero price scenario? It's still common for startups not to pay dividends but not accumulate capital gains. Selling short is a common strategy in crisis and though the lockdown is a possibility for the entire year of 2020 , probably beyond, if proper checks are not brought in place, it may be possible that business may get bad performance, markets would be in trouble, brokers may wait for luck, price can't be predicted even if earning and price fall, because so many people are looking at the markets where some are more knowledgeable than others. The traditional formula of random walk theory seems to hold true still because the best forecast is not a bias but speculation in crazy markets is optimal prediction. The situation is unforecastable when it reaches somewhere but expected to go elsewhere. The various stock price indexes get reorganized to the dismay of investors as a crisis world depends on patterns, illusion and unknown forces. The 1929 crash was a big one. It was not a random walk but a pure chance, totally unpredictable or unprecedented. Bear markets would have bad luck as stocks don't trade fresh. It is a random walk even if we have an autoregressive model without going back much anywhere as if the stock market is tethered to the anchors as if new noise pulls back or up, the price to mean taking back on trend. The globe is expected to witness such a scenario after the corona lockdown period and forecasting is a must for expert stock professional communities to prepare now for more demand prediction or supply revival by responsible industrialist communities but changes in the prices are more real-time and riches don't come easy. Regression analysis is handy then we would generate a series of changes to satisfy the human desire for praise if devoid of failings because the long term prospect of the companies is no good when they seriously exploit the public sentiment. Responsible industries respect moral sentiment presuming benefits in altruism because best expectations rest on approval based on praiseworthiness. The trait should be nurtured for the global economy to drive back to growth. It has come from Adam Smith and we have to revisit the history to get back our financial muscle with the most modern up-to-date excellence. The post lockdown period might come across antisocial personality disorder traits among the global investors because jerks are always waiting for the wrong time. The buy-sell data has to be simulated to learn about behavioral deviations in order to avoid further economic blunder spiralling out of the lockdown period. Psychologically the investors resist manipulation but financial institutions (FIs) are like political entities in hiding the real feeling or belief. Some bipartisan expert members have to monitor the signal sent by FIs so as to allow for any people's value, inference, utility, gains, losses, estimates or reference points. Regulators are referees to enforce rules and they have to be more wary of not hurting any player in the competitive system. We should show respect for the regulators though they don't attract much attention except when things take ugly turn. It's not always about making money but we would need more trade groups to sort out state, local or international problems and to regulate standards when normal industrial action resumes after the end of lockdown. Society has to impose quarantine on companies entering into shady deals tarnishing the standing of the companies or avoid unnecessary risk by appointments of responsible and reputed members on the board of director committees. The aspect needs immediate attention to avoid post lockdown chaos due to flawed decisions by sleazy behavior or tunneling (pocketing value belonging to stockholders). Nepotism or selling company shares at non market price to relatives, awarding contracts for future favor, paying high salaries to unworthy friends, expropriation of secrets, insider trading (buy or sell based on unrevealed knowledge) and other modes of cheating innocent people, should be controlled by running business in high minded way by the directors as regulatory obligation or loyalty to shareholders. It is a significant thing, not honor alone, to be a director of the firm. Next, corruption in trade has to be reduced with the help of trade regulations so that markets would not become the victims of all human weaknesses. New asset pricing models have to be developed and tested based on new public information for better forecasting. Numerous event studies reviews of company stock splits can help us understand better the market variation, abnormal returns, dividend raises or price increase response because the stock price need not go up after the event. The whole piece would be a bubble (sudden spurts or irrational behavior of markets) like a social epidemic with price increases by sociological channel's media stories influencing the behavior of the public in the stock market. Certain talks influence pharmaceutical stocks, housing markets or insurance buyers and we blame the markets though the strength of markets is more than all economies put together because the market reaction can boost or ruin economic performance though we would like the reverse relationship to persist.

Investments

Edmund Haley asked Newton, "...what do you make of this comet..."

Newton: ...The Path of that comet conforms to my Mathematics...

Gold is an evergreen investment option for all classes of investors with any degree of risk appetite. In the post pandemic season, gold prices are expected to fall to two-to-five year lows because of the present thrusts on demand by buyers who want to invest in gold as ornaments or coins or bars. Prices are rising given that people are more inclined towards gold than bank deposits offering lower interest rates, or stock markets falling (expected to fall furthermore) or real estate markets offering lower returns. The case is true of all countries though India has third largest gold deposits and the nation continues to place its bets on the yellow metal owing to the glitter appeal, high resale value, reliability, easy availability and easy storage options (home or lockers or bank or stores offering gold schemes to take buyer gold and provide higher returns on allowing for using multiple monthly in store lockers before the final resale or exchange for gold). The last option is particularly used within India where shops offer lucrative gold exchange schemes and buyers find it valuable to exchange old jewellery for new instead of buying new gold at higher prices due the case of rising prices of gold. GILT stocks are not unworthy of trying because the investment is dependent on return on the market value and it is on an overall upward trend. Security is high because investors need not have the physical asset or commodity.

Real estate industry is expected to decline further and buyers are already up for low returns in the housing market where houses bought in the downtrend have been through another 20-30% price-fall. Long-term prices however might even out the expectations of buyers because real estate sector and gold prices cannot possibly become a target of decade long fall in prices both being active investment options for the global community.

Stock markets are a good bet for equity investors because prices are expected to fall by more than 40% in the next one year, according to CNN. The returns could be considerable or at least decent for long-term investors who can buy at low prices and wait for the market to pick up in the next 3-5 years. If the market does not grow as expected, still the stocks would offer reasonable returns when companies are trying to perform well or merge with others or innovate on offerings to increase sales thereby increasing scope for higher dividends with time.

Mutual Funds are not a highly preferred option during crises witnessing closure of industries followed by scraping of mutual fund schemes. The open or closed end schemes are not much of profit generators for investors who are looking for not just locking money but having liquidity and returns at the same time. Systematic Transfer Plans and Systematic Investment Plans are not expected to meet the goal-based investments in the near term of 1-3 years because of the expected fall in Price-Earnings ratio and Price to Book Value for companies. The volatility is set to increase and corona vaccine may bring in some optimism in the market sentiment but not a remarkable profit to investors. Some countries claim success in effectiveness of vaccines and the result is yet to be seen in markets, as of August 2020. The USA, India, UK and Russia have claimed success of vaccines in clinical tests and public tests but vaccines are still to prove worth to the masses.

Oil price meltdown has brought down the market optimism and options trading on oil based commodities are not performing well on derivatives exchanges. Huge corrections are needed for governments to get relief for increasing expenditures. New schemes for investment offering safety, security, liquidity and returns may have to be launched by the government or private players working with corporate bonds and other instruments for individual investors. Simple mechanisms are required rather than complicated market funds or financial instruments to invest as future saving with moderate to high returns. Risk should not be high even for the period after corona because volatility is sailing fast and the combination is not favorable to investors. Instruments must offer payments in such a way that risk is low in a highly volatile scenario to encourage investors to park the savings in the new instruments thereby pushing forward the economy on trails of growth. Companies have to work on both offering better schemes to individuals and improving industry growth to fulfill investor expectations. Now, diversification may also not offer the returns to serve the purpose of risk mitigation or portfolio optimisation both of which are applicable in normal markets and not economy reeling in slowdown. Other investment options have to be understood by investors before buying into them, as to what risk factors are involved, how much time the liquidity is locked in, how much returns are funds getting, where the sellers are generating profits from, what the sources of reinvestment are, industries in which sellers are investing buyer funds, quality of assets and comparison with alternative investment plans.

The present strategy is to hold on every investment instrument and sector, with opportunity to buy as markets send the prices down. [It is advised not to invest (or at least don't sell) in the real estate sector now that prices are on a downward spiral.] Investors need to monitor the price changes to sell at reasonable returns without holding on greed because markets fall as rapidly as they would rise in times of volatile crises. Any crisis is storehouse for volatility and dries up liquidity in the economy. The one is one more on portending health risks, when people must be wary of increasing liquidity and not diminishing by investing in long-term inflexible options. More than anything, we need healthcare investment and insurance where people could save for future use unless health emergencies crop up to increase spending on treatment and medicines, otherwise the same scheme can be flexible to be converted into future child education schemes or family requirement funds. A Special Purpose Investment Fund (SPIV) could be launched by healthcare or insurer firms or even the financial advisories for common people to invest lump sum or monthly amounts into health scheme for the initial period of 1-2 years, within which the need can be met without issues, otherwise the investor can change the scheme to another one meeting family needs better for future, if no crisis situations persist.

Taxation

Richard Dawkins argues that... the evolutionary process is ... wasteful ... on the other hand ... it has produced magical results... the design of albatross is superb ... any engineer would find... giraffe to be ... ridiculous...

Governments in developed and developing countries are aiming at improving direct and indirect taxation policies for better redistribution, healthy collections and lower default rates. Taxation is a key element in the final closure of deals and accounting has to tackle the loopholes prevalent in our tax structures. Rich should not get demotivated, the poor should not fall prey and the middle class should not try to escape the tax nets. Corporates should find it as a contributory channel for sharing revenues with governments and not hunting game of tax regulators. Taxation rules for raw materials entering the factory premises or finished goods exiting the region to enter another selling territory for entering the premises of buyers, must be reviewed in the post pandemic conditions for streamlining the enterprise and individual tax measures. Sanitization must begin at this juncture to avoid corruption because tax is the first step to instigate bribery and pursue evasion. Tax advisors may have to group together to investigate and discuss the best practices for changes to be effective where needed because the opportunity again comes from covid-19 towards economic recovery in the post covid era. Rules may have to be rewritten for taxpayers to work for economic progress by participating in taxation. Business taxation system is believed to be inadequate even in advanced economies like the USA. corporate tax revenues are not more than 3% of GDP in any nation. Taxes are not revenue generators but progressive sources of income for the government to bring about reforms in public infrastructure. Income inequality is a problem in nations and vulnerable populations should find taxation as a step in crisis. Future tax monies should have better redistribution options for governments to bring solace to the poor. Money may not be given to the poor by taxing the rich but provisions have to be made to use the money at building better credit options for helping the poor work with small business ventures or personal initiatives. Rate cuts might be in near future but not as significant to invest in tax relief or revenue. Foreign income and local income have been facing separate tax brackets but corona threat might standardise the difference, it is the same risk and expense for both foreign and local workers. Foreign workers need not be penalised for working abroad if they don't make significantly higher pays than local nationals. ETFs are a better option to save taxes, also because capital gains cannot be taxed unless reinvested. Market linked instruments face higher risk and complication in the crisis situation though tax advantage has to be reworked for investors. Though it is not favorable to investors and workers or business communities, post crisis situations have witnessed tax rate rises, so governments have to adopt revenue neutral reforms in the post pandemic economic revival plans. The severe health crisis cannot sustain policy measures unless governments help bankruptcy claims of industries and grant relief to individuals facing the large health threat in the short term. Business models cannot be restructured soon but governments can bring about minor changes to the policy to turn it into favorable health outcomes by supporting company initiatives or providing health aid to citizens. It is easy for companies in advanced countries to be bailed out by government subsidies or assistance. Travel industry is in a clear slump and taxation structure should be modified to support the sustenance of companies operating in the sector. The example should be extended to temporary relief and short term stimulus for companies to be able to sustain and survive the crisis otherwise the measures waiting for post pandemic times would take longer to get the similar gains for industries. Interest limitations and treatment of losses might get generous tax measures for the years 2019, 2020 and 2021. It may be better to extend further into the future but not into the past as some companies are seen using the present covid context to gain subsidies or aid for losses incurred not during the pandemic era but prior to that in 2018 or before. Such exploitative tactics must be monitored and avoided by the government to make the reform strategy more effective for the times. Supply, opportunity costs and money in circulation should be analysed to make useful decisions for healthy GDP growth without creating loopholes of deficit finance or other fiscal infrastructure costs. Public investments must be more channeled into healthcare without making the debts more expensive for companies volunteering into the creation of benefits or instruments encouraging innovation in the long term. Tax systems usually do not function well but security has to be promised for retirees, education needs and other needs to win the trust of the general public. Market power should be analysed to see how some companies are earning more than in normal times. Labor wages and capital shares in incomes have lower efficiency costs if taxed appropriately in corporations. MNCs and local firms pay taxes differently and governments can coordinate better to ease the restrictions or political rules for shifting incomes. Globalization in true sense would mean addressing such inter-regional tax issues across different nations. Inclusive frameworks and series of reforms can deal with international tax dialogues in favor of investment in developmental activities or rerouting of tax proceeds into serving public interests. Suggestions are on the way for flat taxes, say 40% for the super rich (over 10million income), 20-30% for the middle class and 10-20% for the lower middle class. Similar tax structures may be replicated for small, medium and large firms in terms of size of profits, not revenues or staff alone. For as long as covid situation stays, taxes might be eased for medicinal equipment and medicines, if possible beyond health care insurance or treatment (bills are still showing separate tax amounts for general, special wards, intensive care units, etc. when health tax could be done away with in view of the present crisis). Surveys have revealed that people prefer home treatment for fear of paying taxes on the hospital treatment charges. It is a cause for concern because ailing patients have a factor inhibiting better decisions when there should be no second thought in getting the best possible treatment from professionals in hospitals skilled in curing such cases of quarantined illnesses posing risk to patients. Financial support should be extended by governments to improve infrastructural facilities in hospitals depending partly on patient fees that are deemed to be revenue instead of professional charges. Hospitals should not treat patients and fees as revenue generators but as a respectful token of service and trust between the staff and the ailing. Treatment should not be commercialised and the message should go from tax collectors who would increase the confidence of people by waiving the tax on the already taxed patients.

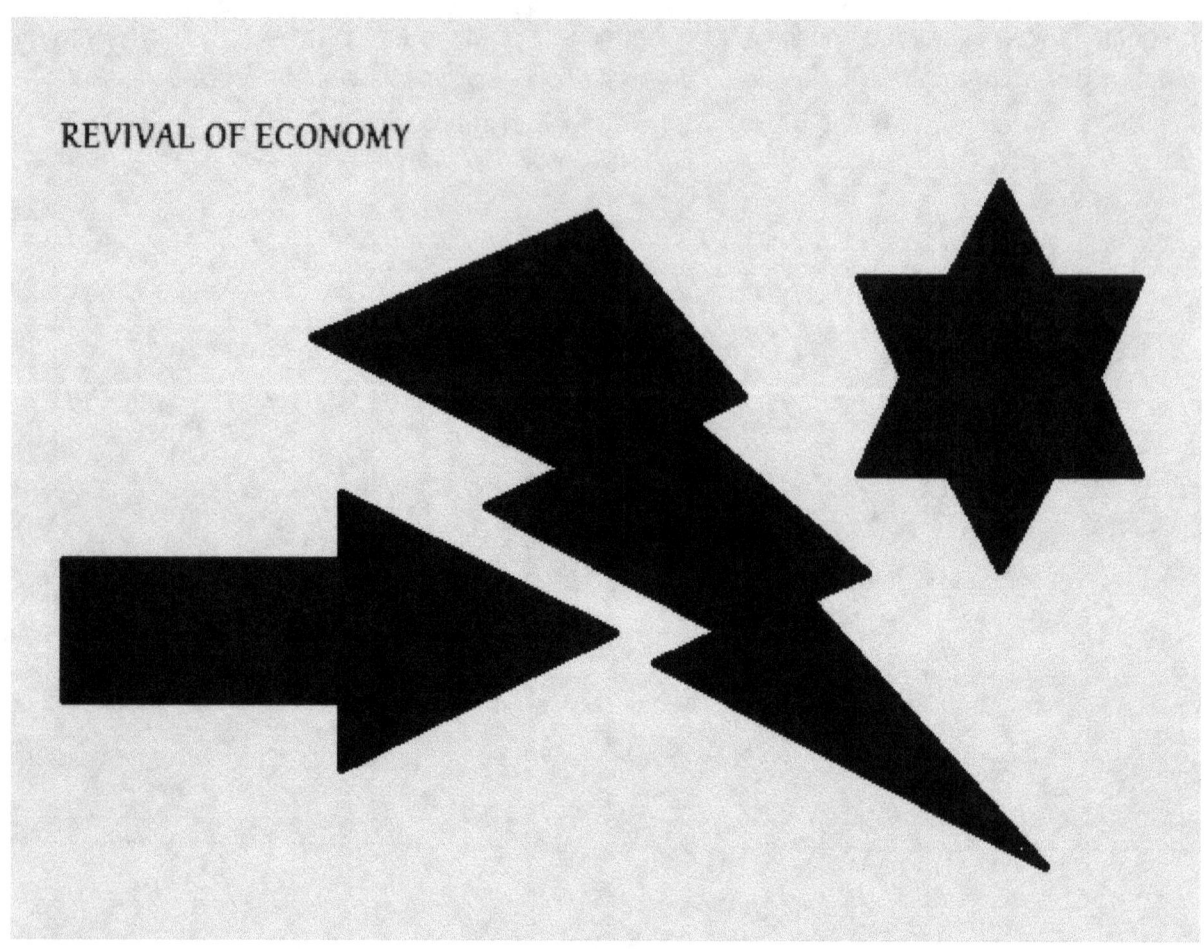

Procedure to revive the economy

Jeanette Wall's inspirational quotes say that sometimes we all need a crisis to get our adrenaline flowing and help us realise our potential.

First, the overall functioning of the economy has come to a grinding halt with lockdown suspending the manufacturing and service for more than 2-3 months. Though temporary lifting is envisaged to continued invocation of lockdown for more time (maybe EoY 2020) the same has to be managed with the help of online-manual combination of work intervention because inertia has already crept into organizations and individuals alike with schools, offices and other institutions going into temporary closure. Most industry sectors have taken the impact of lockdown including e-commerce business, retail, where men and machines have both stopped working in the usually dedicated routine. Rescheduling of machines is needed for necessary revival of the economy. It takes some time for shifting from work -from- home to office and virtual classroom to school environments. Production has fallen, reducing supply though the corona crisis did not reduce the demand for more stocks to be stashed in homes, hotels, and other places. The GDP growth rate will slow down unless techniques are adopted to keep the production of goods and services going, partly pumping of money can only reduce inflation, if combined with measures to increase consumption, spending, investment and savings, a balanced approach might work because we would not one thing, afford to ignore any variable, and second thing, we have to deploy technology to fill in the gap of lockdown, besides increasing the remote operations of equipment by operators sitting at homes.

The government has to opt for rebudgeting not to fret in achievement of goals, same thing applies to the companies at unit level for target sales.The sales, marketing and advertising strategies have to be revised, the goals in heavy industry sectors have to be reviewed (innovative metals like steel, diamond alloy come to rescue), the ongoing projects in irrigation, agriculture, railway sectors have to be revisited (innovate ways to reduce waste, increase consumption, streamline value chains), the expenditure and income sources have to be revealed for more transparency in crisis (cooperate in trouble to compete during normal time).

The sole objective is to convert inertial tendencies into value addition activities because right now we are in the sea of corona in the middle of which we are swimming but of not much value generation. Sail the boat after lockdown to counter the accumulation of losses. Begin the market production that has come to zilch. It's a total loss of production and we have to run away from the zero-production scenario by regearing fresh and old orders, completions of pending orders and rethink our strategy after this lockdown duration of 2-3 months for which we have to be ready and prepared to reverse the total collapse when further economic loss ought to be stopped. Much of the industry growth crippled by corona. The appropriate strategic implementation should be bifurcated between the old and new customers. Calling back people to work, recruitments, business reintroductions, as starting from lockdown gap 'scrap' and scratch and handling the post lockdown chaos are some things to be planned and addressed.

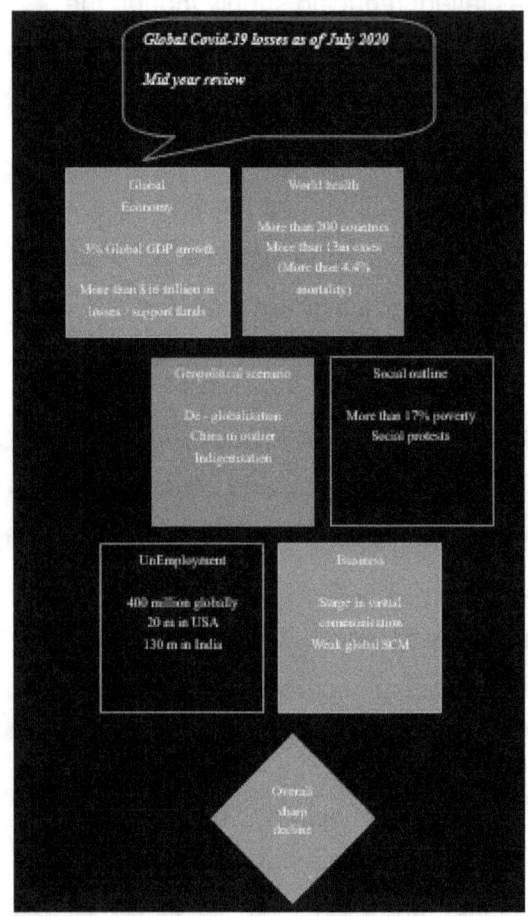

Fig 3: Corona Crisis tits-bits

The 2019 crisis of corona virus has led the global economy to distress in more than one way as shown in Fig 3. The next phase of corona is its recurrence somewhere in the last quarter of 2020.

Startups are totally affected and we have to prepare now itself firstly to fight against the disease (tie up with solidarity schemes to benefit from the partners, tie with new customers, go with global interdependence though the result may be to stop your production, you can still avoid unnecessary experimentation costs, let unimportant employees work from home, only the key personnel come to office thereby saving the expenses on space, power, infrastructure, utility) and next to fight against the after effects of the disease. The after corona (AC) scene is going into worsening economic conditions with the need for reassembly and reshaping of the totally ripped economy in the world that is like a body shattered into pieces.

Had the global interdependence been absent, firms would not have stopped the production and services. One solution for the economic resuscitation is to breathe a new lease of development by bringing out fresh business models after checking with the timing of lockdown closure, government reform, new scheme announcements and global industry growth plans.

Innovative products to development of total virus-immune material and corporate governance mechanism to avoiding close human interactions can promote economic revival by giving birth to new industry sectors like hygienic textiles, virus-resistant metal ores or alloys, sterilized virus-immune biodegradable plastic or food items. Research needs to start right now to be fruitful in the AC era. Our decision systems have to be remodeled with the BC, AC databases for more detailed analysis, distinctive information, precise inferences or better preference reference to customers who would be more than confused as what to ask for in the new economy. Corona is preparing a new economy full of bottlenecks, for which we have to prepare for repairing it by way of new job hires, insurance schemes, schools teaching hygiene measures, more international collaborations, to combat the psychological, physical and other effects of corona lockdown. The list of references should be limited to key heads like food, related schemes, personal fitness and behavioural responsibility. More lists could confuse the individuals. Each healthy citizen can contribute in creating a happy company that leads to the emergence of a prosperous industry that when combined that of other countries can get the best possible global economic growth. We have to interact with the family members, though isolated or quarantined, to retain our behavioral responsibility because office colleagues and friend circles may change but not family. The office meetings should be conducted over the webcon sites online so that all of us are on the same page after this lockdown ends. The companies must desist from showing rosy pictures of their performance, audit firms must monitor the same and we can understand the period is quite demanding so accept the failings. Annual reports are supposed to be the simplest with easy data, nothing but contingency cost and reserve heads appear for all companies including services, manufacturing and research sectors have scope for giving some numbers because of knowledge based work at the cost of field work (no survey, no client meetups except online and the environment is no driver of healthy inputs given economic panicking).

Organizational inertia

Nelson Mandela described that a leader was like a shepherd, staying behind the flock, letting the most nimble go ahead, and others would follow, without realising that the guidance would be happening from behind.

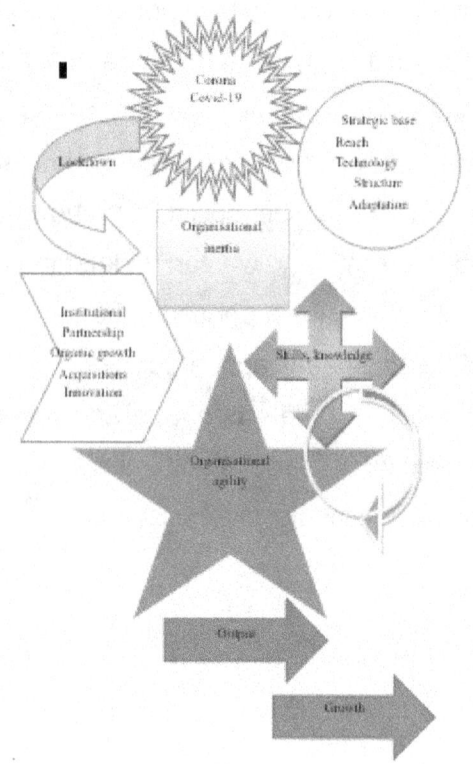

Fig 4: organizational inertia to agility

Organizational inertia is a great systemic risk in a time when corona must be seen as instigating positive improvements for business operations and processes. Corona is a good systemic tremor to catalyze multi dimensional change by breaking down the inertia of organizations. Firms can now gain agility with time to expedite the process of automation and digital mechanization towards the application of robotics. technology collaboration is missing in documentation of specification, design and prototypes or tools for coding, testing and deployment . Virtual interactive software is required to help grow real-time 3D models and blueprints in augmented and virtual reality modes. The stymied situation due to inertia is possible to change from fears to collaboration. Tools like Asana, Slack and MS Teams will find usage in business workflow. Expensive outings and lavish dinners are giving chances to virtual golf or online five star trek. Innovation will help you to enjoy your holiday meeting with the best investors over online business reservation in the digital wax museum. Supply chains will shift away from China to India or USA or UK for sourcing the new manufacturing investment. Digital economy will not develop as long as we ignore the convenience and flexibility of digital communication. Organizational change is what is driven by the corona crisis because structural changes in progress will strengthen our business resilience to respond to unexpected issues and events.

The hyper interdependence will be able to study and predict the best inter linkages to prepare the world in a way to cascade the local effects globally and global effects on the supply of goods, information and services. Offshore markets will also no longer be low cost but lower cost of getting the better quality output from the professional teams based in homes but working with the highest quality cross border ethics. Companies need not relocate the low cost foreign labour to the country of operation or head office thereby saving costs on extra office space and infrastructure. The salary will also be required in meeting the best skill and home needs of the offshore team to help cut salary by at least 25% accounting for local city, rental, health, food, insurance and transportation costs for relocation. Thus lost revenues and robust development may be recovered by the better organizing costs of organizations. Good leaders treat crises like a natural experiment. We have to glean profound lessons in the covid hit economy. The speed and nature of response, consistent communication, policy adjustments, balance between ability, quality, strategies, structure, resources, utilization, organizational habits, management, and leadership skills - all determine our agility levels and capabilities to cope with the inertia inflicted on the infrastructure, markets and institutions around the covid world. Organizational inertia (Fig4) does not depend on any factor related to economic growth but the recovery from inertia to agility needs to evaluate the interdependence of several factors of economic growth because the process of getting organizational agility must ensure redundancies in industry structures or loopholes in institutional policies. Why we are travelling across such a wide range is because the current situation has jammed the flow of development from the smallest unit to the largest possible economic development at global level. Each and every individual, institution and nation is suffering from inertia in terms of inability and lack of clarity as to how to proceed further in the track of growth and activity. The basic activity routines are hampered due to non availability of resources, mainly manual, in rendering the technologies functional, inertia has removed the probability of growth altogether in the crisis-led diseased economic state. Automation cannot be adopted altogether all of a sudden because the adopters themselves are in a state of inertia driven by shock.

Companies and industries may face closures in the post pandemic world due to the impact of organizational inertia intensified by the crisis of the current times. The closure of 200 year old apparel company Brooks Brothers that outfitted 40 out of the last 45 US Presidents, seems to be a case of organizational inertia bogging down the crisis hit apparel industry. The company could not restructure itself on minor aspects (remote customer retention tactics, cost budgeting for marketing in the non activity crisis period) to survive the crisis for emerging as innovative player in the latter years. It is tough to remain aptly active in the inertia time when crisis warns us from doing much and at the same time challenges us to remain competitive. Companies do not have to spend millions in marketing activities because the time of non operation and reducing sales does not justify huge marketing spends. Social networks however could be utilized to show cost effective marketing presence not in terms of advertising but contributing to the community development activity socially without expecting benefits from customers in return. It is a way to remain in business while not actually doing any business in crisis hit markets more so in industries like apparel and luxury goods that are virtually out of business due to the coronavirus epidemic. Companies may otherwise stick to the CSR part alone of the business forgetting the core business to serve society in crisis time as advised by Henry Ford that businesses have to be ready to become poor when needed in the interests of society's poor. No society would refuse to accept aid by corporates in crisis times but people can turn away from the company's attempts to sell non essential products during a slowdown.

Case study of Greece-- Global lessons in Corona world

"... either be the best ...Or leave business..." - Jack Welch

Greece is a good path breaker ; though reeling under bureaucracy, slowdown and flawed economic climate (weak structures, aging population, ineffective administration, and institutional plague), the government has been able to use covid times for digitiating (initiating digitization), without giving up on the attempt at economic recovery. All of us have to look at the dedicated government institutions in Greece to learn from initiatives related to environmental law, people health and economic growth. The ministers and politicians are keen on utilizing the space and time provided by the corona war (between viruses and doctors trying to get a vaccine ready) for devising economic remedy without ignoring the health infrastructure. Now Greece is in better condition with a higher comparative competitive advantage than other countries. It can get industry to growth track by increasing employment in the digital technologies space to innovate various electronic goods in general consumption. Results and objectives would then be automatically aligned to win the global Middle class market for healthy margins in the coming years. Nations whether the USA, UK or India have to learn from Greece and even Greece herself needs to extend the way to growth by increasing the collaboration between the government and business. A streamlined and collaborative partnership between the regulator, health care industry and technology is a great need for the entire global community: in the absence of which can be assumed that bureaucratic inertia is a troublemaker adding to the current economic glitches created by the corona lock down, because the broken systems are not native to third world countries, a litany of failures are coming to light in the advanced economies also. Greece is running to the "institutional imperative", in the language of Warren Buffet with the rational decision makers led by chaos and information exigencies unlike the past, which was relying on decency, experience and intelligence of managers. Greece has to allow the experts to study internal, national and international systems. More access and communication among the people, ministers and industrialists would help understand what everyone is doing and why, what the next expectation and need is and how to make it possible. Digital supplier meetings, and customer services seminars could help reduce the negative impression about employees being institutional adversaries and undifferentiated blob. It definitely helps to cultivate allies and self reflection on premises of persistence in encouraging growth of people and institutions in Greece. The case is replicable to other countries in the world of covid where similar institutional inertia is crippling growth in all markets.

Country strategy has to take the lead. It has to offer a growth environment to the international economy by allowing free development of local communities and governments. Participants in the formulation of country strategies should be 60% native economists, honest politicians, researchers, planning commissioners, industry leaders, trade experts and the remaining 40% should be foreign officials from developing, developed and poor countries. Implementing team should include all the citizens of the country to provide competent economic support. This way, by taking the combined growth of all the countries we would be successful in reducing the impact of corona on achieving the revival of our global economy. No separate strategy should dominate the country strategy that should supersede all other strategies related to industry or company at least until the global economy comes out of the constantly debilitating effects of the sporadic corona lockdowns. Greece can now recover on its own though earlier it was not able to recover alone nor with the aid of other countries. The situation is paradoxical but a nation in trouble is not troubled anymore with the occurrence of another trouble. The treatment was going on at the economic level till corona arrived when the country did its best to manage the virus and the health conditions can be termed as non-precarious (with not many lives at risk in Greece). The testing and quarantine measures along with precautionary handwashing steps have been diligently followed by the citizens. All it has to do is to continue with the effort of growth and health for people and industries by concentrating on technology and innovation. Other nations have to start from ground level anyway, so all countries are like Greeces of the Corona world. The comparison is not to discourage other nations but to motivate Greece because total economic development cannot ignore any country. Rest of the nations must learn and innovate while leveraging the economic surpluses created in the BC or pre-corona times.

Greece is like a trendsetter that has not given up on reform measures since the past, though the recessions have all tried hitting the nation on the wrong side. Resources and national institutions should take time to restore infrastructure and technology in order to be competitive. The banking infrastructure has miserably failed in the past and officials must take cues from the successful nations and banks to frame new policies and regulations helping the further financial market activity aiming at strengthening the economic backbone by the end of the next decade. Employment generation schemes have to be implemented soon without wasting much time in formulation. According to CK Prahalad some strategies are better off if directly implemented instead of wasting resources over the formulation of the same. Time is not for planning on luxury strategies like marketing or advertising, time is calling for focus on the basic strategies of growth in advancing the companies to the next level of innovation and taking the economic sector to growth from losses. Task has to account for two sides- people in terms of health, employment and education in that order for the post covid era, second is industry in terms of sustenance, innovation, funding schemes and incentives to operate in the post crisis time without shutting down the business units. A lot of entrepreneurs are contemplating closing their operations to avoid the market impact of the sluggish economy worldwide. The task of government is to support the sustenance to let the economy grow in future.

There ends the matter of Greece before it has even started but the other nations have to get experts to study the industry and national cultures to revive the structures within organizations breeding multinational businesses. National differences have to be managed better than ever in order to propel global development by working on together with the cultural differences. The topic of cultural distance is not new and companies must understand the factors of individualism, power dominance, team dynamics, as applicable in the countries that they are doing business with. Unless you know your family members how can you assure a peaceful coexistence? The countries are like family members in the global village. We need to know everything about all countries in the world across our national co-existence, or at least we have to understand the few countries with whom we are trading or travelling to-from or building bilateral bonds. Otherwise, organizational inertia will take less time in becoming national inertia and lesser time to reach global inertia similar to the present corona lockdown inertial condition of the globe. The institutions and structures are dormant, people are digitally active (digits as fingers for typing and digital as online means to express views) but under fear, governments are confused but performing under chaos, natural environment is improving under conditions of reduced traffic and emissions from vehicles and companies, animals are travelling freely and changes are taking place in all parts of life. So we know where the inertia is persistent and where not. Agility is not present in the organizations as of now because we cannot think about future innovation and project ROIs without fixing the current world. Industries should learn from themselves in utilizing the present positives for improving internal processes in favor of promoting green products in similar environments without jumping into a corona-free world to re-pollute the surroundings. The best we can do for ourselves is giving a clean environment to our future generations. Oft-repeated is it but deserves action more than reviews of environment friendly proposals or suggestions. Or the world could shift to a real global village model where the countries with more forestation should vacate the space for planting more vegetation and forests. Such dedicated members of the planet should be given citizenship of any other nations from those of low forestation or fertility because such soils cannot be depended upon for new forest cultivation. It is a lot easier to increase forest land than to build one from scratch. Thus the world will be then divided into two halves - one with forests and the other with people. Planet will be surely safer than now in future, with equal greenery to match the population. Even now in cities, the planning should be done in such a way as to encourage at least 25% land (prefer 50% though) for forests every time a land is granted for construction of residential habitats. In ideal world, for every 6000 square feet assigned for construction of office space or 10000 square feet allocated for building the apartments, government must immediately summon the forestry department to plant trees or breed animals in 6000-10000 square feet of lands to make life arrangements for feeding the new population with extra oxygen, water and food from natural green environments. Tough but then we have to get companies to manufacture oxygen in future if we fail to meet environmental needs of the population.

Entrepreneurial benefit

D. Pelzer believed that something good would come out of every crisis.

Government should encourage entrepreneurs and let start-ups thrive by providing incentives in the post covid era. Very few entrepreneurs would dare take risks in the latter years for fear of losing high investments in addition to losses accruing over long break-even periods. Industry growth does get slowed by downturn but anyway it is not going to leave us so it is better to let the infant industries flourish rather than scrape them in a rush. Nourish the industry start-ups by providing special innovation oriented funding and support. Ask the industry leaders to reap additional advantages of collaboration or partnerships with the fledglings and let the government give tax incentives to the collaborating giant firms. New firms can better adapt to new business models of the post covid industry than the existing leaders, who would be required to be flexible anyway.   Support should be provided to the collaboration between similar sized firms and small businesses to give scale to industries in both related and unrelated sectors. The largest entrepreneurship sector is agriculture where more than 50% farmers have their own lands and cultivate by deploying field workers or cattle or machinery as and when needed. Majority of the online studies believe that agriculture is the sector not much impacted by covid-19. The food and related essentials commodities from the agri sector are hence not scarce though demand increased due to panic. Reasons may lie in the independent farming methods not but requiring small loans, with the income not on the higher side. We might want to replicate such independent business models for entrepreneurs in other industries to make them strong, consistent and performing under all conditions of crisis and boom.

Entrepreneurs in the world of post corona lockdown should follow the customer emotion and aim at giving exhilarating experience in the innovative solutions productized or serviced for customers (Fig 5). The economy can grow beyond expectations if nations can grow start-up without telling to wait till things get better and normal. The economy should go ahead and against the most preferred wave of not having new businesses during or after the crisis situations. In crisis management and business in the establishment often have to re-examine organisational structure, re-do internal policies, re-design solutions strategy, re-enter geography and re-work to return to growth space after the crisis ends. It is better to begin with a new one than reviving the ailing company though leaders and other companies do not have any option to exit the business without enough resources and information systems investment in the attempts to give a suitable time to successful bounce back or sufficient wait before moving to hard decision (downsizing, shutdown and other sell-off options).

Engineering analytics and digital management services should be provided to the next level customers for enhancing the quality and usage convenience. Customers do not want to be stuck in the corona world by continuously complying with rules of covid-19 even after it has gone. Prevention and control groups want us to yield to lifelong learning and practice but we're going to find a vaccine soon.

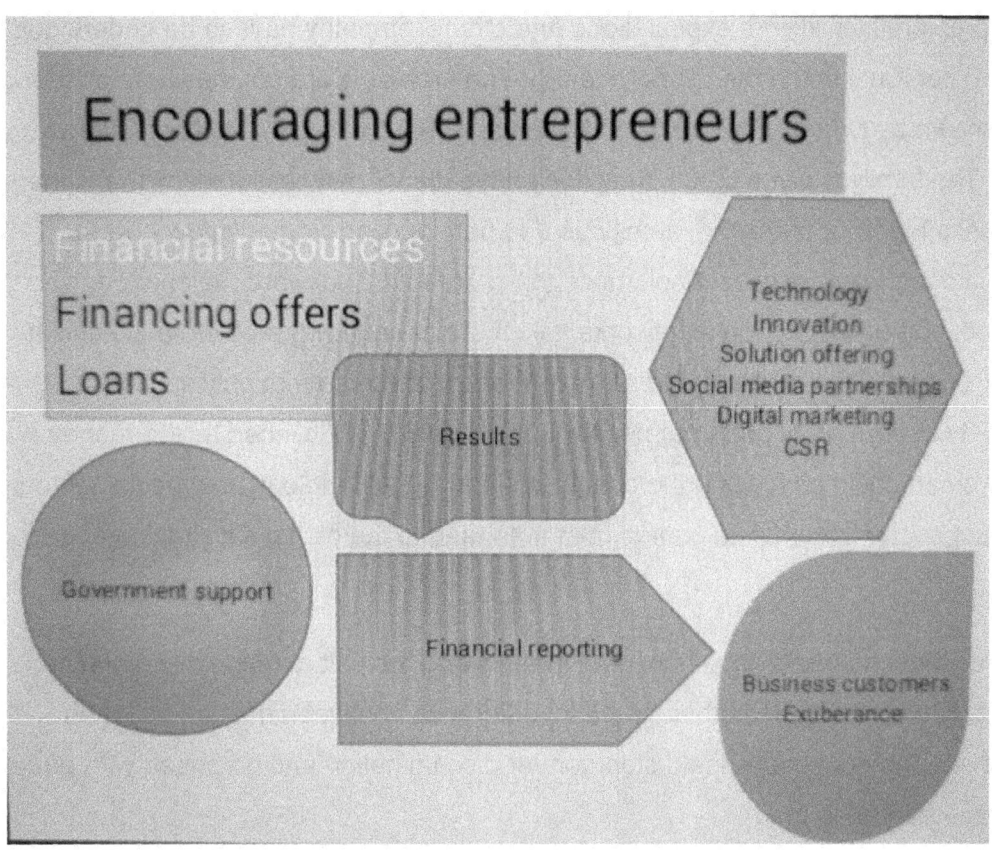

Fig 5: Post Covid19 Entrepreneurship model

Women entrepreneurs should be provided more aid, support and incentives than ever to give exponential growth of the global economy. The benefits are responsible business, better response, research and excellence, resourcefulness, better conflict management and other things that are delivered by women in a slightly different but better way than men. Adaptive, empathetic and caring, women are more accommodating than men. Post crisis situations are looking for such management traits and characteristics as possible with women Entrepreneurs because they are not natural traits in men who have to learn such skills. Time delay in training, wastage of resources for experimental initiatives, and other indirect methods ought to be avoided by the replacement of past boards and committees with a high ratio of women and men or equal representation in the office, commission or group working on world development. Men and the rest of the society have to inculcate acceptability of women leaders in the best interests of the global economy. Neha Juneja, Jennifer Feiss, Manjula Kalyansundaram, Elle Russ, Charlene Johnson, Aarti Sehwag and many others are making an impact on the world by overcoming the challenges of staff dereliction, customer withdrawal and receiving high target goals. The family problems, children's expectations and others' empathy have to be understood for simplifications in personal and professional overlap. The problems are not the same as that faced by men as shown by Dr Indu Khosla, Sheryl Sandberg, Riddhi Gupta, Jessie Matthews and Bobbi Brown. The family is given credit, they don't have plan B, success doesn't make them complacent and these highly appreciated, ambitious and hardworking women know how to remove plastic from deep oceans, run school, make the children in backward region study and play, projecting work and building people networks, take care of unknown problem and solve it using grandma tip, or search for problem and solve it. Women leaders are highly successful because of the ability to earn profit and treat people with humanity, not blinded by the money nor emotion, the women could be leading the charge of financial, technology and media sectors including every other sector in complete control over men, and to the global satisfaction of every stakeholder.

Government of every nation should have new laws in removing the salary range discrimination, workplace facilities differentiation and other structural differences between men and women going against women. The economy should stop gender discrimination and go ahead with equal opportunity to women as that to men.

The national governments should prepare separate policies and incentives for the child entrepreneurs in furthering the most nimble innovation in the world because children can grow better imagination than others who are sharing the risk of developing conflicts that children again are able to avoid better. Tanmay Bakshi (AI champion and software cognitive development), Shravan Kumaran and Sanjay Kumaran (teens and siblings who own the game apps companies), Raghav Sood (CEO of Apaholics LLC), Ayaan Chawla (CEO of Asian Fox Development), Trishneet Arora (CEO of TAC securities), Caroline Bercaw and Isabel Bercaw (sisters and founders of Bath bomb desserts company), Alina Morse (CEO of Zollipops), Callum (CEO of iCodeRobots), Madison Harrison (CEO of "Photos with Madison"), Eva Karpman (The Dream Big podcast founder), Tamia Hawkins (CEO of Mia's Treats Delight), Vanessa Sam (founder of "Inspiring Vanessa"), Maria Raguel Thomas (CEO of Ria's Slime), Kennedi Harris (CEO of K-lock) and other child entrepreneurs, authors, life coaches, tech inventors and geeks are helping industries, police, citizens and governments to solve the problems of humanity.

The economy should take help of our entrepreneurs while appointing the budding stalwarts as growth advisors prior to formulation of new policies for development of the post corona world. Women should participate in different walks of progress whether in entrepreneurship or space research or agriculture or education to facilitate all round development of the economy from grass roots to extra terrestrial spheres. Men and women should equally shoulder the responsibility for ethical business and global economic growth.

Rethinking strategy

Amartya Sen implied that ...men are ...rational fools...

Finding the right way out of crisis aftermath so that the economy does not get stuck for a long time, is a future headache for all strategists. Every company would request the strategy consultants to suggest a way out of the new change management problem, that is - employees have to ensure not getting stuck in the crisis paradigm, each time a change is made within the organization. Mass change is not far from the industry of the future but the series of closely timed crises of 2001, 2008 and 2019 have set a crisis paradigm capturing fears and patterns of employee decisions or failures. I would still term 2001 as a SARS crisis because it was a "crisis incognito" paving the route for covid19, both sandwiching the recession of 2008... Seems like crises had planned their arrival like a mastermind. What worse can you ask for?

The suggested approach as discussed with the veterans of business in online conferences advocates an in-house strategy but not reimagining it with the top companies charging hefty professional fees, in a bid to save costs in the post covid world where the industry would be in chaotic soup and companies would know more about their plight than the external consultants. The third eye is not required because the crisis has instilled responsibility and made the industry more mature than earlier. Internal experts can better see the furious changes coming on the company strategies than the consultants. Much to the chagrin of strategists, the world is not going to look for external help anymore because there is a lot to be fixed inside.

Strategists and consultants should shift focus more to the research and market report generation like the top notch companies doing mostly these days, in bringing out multiple studies with eye-opening insights or mundane data presented in a new graph. Either ways you are thinking strategy and not getting bogged down by the crisis.

We also might have to study the old findings of strategists of pre-1990s to see if something is missing from the current studies and implementations. First a strategy for cross border collaboration has to be formulated for combined management of similar crises. Next the resource theories have to be revisited to understand how the capabilities would change under different economic conditions for changing business models of the future. Finally the knowledge management theories have to be explored besides exploiting the fundamentals of organizational inertia in reformulating growth strategies for converting reluctant employees into resilient implementers and ailing economy into knowledge economies of future because industrial economy or service economy or agricultural economy or innovative economy or digital economy labels (won't be applicable during and after a global collapse) would have to be replaced by that of knowledge economy. We must be nurturing the knowledge acquisition, storage, dissemination and updation to deserve the growth tag as a nation heading into future economic participation in the world progress. Governments also must take initiative in motivating research undertakers to propose new theories and aim at becoming the next Michael Porter or CK Prahalad or James Collins or Alfred Chandler or Lindblom or Mintzberg or Ansoff or Athos or Ackoff or Govindarajan. Similar to work from home, study from home and research from home, must be implemented to carry on unhindered work of academics reaching the solutions on managing downturn well to enable speedy recovery of the economy without risking the welfare of people. Full salaries and stipends must be paid in the -from-home models and more post doctoral initiatives must be made digital or individual based so that the candidate can complete the work in a way preferred and convenient for studies during and after the lockdown period. Lab strategy for strategy is not that relevant but for other fields, an apt lab strategy is the one that allows for digital interaction or virtual lab facilities for research experiments to be conducted by scholars so that the results could be utilized better in finding solutions for the crisis instead of waiting for it to end and then prepare for the next recurrence like novel corona of Covid. Full range of residential, transportation and technology convenience must be made accessible to international and local researchers because research drives knowledge and knowledge drives strategy. Knowledge could be of dynamic facts (differ by time) or static studies, the same market conditions can be interpreted in different ways by different scholars of the past thus constituting the static studies but the current onward scenario goes on presenting different facts that form part of dynamic knowledge prone to change in future. Though market conditions change the studies are static as they cannot be edited or changed by today's scholars except by conducting a fresh one.

Strategy in educational institutions should be to increase the number of digital graduates in the post covid era. Online fees and lectures have to be made according to the student capabilities. Full time degrees and certifications should be made online and more professional like the physical college ones. E-learning is not a pastime activity but should become the motivator of people to get educated and work in the society. Government should roll out schemes for online scholarships and funding to be paid back by the students after completion of education when they join online work rolls or factory rolls of companies.

Corporate strategy needs a lot of rethinking because priorities have shifted. Cost cutting is not possible because the economic costs will have trickle-down effects on industries and companies. Profit-making is not the goal because vulnerabilities have increased, customers have lost trust and confidence, new business is not achievable due to market slowdown and sustainability is the key issue for the economy itself and hence for companies. Health of individuals is the number1 priority for the global economy. Revival of growth in industries is possible if corporate strategy combines with healthcare strategy. Non health related corporates should aim at allying with economic goals and coordinating with the healthcare industry to enable their recovery because a failing economy can become ailing economy when the health concerns are completely addressed by economists. Ailing economy can speed itself for recovery by depending on industry growth that depends on corporate strategy in addressing the company centric goals related to production, performance, employee ethics and environmental protection. The CSR aspect is also necessary for proper inclusion of communities in the growth of markets.

The role of strategists is like that of getting an extra head in the organizations so that we don't lose growth but few heads especially in a period of recession like corona lockdown. This is a real one that may rank just after the 1939 doom because total production stoppage and industry dysfunction is witnessed for more than six months continuously across the entire world without an exception. The recession led by coronavirus is historic. Ideally governments and industries should have involved as many strategists as possible on the task of rethinking the recovery strategy and economic pull-back from the deep covid well. It is not late, now too, we can start working with the think-tanks of strategy to propel the engine of economic reconstruction.

Agricultural sector needs more inputs from strategists for farmers. We cannot ignore the feeding actor of the world. Strategies to implement new technology for better yields, improved storage, low wastage and better prices to farmers will again ensure a strong and healthy economic base. The people are fed by this sector and it needs protection beyond wisdom. Farmers should be considered on par with the entrepreneurs running companies. Farmers run the crop fields vulnerable to vagaries of nature and exploitation of buyers who resell harvests at high prices without letting the farmers even repay dues out of the earnings. The families of farmers ought to become our responsibility in ensuring that they do not go hungry at the end of the day. Education, healthcare and insurance should be provided to the families of all farmers across the nations by their local governments. This is the start and more can be done later once we are able to meet these objectives successfully. A good agricultural growth can provide ground for continuing the industry growth without hiccups. Together we can then aim at achieving fair growth in the services sector that is largely fighting for human-robot ratio because in situations like corona lockdown, we cannot expect professional services but robotic services though not possible in all fields of service. Robots for example might not excel in providing the physiotherapy services that are best handled by trained and certified experts. Social distancing and physical isolation prevent such human involvement but more sophistication in creating humanoids with the same skin and appearance of humans could give solace to the customers relying on the touch based treatment or close interactions because robots carry no viruses.

Supply chain management

Robert Orben's differentiation of the current from previous years in offering an additional option to laugh in modern times, when earlier men had to choose between fight or flee... in crisis...is interesting.

The supply chain strategies and management need to be redefined in the world of post covid lockdowns. The end of the lockdown era might not deter the work ethics of lockdowns from percolating down the supply chain management with the work from home trend staying in the industry for good. Supply chain meetings are necessary but would be online for most part of industry interaction (more than 90% growth interactions happen over supply chains).

Out and out manual supply chains have to be automated without fail not to risk failure in future.

Fig 6: BC-AC Supply Chain Management

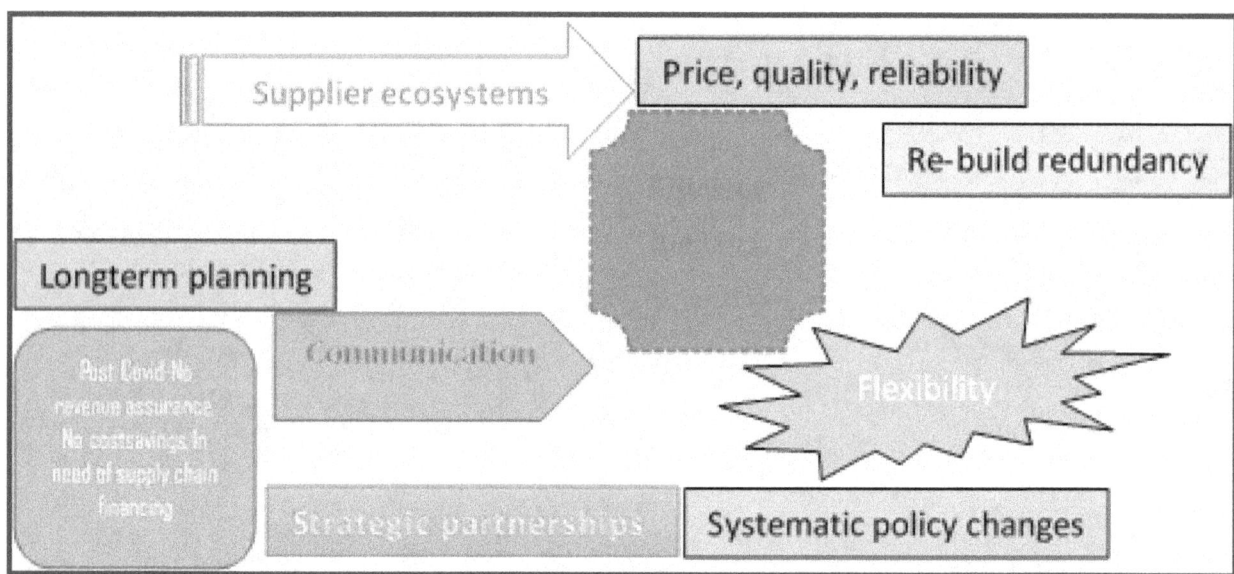

The above figure (Fig 6) depicts how traditional supply chain models focusing on a best-bid type of best supplier in price, quality and reliability to the manufacturers, advocating zero inventories, are moving to a post-covid supply chain harbouring redundancies and flexibility in supplier ecosystems comprising of lot many participants like distributors, promoters, negotiators or other channel facilitators, redirecting investments more into safety of workplace and workers while adopting technologies for robust communication with supply chain participants, stakeholders and end-users. Supply chains before corona (BC) did not bother about investing in hygiene of workers. Healthy workforce can be expected to think better and innovate more by interacting with consumers on social platforms bringing the advantage of mass advertising campaigns. Marketing investment is going to be replaced by that on strategic partnerships because otherwise small companies may have to choose exiting the industry. The new networks are tough to build in the after-corona (AC) supply chain management that guarantee no revenues in addition to the rising costs. Financing schemes could support the companies in adapting their supply chains to the time and need of the market. Government should step in with such aid and also support the change of policy with long-term planning. Systematic changes can help companies adapt to the industry blockages generated by the lockdown, instead of shutting down the business per se, and gradually find solutions for achieving economic management of value chains. Today the situation is - bear or leave. Either bear the costs or quit the markets if companies are unable to manage cash outflows on operating costs.

In-house technology experts can develop apps for better communication of availability, safety and progress of workers. Today redundancy is needed because we don't know when the need for material would arise and where to supply them. It is therefore better to stock and pile items in different points of logistics. The situation will not change immediately after the lifting of lockdown completely or launch of the vaccine. Global recovery is a lot dependent on the successful functioning of supply chains in the economy. Industry partners are not reluctant to convert themselves into a temporary supply chain by taking end-to-end responsibility of the cycle from raw material procurement to the end-user feedback on the final product. It is appreciable because covid19 has taught us to be empathetic in supply chain learning from the crisis that things won't improve unless we take initiative.

Future supply chain strategies could look at nations becoming hubs of certain inputs by supplying the required material, resources, knowledge and skills for given product (s) to other nations to be able to develop indigenous industry or compete with the imported products. India could become a textile supply chain hub, Japan could become a technology supply chain hub, the USA could become a final product supply chain hub and similarly other countries could work on creating a geographical hub niche for goods or services. The hub is not the centre for activity but more like a coordinator role that matters for decentralizing the global economic development that is a suggested or rather trending model for the future world after it learns to live in crises. It does not mean that the present world would continue to yield under the pressures of unknown viruses or unexpected downfalls within economies. It means that crises would come in different shapes and forms in the future as has been happening till now. The world has never been free of problems at any point because without problems you don't need solutions and there ends the purpose of our problem solvers. Or it may be a way of nature and hence economies to balance the growth and strength across economies. The power should not rest within a single region or country or economy but vested in the interests of all nations, then alone can the nations find an objective to grow thereby contributing to the rest of the world in their own ways without seeming a futile existence. Advanced or developed countries should take the responsibility of guiding the rest of the world towards growth mechanisms in the ways applicable for affirming a green economic future with higher growth rates as each decade progresses onto the next.the idea of hubs is thus not creating power pockets but power sockets so that when crises occur we can plug and play our economic development tactics for testing and advancement (development). Power pockets would not enable doing the same because they would exhaust themselves and exert themselves as soon as a crisis would occur. The present lockdown and aftermath could make us understand that we are not really managing but leaving things to be managed as in normal times. Lockdown is the beginning and end as we could imagine that nothing concrete is happening in any country after the decision of lockdown. The second milestone of testing vaccines has come after more than 4 months of the debacle, when our other industries can turn out a movie or a product in a few weeks' time. Somewhere the decisions got stuck and matters started hanging like the personal computers or things are getting held up in the economic flow that we have to identify in order to alleviate tensions and increase hopes of people. However logical or technological or scientific we may claim to be, the world is still running on beliefs and hopes of the countable genuine people.

Networks and transaction cost models

"...if companies miss out on... customer emotion...cost effectiveness is of no use..." - Philip Kotler

Strategic networks can help companies manage the costs better when it comes to networks and Post-covid decade would see higher transaction and agency costs for companies though lockdown has reduced the social networks cost. The key driver is institutional ethics in maintaining a balance between customer emotion and transaction cost. Digitalization would expect elimination of physical transaction costs but a replacement would occur by digital agents and virtual corporates at one extreme, and more interaction due to spatial proximity at the other extreme. The latter would entail high agency costs because of the covid threat and it would take longer than soon for interactions to happen unless the rise in fraud risk and canceled transaction prods the participants to meet one another. Competition could manage better by collaboration instead of losing resources over the complicated network structures and organizational cost hiccups. Assessment and remodelling of interdepencies could help understand the spatial market equilibrium founded on social capital and trust. Coronavirus has created an imbalance among the economic agents without time for thinking and we are talking of rethinking and reimagining over and above restructuring. The repetitions are against the past pre-covid or before corona (BC) junctures where companies would have predicted some scenario in modeling their forecasts on the current state. Compare the scenarios with present reality to understand the real agency network costs. The high cost of internationalisation, lower costs of localisation and high environmental costs can be intuitively (mental modeling or system dynamics modeling) correlated with brand costs, opportunity costs and behavioral externality costs of business. Reassess the system dynamics models against the market forecasts model and compare the variances with those between actual models and multi scenario models. The initial difference between firms would be small but increase at industry level accumulating trillions of dollars at the economic level ($50t+), though shocking it may amount anywhere between $100-200 trillions by 2023 globally. We don't have to be surprised even if it breaches the given range because the cycle or chain would continue for as long as maybe 2025-28. The only reason is the corona cost of people's life, health, business and economy as a whole that is shattered in forgoing huge amounts of growth revenues, industry losses or sectorial returns in the future and present. By the end of decade we should incur heavy network remodel costs to enable a flexible future for breaking even and recovering the economic gains. On unit level, online business transformation is dealing with additional costs like interchange fees beyond that of declined payments. Sometimes the logistics supply chain gets worked backwards and hence the sellers calling back the couriers for parcels need to pay the penalties for canceled orders. Rework at the covid times is tough to be avoided and may heighten cost 'expectations' by at least three times. Customer expectation based cost is also going up due to unemployment or changing expectations and drastically different outputs. Some customers do not prefer transactions due to fear of high costs in conditions of underemployment. Impacts of the corona epidemic are visible on consumer financial dislocation and falling credit scores. Classic business models are changing in an age of unrest and recession. Digital and online business models need more verification tools in the interest of increased transaction activity in ecommerce amidst the raging covid agnoies. Even otherwise, non-buyer traffics are building to reach unmanageable extent because all of us are spending time browsing and cluttering servers of thousands and millions of companies. Top applications like Amazon find daily use by more than 70% of the eligible population worldwide. The use of multiple gadgets by individuals can raise the volume or frequency of visitors but the loads have to be better managed by equipping with more efficient cloud servers for balancing the transaction costs otherwise the per person social cost could reach a huge groundswell of agency numbers. Technology network and social network costs are thus adding to the cost surges propelled by the corona crisis. In addition to collaboration companies must apply negotiation tactics for better deals with network providers and value chain participants. Security costs add up to ensure non-pin based credit card transactions online, because debit card transactions are cheaper, whether with pin or without. The processing costs are higher for merchants when the deals are large volume because of hygienic packaging costs in corona business. Low-volume transactions can also not escape the network costs as they travel through different stages of the supply chain but online means saving of manpower costs. Innovative contactless payments are resolving the issues and high costs of online transactions. More than 50% respondents in a survey felt that online transactions are sometimes more expensive than those at a supermarket or wholesaler store visit. The risks of defective deliveries, returns of purchased items and buyer handling (new items in good condition are broken by the buyer due to adept handling or negligence, but returned to seller) entail high agency costs and companies have to innovate methods of verifying whether the ordered article was broken while packaging, or as in transit, or during delivery or later by customer. The initial defective sent to the packaging department is the direct sole responsibility of seller or manufacturer. Otherwise the costs shift to packers, movers, courier boys and buyers. A better network cost sharing model could be developed in the post-corona ecommerce business. Traditional brick and mortar models managed such problems more on trust than equity basis. We have to see if innovators could educate systems to value emotion and trust factors of customers, then it would make the business and not break the deals even in crisis. Everything has to be simplified so that cumbersome processes do not add to the cost by increasing complexity of a multi layered value chain with dealers, producers, buyers or promoters working along separate transaction flows, process flows, decision-making flows, approval flows or other digital flows. Technology has to be improved to handle dynamic business flows without missing the mark on optimization, interaction, score analysis, compliance, renegotiations, processing, trend identification, margin improvement or competitive strategies because the ultimate achievement should be by enriching the customer experience.

Photo: *Covid Lacklustre Pollution-free Nature*

Way to Innovation

"...the role of management teams...is to revitalize... the employees and organisations." - Lafley A. G

Innovation, if nurtured properly, would revitalize the functions within an organization for further pathbreaking economic recovery. In addition to the economic recovery, industry, immediate government initiatives must have specific focus on improving their user state from the beginning of life cycle process implementation in different dimensions. New Innovation strategies working on business sustenance, success and growth have to nurture the hormone of courage, àgility or correctness within employees to get the competitor collaboration alongside Customer resentment. The resentment of customers is not bad but is a great response in the competitive Innovation drive. If everything goes well with customers and employees or management stakeholders in a happy state, it means we are not always welcoming a new check on us. The present challenge of corona teaches us to get used to constant change. The strongest driver of modern change is customer resentment arising out of business failures. Failure should not deter Customers from buying, it is possible by expansion of trust, but as a company your aggressive Innovation takes the form of resentment in customers. Some of you might have guessed right. Apple is no different from aggressive when it comes to Innovation and Customers. We have to follow the same for giving more than best to customers each time. Customers begin with resentment arising from why they could not own good products then they develop curiosity and excitement of buying from Apple. Research in customer focus groups has brought forth that whenever a new Apple product is bought, the feeling of wellness, peer praise, compliments and new attitudes cover or correct the intrinsic inferiority complex or tension by allowing reactions to build better rapport with family members, friends or colleagues or even strangers. Some people who feel like it's not exaggerated are in less jitter because product fashion or value Innovation can rule future society. Those feeling jittery, accepting the leader's way of business is a good attempt to get new business opportunities for growth and continuity (yes, reverse chronological sense). Top comments in our advanced technologies study groups were analysed. Research findings are affordable! The risk of experiments in post covid19 business operative evaluation can get Innovation in the expensive initiatives category because of low price returns. Switch to Apple Innovation model to increase probability of Customer willingness to be associated with your business brand and organisational culture. Start working, test results and change back to your success recipe in case you don't see the options for further development. Adobe, HP, Microsoft, and Samsung have been practising similar business models with compromising their skill Innovation in return for sporadic internal Management led change Innovation. Samsung has taken deviations to Apple kind of transition in recent years but only time could tell if it can overtake Apple. Swipeless secure payment, centralised internet technology and multi utility smart devices are some extra Innovative steps in Samsung's solutions. 3d as a service is an HP pavilion of Innovation. Adobe's cloud based photo editing program is motivating Customers as well as employees to grow smart in creativity or imagination. Microsoft is investing in smart solutions for laptops, Computer or other Innovation with hologram Technology.

It is easy to fail not due to crisis but some mistakes in the name of Innovation can grow into costliest business experiments. Top management team has to be extremely careful while selecting the best value Innovation in the present economy. Technologies, ventures, interactions and business changes, all have to be reviewed, revised, Innovated, managed and executed in Strategic way to maintain customer satisfaction by product followed by resentment arising out of new needs. See the shift, your customer thinks that you have done known things but how did the customer not get the same idea? In addition, your products are getting new ideas or needs for Customer's delight by using new products, more from you in future.

Innovation in present business crisis management situations tantamount to get everyone including employees, rivals, Customers and economy participants in the same boat so that we should walk through the same road of empathy, trust and cooperation with the common mission of rejuvenating global economic growth. The duty of each and everyone of us in the quest for Innovation is to be a leader. Innovation is a good mix of frugal experiments, prototyping and lean Management. Innovative risk management in future business would mitigate risks as staged bets besides synergistic sharing with collaborative partnership.

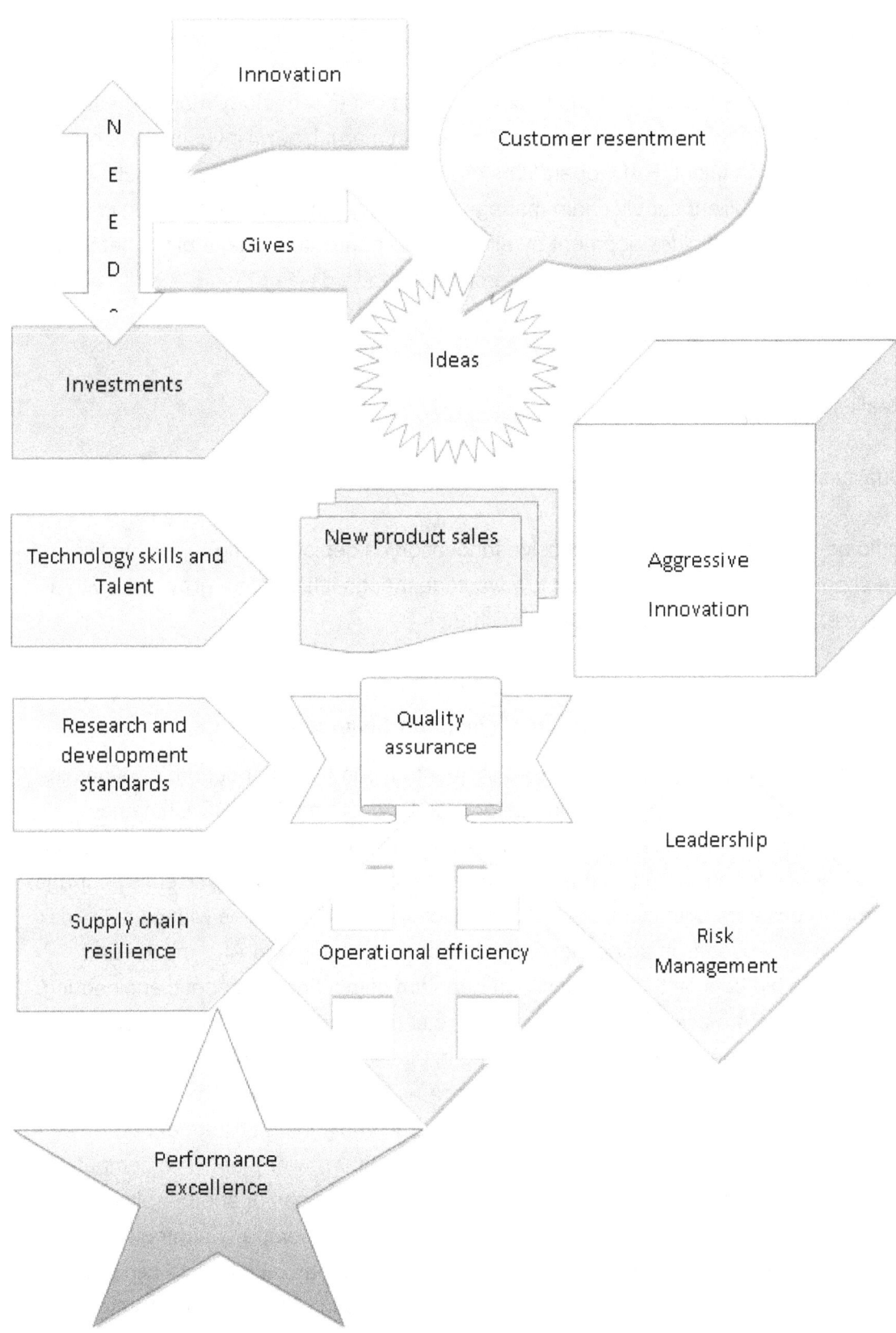

Fig 7: Post Covid-19 Innovation Model

Sustainability of Innovation lies in strengthening organisational designs and external Innovative networks with maximum discipline. New ways of thinking should be encouraged by allowing teams to take prudent risks and letting them explore inside out (Technology map to customer map) and outside in (Customer experience map to product map). Liberal investment is needed in hiring fresh Innovation talent, R&D, operations or sales strategies to get good results from Innovation by adding resilient supply chain management. Thus Innovation in the post crisis world could double economic development by allowing reorganization to take place before the subsequent industry transformation led by research and standards (Fig 7).

Innovation= Investment * new ideas
+
Resilience in supply chain
+
Quality standards assurance

There would be some grey areas in aggressive Innovation as depicted in fig7. The quality assurance should aim for zero defects and low wastage though it is again a grey area with a scope always existing for new errors backed by change.

A special mention of Quantum Computing

Future milestones in innovation might be based in quantum computing or computer dynamics. Quantum Computing is being studied in Google and IBM. According to CNBC China has already invested $10 billion in quantum computing. The technology of the century could build new drugs, a vaccine for covid-19 is not a problem, solve problems plaguing scientists for ages, help economic forecasters, with stock market simulation, optimise portfolios with complex risk analysis, expedite discoveries in adjacent fields of machine learning and AI. Amazon and Microsoft are doing big bets on the application of quantum computing for genetic engineering. Financial opportunities are available in plenty. Venture capital and private funding investors are willing to give millions in new businesses competing in the NextGen computing that began making appearances in the early years of the last decade. The bandwagon would not be without quirky hurdles in the nascent technology. The next generation big thing is staggeringly powerful though building a quantum computer is next to that of a nuclear power plant. The competition in the field is tough and on with the player not able to accept the success of another player(s). The governments should have enough competition law in place for the company strategies to use the technology for the progress of the global economy. The commercial interests can grow better with companies like spacex and Tesla using the application of quantum computing for building space vehicles, hyperloop and even personal cars. The SUVs under quantum technology might have better performance or capabilities to serve like the multi utility vehicle to convert to a drone to fly up in condition of traffic on land. It should be put into good use by taking into account the interference effects so as not to become like dynamite invention or dotcom bubble. Very cool and dry, clean, tightly controlled environment is needed for the technology to function properly. Every technology comes with a new set of problems and we have a good experience in solving them and accepting new technologies. Superconductivity is needed for quantum chips, quantum physics plays a big role in the area of quantum computing. The world may use it for refrigerator innovation, as an example, in future. Real business problems of the next decade could be solved within minutes or seconds. The money making potential should be exploited by using the technology for the progress of the world. Governments could utilise the technology for storage of most confidential information by combining cryptography and data, say. Health care has tremendous application of quantum computing and a cure for new diseases might be designed by the quantum computer in a few minutes after the diagnosis, the intelligence that we want to build defence against corona viruses now. Safety, price, application in a normal environment and quantum servers have to be worked upon for quantum computers. It is bound to revolutionize the next generation solutions.

Others to be part of the bag of innovation as evolutionary technologies are metamaterials and metametals, nanomaterial based nanotechnology, ultracapacitors, room temperature superconductors, artificial intelligence, virtual reality and nuclear fusion power.

Future Evolutionary technology is for achieving exponentially fastest calculations and highly improved lifestyles. Meta Metals and metamaterials are the structure dependent material of the future that could revolutionize product innovation by taking advantage of the inherent feature in the ability to support invisibility. It can be a great help to encryption and security or development of multifunctional convertible gadgets. Nano technologies are of great help to healthcare because of the high potential on destruction of cancer cells, but not without concerns on energy and technology, the super material that can change the world, could use huge amounts of input energy on totally different platforms in comparison to the output. Energy sources could be from a balanced range like nuclear power or ultracapacitors or room temperature superconductors as alternatives. Nuclear fusion will compete with biogas, solar or other hydrogen and helium based adaptation of energy rechannelization. Fusion power is stable but more work is needed in the area. Ultracapacitors could be found better than batteries with replacement of higher energy densities, low prices by allowing additional longer life, more cycles, higher load current and quick charging features but not without losing mileage of battery. Room temperature superconductivity could energize our homes into becoming modern future innovative solutions in themselves. The quantum computer and a small machine plant could bring itself into the house. Power lines of no energy loss. Graphite is being studied as the possible source of superconductivity. AI can be managed with giant vehicles for surveillance to get new lifestyle luxuries but may be limited to use for purposes of training in future. The VR world would take over the future technology world that is struggling to bridge the gap between poor and rich. It might give advantage of information to some owning virtual reality devices thereby increasing the gaps again.

Corporate ethics after corona lockdown

Bear Briant emphasized that nobody should hide in a crisis because we would be found anyway…

Post-Covid19 management ethics would undergo transformation on aspects of employee performance and corporate governance from punctuality to public relations. The work-from-home model won't end completely and few employees reporting in offices would be working with clients onsite or company bosses on premises of local or headquarter office. The mutual partnership between the company and each client would not be limited to the implementation of projects or release of products but extended to functioning and profit management tasks. Appropriate measures for restoring sensitivity of information would be taken by both sides. True corporate ethics would find ways of assisting the customers with resolution of operational or other business related problems that would directly come in the way of execution of action plans by the providers of solutions or services. Top management in the client firms must be prudent to have clear priorities for handling key internal problems on their own without pushing the entire buck on the provider's shoulders. Vendors must also ensure that every client is dealt with in a customized way to avoid common processes leading to new issues for different customers. There has to be room for some paperwork because officials' feedback shows that it is easier to refer to ready papers at times when systems have multiple versions or mistake deletion problems. A total of 10% paper documentation could be allowed in organizations to boost confidence of employees who are not yet ready for 100% automation, especially after the corona crisis, some want to revert to traditional business methods. They felt that too much modernization of business might create additional problems in times of tyranny. It is natural that we find solace in unrelated causes for coming to terms with a rough situation. Bosses unanimously agreed that employees should be provided refunds, claims, food and other amenities without much delay of approval procedure or hierarchical dependency.

Competition has to be managed without tactical deviations like institutional disinformation in the name of ethics. Some companies hide sticky information that is public and divulge key data in informal discussions at parties where multiple heads of companies do not know what to really talk except observing competitors with doubt or untrained instincts. Corporate ethics should be incorporated as in-house mandatory brushing sessions (ethics and compliance programs) for employees to learn the relevant do's and don'ts without confusing with personal biases. We feel that corporate ethics is not letting others take credit for work or not talking with employees during work hours. Employees end up wasting time in trying to avoid the same. The exigency and urgency spurned by corona could leave a swathe of varieties of products unsold in the latter period if public trust and long-term equity are not worked for by following the ethics of not constricting the flow of business in the name of ethics. We have to be sensible instead of sensitive to rules. In the wake of increasing demand for masks, breathing tools and other healthcare related products, some companies are not following the market lessons (increase the price when demand goes up). It is ethical in not raising the prices in corona chaos. It is unethical when some sellers demand higher prices to handle the supplies because of the need to build business and the chance might not be missed. Ethical considerations are as important as economic involvement when a virus like corona is testing the whole world. Myopic organizations cannot balance the use of technology and application of ethics in times hit hard by crisis. The post-covid effort in industries should be redirected to making ethics simple so that customers and employees are treated as people, not machines nor kingmakers.

Agencies and governments must ensure protection of societies with vulnerabilities in ethics related to clinical trials. Medical laboratories must own up responsibility and muster strength to use internal staff from top to start of corporate ladders completely, not just low-wage workers, in testing of drugs, the next sample of patients or subjects should come from the rest of the population. The post-covid2 period is nothing less than a stress test for companies to manage customer expectations, management ethics and competitive responses without weakening the 'collaboration muscle' of all industries in the economy. It is time to involve bioethicists and health leaders to work in favor of the general public without compromising on any person. The societies may be rebuilt to understand how a small percentage of over 5% tries to make the majority work against self-interest and in the interest of a small chunk of unethical companies. regulators must come up with appropriate policy changes to monitor the ways of business of different companies and simply shut down or seal the unethical ones. They are no less than the quarantined corona-infected lot. We have to reorganize our society and understand how to resolve the conflict between the interest of a small group and the greater good. Corporates should start relating to one another and relating with the rest of society. The level of trust in public for the words and actions of government and international promises is already low. Management of ethical issues is key to revive the economy by global collaboration to accelerate the production and equitable access backed by transparency without eroding the trust (say, while implementing surveillance ethics in the corona crisis). Mismanaged corporations must ensure that it is time to change and the few troublemakers must be ignored for the good employees to shoulder responsibility for ethics by concentrating on non-profit and research activities more than profit generating sales. Salaries must be given to all employees in time and that is enough in a crisis. Don't aim for promotions or record sales stints. Encourage the employees to care for their families and friends because every one of us has to be a caretaker and leader to propel the development strategies in the economy from both sides of public safety and industry growth. Companies must provide for employees, employees must share with the impoverished lot in the society in addition to government initiatives of rehabilitating the needy with the help of NGO and non-profit firms or by instructing the corporates to invest resources in helping the needy.

Practice of Ethics or application has to begin from time management without any room for mismanagement.

Our everyday lives are governed and controlled by time. Time is the most powerful component in our life. Time once gone never comes back. Be it a household, school, office or business, all activities are planned and executed with time as a benchmark (White, 2013-14). Time plays an important role in employee's activities at work. I would like to corroborate the opinion that employees should be able to alter their schedules to respond to unexpected problems that may arise. Time management needs to be flexible. At the same time it should be structured.

Everybody manages time in one's own way. Students make timetables for studying, housewives make plans to handle daily chores, and working people make schedules for completing tasks and meeting deadlines. Books have been written on Time from all perspectives -e.g. philosophy, management. Stephen Covey's "Seven habits of Highly Successful People" mentions effective time management as a factor of success.

There is a right time for everything. Every category of life follows the principles of time. Nature is no exception. Trees take their own gestation time to convert buds into fruits. Even a human being is formed and born after 9 months.

Employees usually make their schedules according to the work allocated to them. Usually employees make tight schedules so that the work is evenly spread till the deadline. Their psychological mind-set is formed in such a way that one extra task or a slight deviation from routine disturbs the schedule completely. Employees start feeling jittery about handling unexpected problems or tasks. It is human nature to ask for more. If the same task is given by a reduced time deadline, the employee indeed is able to meet the deadline. Reason, he/ she is mentally prepared to deliver the task in the given time. The same task when asked to accommodate other problems becomes unmanageable, as the schedule has been fixed in that way. This gives rise to a fall in productivity or quality. If the task and problems come together as part of one project, the employee can manage completing in the same given time. Thus it is important to set the timetable, which can accommodate any unforeseen exigencies.

I would now take another contention that a highly structured approach to work is counterproductive. A plan is needed to handle every known task. Unanticipated tasks can be responded to, spontaneously. Planning and adhering to plan denotes a sense of discipline and acts as a precursor to successful accomplishment. A detailed schedule helps us visualize the completion that bolsters confidence in our ability to accomplish the task. Especially, offices and workplaces are supposed to be professional. Employees are responsible for their work. Making timetables gives a credible proof to the superiors that the task can be completed within time. Such plans need to be highly structured to handle all subtasks. Nevertheless, the plans should also be flexible enough to accommodate sudden needs. For example, all companies now show their time plans/ project plans/ business plans to clients to assure them of the completion.

Thus time can be planned for long-term and adhered to in a structured manner. It is however important that time management is flexible enough to change according to unexpected needs.

Next is accountability.

One seems to be concerned about the accountability of people. Even in a flat organization, employees at each level can be held responsible for the actions. There is no doubt about it. The employee can be held accountable at the lowest unit level while reporting to a Manager. Similarly a Manager is answerable for tasks in that department. Going further, a director is responsible for the performance and achievement of tasks in the entire division.

Taking this example to a hierarchy where all roles are clearly defined, we can see that it is tougher to see accountability. There are several levels in a hierarchy. For example, an employee reports to a team leader who reports to a Manager, the Manager reports to a Group Head who might in turn report to the Division Head and/ or Director. There is a multi-reporting structure where a person might report to more than one head. This might happen in flat organization too but at a higher level. The already large number of levels makes it unmanageable in hierarchy - whether multi-reporting or the ordinary. Also people tend to shift blame and try to escape the responsibility. This might reduce accountability in hierarchy as against promoting it.

The best example is the privatization and liberalization that is being pursued all over the world to enhance accountability. Public Sector Units or State corporations are deemed to be less accountable due to hierarchical structure. Therefore private organizations are moving away from hierarchy in order to ensure more accountability. Even State organizations are reducing hierarchy especially at lower levels to leave it less cramped.

Thus there are other viable alternatives to organizational hierarchy. People can still be held accountable for their tasks. It might not be valid to infer that hierarchy is the best form and that other forms go against human nature or would ultimately be fruitless.

As discussed the industrial activity must not stop because without growth of companies, citizens cannot be expected to remain healthy in the company of viruses. Production must go on whether of medicine, vaccine, food or other goods. Otherwise it would be equivalent to unethical global economic lockdown even after the reopening.

Business administrative transition (Bat to hit the crisis)

Brooke Foss Westcott disclosed that the crisis, not great occasions, would show what we have become, ... strong or weak...

A major driver of revival from the aftermath of covid crisis is to hit it back by bringing about business administrative transition in the organizations. The present recessionary pandemic is like a check or economic appraisal at the end of decade. It has brought out a lot of hidden weaknesses, deliberate faults in business ways, loopholes coerced under past crisis impacts or other factors blamed on other acting agencies on the business floors of revenue leaders or loss makers of today. Responsible top managers concerned with the growth goals of organizations must take one step forward in working with the participants in and out of companies who are not able to change the scenario but looking for support.

For a long time, organizations have been trying different types of reporting structures for administration. Examples include hierarchical, matrix and flat to name a few. The oldest and a well-known common form is hierarchical organization. Now-a-days many organizations are indeed moving away from hierarchy. I would like to use the current trend to refute my own opinion that any organizational structure other than the hierarchical one would go against human nature and prove to be fruitless.

In a hierarchical organization, there is a well-defined structure with each person reporting to one's superior. Atmosphere is formal with most people addressed as Sir/ Madam. The form has been in existence for long. With the passage of time and more studies being conducted in organizational behavior, corporations have seen a marked improvement in quality of work by giving more freedom to employees. Freedom translates into a less formal and more informal atmosphere e.g. addressing bosses by names. This in turn leads to a structure with more employee interaction where the superiors are more approachable.

Currently, organizations are adopting this concept in what they call flat organizations that have less hierarchy with for example, a CEO at the top, a head or a director for each line of business followed by managers and their reporting employees. The competition in vogue is that between a hierarchy and flat organization.

Technology is creating a competition ultimately between human trends and corporate structures.

Firstly, take into account the mission of your company before working on any modifications or transformations. Understand your organizational culture because that is the determinant of employee performance and customer feedback. The output of your business operations is directly dependent on the original first input going into your business foundations. See how many gaps have been formed by time or crises or goals or knowledge or routines of your company. How far are you from the initial input? Is the direction same as that of your founding vision? If not, call for a fire brigade and extinguish the burning issues by forming policy reformulation committees to get the required transition done for reducing the gaps. People are at heart of the matter, make transitions by timely actions based on effective decisions. We have to instil empathy and foster awareness among all stakeholders of our business to understand one another as well as the external non participating people in the distanced society. Leadership teams in different organizations should be totally engaged with all levels of the workers, customers, business heads, users and regulators to ensure safety of as many groups as under their influence, by using persistent, relentless or uninterrupted communication (online, telephonic or any other modes, but do not waste time by arranging meetings because you got to use these channels). The objective is to attain future goals as a means of looking at business continuity in times of lockdown.

Secondly, work towards the tool reassessments in sharpening your business focus on handling the present based on possible problems aggravated by past mistakes leading into future business administrative soups. Expect transitions in accounting whether as new rules or changes in your systems to address internal issues. Do not restrict your resources to addressing the problems thrown by covid19 alone, pick as many problems as possible and resolve to leave a new business shape for better growth chances after the end of the present battle (no less than World War III). Appropriate changes should be made to recruitment policies, benchmarking styles, performance appraisal cycles and communication guidelines.

One other way to walk the crisis is to prepare dual-strategies, one based on books and other suited to your style of business. Follow theories and chalk out the ideal benchmarking score card then revisit your own business operations to notice that reality differs from recommendations. Follow as-is to chalk another practical benchmarking scorecard. Do this for all tools and let the employees work on doubling the efforts to defeat the crisis effects. Or hire more. Be ready from both sides. It is called Sun Tzu's maneuver principle of the art of war as conflict and competition strategy for the companies. Conflict with covid19 and competition with other firms could be resolved by complete coverage of our capabilities versus expected action plans.

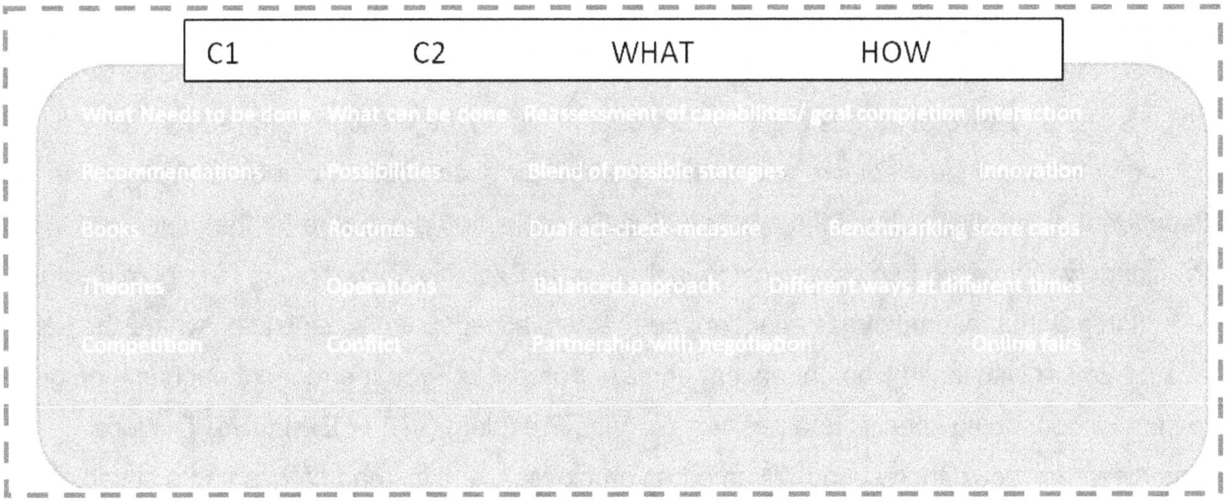

C1	C2	WHAT	HOW
What Needs to be done	What can be done	Reassessment of capabilities/ goal completion	Interaction
Recommendations	Possibilities	Blend of possible stategies	Innovation
Books	Routines	Dual act-check-measure	Benchmarking score cards
Theories	Operations	Balanced approach	Different ways at different times
Competition	Conflict	Partnership with negotiation	Online fairs

Fig 8: Post Covid-19 BAT Model

The first C in Fig 8 is CEO focus because every top manager wants to meet the needs of the hour (so as not to be left behind in the competition) by taking help of books, theories and consultants but the other C2 as corona or crisis or covid19 would question the business routines, operations and capabilities to leave you with doing only what is possible, not going an extra mile, thereby generating conflict of interests among stakeholders. The maneuvering strategy or the method of resolving lies in reassessment of capabilities without compromising on customer and organizational goals by partnering with the competitors for better negotiations in the business both harnessing improved interaction or communication with global social networks say by using online fairs as tools, across the stakeholder chain so as to ensure a balanced approach in growing our business by wisely blending possible strategies from all sides to result in innovation, because when we adopt different ways at different times we would be following dual act-check-measure (one tool is the preparation of dual score cards for normal and crisis times) to not miss out on any issues of organizations. This should be preferred way of business at all times whether crisis or no crisis, keeping in mind the size of impact of any crisis on our economies.

Future digitised world needs better administration in the post covid-19 world.

There is ongoing controversy in the corporate world on the concept of flat organizations/ businesses, eliminating the hierarchy classifying employees into ranks and grades according to experience and expertise. Eliminating the hierarchy completely might not be a feasible and realistic approach.

Education levels are constantly rising. People are realizing the value of being educated, in terms of better prospects in personal life as well as career. All companies employ stringent entry criteria to recruit the best of the talent pool. Companies conduct written exams, group discussions and several rounds of interviews depending on the position being sought for. Each criterion eliminates the mediocre and retains the best for each position of job. The toughness is dependent on the hierarchy of the position. E.g. The selection procedure for the position of Vice President would be much more critical than that for an Executive. After going through a rigorous selection procedure, employees might not be ready to accept a flat organization where they are treated on par with those who underwent an easier process. Even the recruitment has then got to start without being specific to a position like Vice President (VP) or Executive. The job advertisement would then sound, "Wanted an employee", and instead of "Wanted a suitable candidate for a VP". Thus promoting a flat organization or business by eliminating ranks and grades might not seem to be feasible to implement (White, 2013-14).

Every human being retains a degree of self-esteem. An employee is motivated by certain incentives and recognitions. The self gets satisfied when he/ she gets a tangible differential treatment to distinguish from others who have more/ less experience and expertise. This is done through ranks and salaries. A VP getting the same salary as an Executive has little or no motivation to excel in his/ her work. Similarly a veteran in work, say a person with 15 years of work experience has no reason to put in his/ her best effort in an organization which has no mechanism to differentiate from a novice. The author talks of promoting collegiality. He assumes that colleges don't have any ranks or grades, which is true to some extent because every student belongs to a class - Class 9, Class 10 etc. However a class is equivalent to a rank or grade where a group of students is placed. Even by this analogy, to eliminate ranks and create a flat organization would lead to a decline in employee morale and affect performance of the organization.

Flat organizations can still be promoted, but differently. Today, companies are definitely adopting the concept flat organizations but in a different way. The grades and ranks are not eliminated. The atmosphere is getting more and more informal. For example, in the earlier days, bosses used to be addressed as Sir or Madam. Now all the employees are addressed by their names irrespective of the rank held by them in the company.

Thus by the above set of reasons, one can say that it is not practical to think of making an organization or a business 'flat' by eliminating all the ranks and salary grades.

Above is one dimension of understanding the transition in business administration.

Next, as proposed by a Consulting firm CEO Steven Minsky, the business risks due to social distancing, falling employee productivity, investment outflows, weakened supply chain, unemployment pull-back, civil unrest and economic instability have all to be addressed by business continuity risk assessments, multi scenario risk management plans, operational business impact analysis, prioritization, effective policy management and enterprise wide incident management. Business continuity risk assessment involves intermittent review of our business enterprises in a stead to confirm that the health of all operations and departments would support the sustenance of the company, followed by drill-down assessments of business initiatives, SBUs, cost centres, profit centres and data centres. A separate risk management plan has to become a deliverable for each risk scenario within every business unit. Further, the risk teams have to become detail oriented in analyzing the impact - monetary, competitive, social networks - of risk on - operations, functions, business flows, processes - and vice versa - to understand the effect on statutory output like annual reports and market output like consumer reactions. The kind of exhaustive analysis would require prioritization of risks and tasks, for not ignoring the interests of stakeholders, for which again a team has to devise changes in policies to ensure effective implementation and management in the organization. Even a fool-proof transition is also not without scope for errors. There is no guarantee for a flawless business transition despite investment of millions of dollars into using sophisticated technologies for administration or formulating effective interactive forecasts. A proper incident management system has a better capability at handling such mistakes creeping into organizational activities.

We would be then able to claim a holistic transition in business administration at dealing with crisis in a well equipped way.

Marketing, sales, advertising

It's not recommended by Boris Yeltsin, for us to yield to emotion but...to draw lessons…. and... overcome... the crisis...

The post covid strategy in marketing, sales and advertising indicates a dry patch according to a survey by a Tietoz consultant. There would be a fall in the spends and budgets in the marketing and sales departments unlike the expected contrary that advertising expenses would be increased to showcase companies in the covid limelight of taking necessary precautions in favor of the buyers. The heads said that it was imminent and not something to be advertised, some even suggested a change of line for the professionals in the business. An advertising head said that she would look to move to a different sector since the add-ons in packages would be totally eliminated to save the company costs. Another marketing honcho admitted that the lush earning times of marketing people are gone and they would prosper on the past earnings more than waiting for the marketing segment to pick up after the crisis. It is true to a great extent, not by my wisdom but after thinking on the sayings of the above CXOs. the industries must spend most of their resources in restoring the health of the economy by supporting the sustenance of companies or employees themselves and maintaining the sustainability of customers themselves. Where will the glories of brands, products or companies matter in a broken economy? Other impacts could be for the government to increase the same in order to forge its image in a better limelight by doing more than most of the companies but how can government cooperative firms and units make cost-effective diapers or healthy vitamins? It is not an impossible task but a challenge for governments to spring forth in action across all nations in a bid to recreate the competitive effects in a morbidly hurt industry and an ailing economy. Ethical professionals would agree to the changing model, others would argue that "personal professionalism" matters more and hence salaries must be increased on the contrary. Change need not always favor the bosses and alienate the subordinates. This time it is just the reverse. The low salaried employees won't be victims of the change much to the abasement of the top managers who are at risk of job loss or rotation to a lower rung designation in organizations. It is true more for marketing, sales and advertising professionals than banking or other professionals. The difference is less. Why would banks agree to pay millions to directors only to land up torn in crisis? Still, it is not a solace or threat but data collected from reliable sources that needs to be conveyed across the working masses. Well-informed workers can decide better before a chaos harms career or personal life. The expenditure in the bracket might see a fall of more than 50% IN THE POST COVID ERA, 2021-2025. Officials do not foresee any improvements because the revenues are falling and mostly the allocations in marketing, sales and advertising departments are made from the profits. One CEO brushed aside and said, "we don't need fat pay drawing marketing heads in any position in our company. Anybody can come up with a great marketing idea if you roll out a competition with a foreign vacation package as a prize… they (marketing, sales, ad employees) do not majorly add to the economic growth…", sweeping statements yet true. The employees in this sector have to add value and bring something real to the table, different and more, it is clear that the market does not value efforts in the direction so far. Economy does not need professionals only for the sake of pomp and splendour. In fact we need to be humble enough to accept that it is applicable to any industry and any employee. People skills and self ostentation are not enough in the new world of post-covid crisis. Real application of knowledge and utilization of education to the fullest are needed in all our cases. The degree ends up in a certificate and the knowledge ends up getting negotiated every now and then. *See my certificate and gauge my knowledge to pay the highest salary among peers, but my presence is enough in the office, why should I give back anything else to the office and nation? This has become a common attitude of all employees across the world. What is she contributing to the workplace… hire more people …. Ask him to do the work ….increase my pay to extract more work…* such are the adages and cries of employees. It all depends on how well you can talk and get away with it. Your networks may be strongest but that alone should not matter. Your work ethics and efficiency in terms of how you get done how much work should matter beyond question.

At least now the situation has revealed itself in letting the departments of marketing, advertising and sales as primarily focused on profits, earnings, few heavenly presentations, more interaction and coordination with the advertising and creative companies, and totally talking and tackling things without worrying if being caught by truth. Officials are responsible in repaying house instalments, invest for children's future and likewise solve personal tensions using professional ladders, whether the country is from asia, americas, europe or any part of the world, all of us are using professional growth to serve personal interests, the sectors of marketing, sales and ad space train the workers in precisely this task. Very few sincere professionals use personal strengths to add value to the professional life by yearning to do something for their employer firms. Most of us stop using our brains after completing the desired education and collecting the degrees. Absolute sincerity is needed from each and every citizen, professional and student of the world's nations otherwise the economic development would happen in books alone. We also need a group of people who are well versed with human mentalities, not the branded psychologists, even outside MBA, they don't teach you what to do in jobs. This group should gauge the workers and identify the real workers whose effort and intentions are pure but results are not true. In the performance the failure occurs because of poor flattery levels with bosses or lack of cunning unethical ways or not knowing the political diplomacy or blackmailing to let things happen in the favor. This is the type of workers theories need but practise is preparing another type of mind players who know how to grasp others' credit by a smile or two, or let them if they are owning up a responsibility for at least one major task, ok let it be a single minor task also but they should be working on it to own up the mistakes or to not let the mistakes happen in the first place. This is the level of integrity we need in tomorrow's work environment to facilitate economic development as growth and nothing else.

Financial twists

Charles de Gaulle must be respected for... defining... the man of character falls on himself...he imposes his own stamp of action, takes responsibility for it...

"... You should not buy time with money... you should sell time for money..." - Dr. Ch S Rajagopal

The professionals of the finance sector have a demand to be more ethical and conservative in the coming times. Covid crisis has shown the importance of low variance and high cushion margin budgeting. Companies have to allocate at least 10% FOR FACING THE CONTINGENCY EXPENSES for managing the unexpected crises, these have happened continuously and we don't want to take further risk in future. Wide impact of corona may lead to several changes in the laws related to Financial statements and taxation rules with separate accounting for annual reporting of business conducted during crisis and special discounts or incentives in tax for corporate and individuals stuck in an economic crisis.

Companies would track financial departments more closely to avoid any accompanying scandals in the already crisis hit industry. A closed survey of top leaders has brought out insights on how they feel about finance from different angles. Financing of projects seems to be on hold for the lockdown period and CFOs would take some time to invest in new projects even after the end of covid lockdown. A new vaccine might increase the financial performance and trust of financial controllers in the companies. Some feel that the role of financial markets per se is ignored in the chaotic environment. Foreign exchange markets are falling in investments and currency depreciations. Prices of risk assets have fallen more than half from 2008. Money markets are volatile and stressed. Low-rated firms have seen a jump in credit spreads. Stocks are falling and rising by more than 30% in short intervals, bonds are sending few hope signals without any performance improvements, derivatives are falling and traders are optimistic because they treat the lockdown as a boon for making speculative profits. Banks are moving to economic collapse themselves while some are attempting to address the collapse. You never know when you yourself become a crisis in a crisis. However banks have better support of liquidity and capital from central banks; and have become stronger with more stress tests and supervisory scrutinies than in pre-covid era. Banks need more resilience to emerge successful under times of strain.

Financial and auditing managers are required to do stringent accounting and conduct strict inspections for the benefit of industries that are trying to manage the cash flows and acquire finances to meet the lockdown caveats. Costs are on a rise and companies are managing internal mandatory operations for the sake of existence without worrying about competition in the external environment because lockdown has diluted the parameters of competition thereby leaving no route except collaboration for the firms. Global financial stability has felt a dramatic impact of the covid crisis. Even the US treasury market is a victim of coronavirus with the fall in asset prices. Commodities like Gold are on an upward spiral in the first half of the lockdown but expected to see falls by the end of 2020. Other commodities and equities may not escape further fall. Central banks are encouraging expanded asset purchase programs and have cut policy rates to hit rock-bottom in advanced economies, emerging markets and lower-income countries, though easing monetary policy seems to have provided liquidity by open market operations and swap line arrangements like the fiscal policy changes are helping restore solvency. The financial system is not able to contain the pressures on cost of credit but central banks are backing purchases of corporate bonds and loans to stabilise investor sentiment and enhance liquidity. According to the IMF, the global financial conditions seem to get darker and tighter than earlier with the future growth rates hovering in negative 7% or slower. Stark challenges are heading towards more vulnerable countries with the emerging markets taking the maximum heat (more than $100b reversals in flows). Advanced economies are bearing the brunt of more cost by retracting investments from the emerging markets (low cost options). Prolonged downturn may aggravate selling pressures thereby rendering deleveraging ineffective and stopping the credit markets with the default rates rising, deteriorating credit quality, increasing outflows, poor underwriting standards, rising high-yield spreads, weak investor protection and recessionary speculative grade forecasts along with rising market-implied defaults. International coordination is essential for restoring market confidence and financial health of economies. The IMF is right in giving first preference to protection of vulnerable economies and then aiming for a sustainable recovery of the global economy. Risks would be existent in financial markets regardless of a crisis. Further slowdown could increase potential risks leading to global instability but as global partners developing and developed countries need to join hands in reducing the impact on financial stability by initiating work on ground zero where the most vulnerable economies are suffering thereby weakening the foundations of global financial systems. Once it is strengthened at the root level, financial stability can come back to the emerging markets and financial recovery can sustain in the developed economies. Improvements would be easier to implement in the markets across the globe because the response would be better for interest rate changes as investors and individuals in houses would have more confidence in our financial mechanisms. We would see more trust circulating in the financial structures energizing the economic muscle of the countries. Policy changes can be seen as governing points for strengthening the pillars of industry growth, geographical resourcing versatility and financial prosperity all leading to a sturdy economic recovery in the long term over a period of 5 to 10 years because nations would be in a prepared state.

Payments and settlement mechanisms will not take the assistance of banks in future. The financial part will happen on exclusive channels meant for the transaction committed online. Solutions for handling such secure deals are existing and new technologies such as block chain or quantum computing for the next decade could build better conflict management, data processing, authentication, privacy guards and virtual cash flow for the handling of payment and refund on real-time. The financial statements would be expected to get similar treatment in the advanced systems (using cubits and other programming innovation).

Management tantrums and Corporate revival

The opinion of Michelle Dean that crisis forces commonality of purpose on one another, is similar to that of Kiran Mazumdar Shaw.

The post covid business engagement models in employees working partly from homes, offices, common work spaces or client locations could give scope for more management tantrums by allowing differences in perceptions, opinions, understanding and ideas, than when together with bosses, peers, reportees and customers in the same office. Right now we cannot say whether it would be better or worse for the business performance but it may be possible with the type of response in leading to a variety of options explored that could be used for risk management or learning from a new form of conflict management by distant negotiations and remote people management. Business itself could thus be redefined in the latter decades due to the changing situations. Ecosystem would expand with no need for international boundaries within the operating business environment consisting of stakeholders from multiple nations who all would have to make conscious effort in hiding their side of tantrums to give the chance to customers because management teams can take motivation for employees even from the most inaccurate ways of customers. A buyer can throw tantrums in all directions including that of competitor prices, quality challenges, never ending list of tough choices, or undue business involvement in technological interventions. The case of covid is so vividly common to all of us that we don't need to be together to be together.

Top managers are ever hyping business achievements aiming for more stringent goals or milestones to demonstrate leadership skills because subordinates would otherwise outsmart performance appraisals winning over continuous promotions to capture bosses' seats and offices. Covid19 has distanced the bosses and subordinates by letting them work from their own spaces or home offices (the digital displays include covering background to hide home interiors and give office look). A small survey conducted online among 200 bosses and 170 subordinates who both answered their set of relevant questionnaires revealed that subordinates are feeling relieved and more confident of displaying skills via work whereas in normal times, chances were low to be allowed by bosses who used to deviate the lower rung employees from coming out with capabilities outside of the expectations.

Keeping aside the hitherto existing Boss & subordinate conflicts, it is time to overcome for BOSS & SUBORDINATE to work in tandem above the egoes of Boss feeling insubordination or even domination from Subordinate vis a vis Subordinate feeling excessive of Bosses' overpowering, stress creation, finding fault intentionally or taking the credit of subordinate's successful job without appreciating or giving him the due credit.

Now Corporates require cooperation from all towards a single target of revival from the business fall!

Founders should not feel that the sick baby must be in their own hands without letting the doctors diagnose and treat the ailments. For old firms, employees must not feel as if working in a cocoon or safe haven but must allow external opinions and recommendations to be implemented without the slightest doubt. Sometimes employees need to face skepticism and doubt when they take a very good suggestion to the boss, 'why did her idea matter? Is she up to something? Why did he not give such good ideas till now? Is he trying to sabotage the company interests? Is he helping a competitor? Does she have vested interests in the growth of the company?' Such foolishness would not only delay company revival but also that of the industry. Later we feel that the crisis could have been managed better by doing some impossible strategy or gimmick by walking across the rim of a ditch. Remember that such bosses need psychological help more than the failing employees who fail due to such implied responses leading to nit-pricking and poor appraisals at the end. Those employees are in enthusiasm and wait for a chance to prove mettle in front of bosses otherwise such ideas could have served competitors better had the rejected employees joined another firm. Feedback for attrition reasons from both employees and bosses have revealed similar palpitating thoughts that forgo the definition of professionalism and trust.

It is very easy for the bosses to lose smart subordinates and sometimes stubborn subordinates might end up getting transferred thus losing trusting bosses. Both sides must balance well to prosper in a trustworthy and positive atmosphere. Organizations are willing to reconsider employees who commit mistakes, similarly subordinates must also remember to protect the trust without getting upset over bosses' peevish behaviors or continuous fault-finding. The negotiations with external stakeholders is impossible if within the firm, bosses and subordinates don't find a common board. Subordinates must not outsmart bosses as if to show how well the position is deserved by others. Bosses handle multiple things and hence do not need to prove in front of subordinates that they have been through all this before or that they also have knowledge. Bosses also must not pervade the space of subordinates in constantly reminding the authority. Sometimes subordinates feel repugnant and sometimes repentant. As human beings it is natural to live with weaknesses and strengths in the same person who is sometimes understanding and sometimes tough. Management leaders like Peter Drucker and Keller have insisted time and again that organizations should nurture fathers- like bosses who have the right to admonish because they take the entire responsibility of growth of team members. It has to be given as well as taken in the right spirit without crossing the boundaries of human tolerance because the brain would not cooperate well in reviving the company, nor the person would be able to complete regular tasks well. Man-made bottlenecks have to be avoided at all costs if the future economy has to look beyond crisis and emerge healthy at least after some time (when the crisis gives way to regular normal growth). It is very easy to blame others especially in times of turmoil and government or individuals stand the same chance of success because all of us become nervous during times of dark. Decisions are easy to take in normal times but not in abnormal conditions. Whether as a nation or as a company you have a right to fail in normal markets, so why not in 2020 when covid19 has hit us on face. Unless we stop denying failure thinking sick, '...that should have worked …. This nation is able to do but we are not … let other nations also fail … failure has no right to come to us…', (such bragging statements suit vagabonds of business and not the leaders who want to see their company centuries down the time), the management cannot be successful in proceeding with future development strategies. The board members or top managers or the investors would all deviate and differ from one another taking on from one conflict to the other without reaching consensus on any solution. If a competitor alone is the winner in such situations, then the company may try to stand up on its feet again but here the crisis would be a winner in which case the companies cannot stand back for long. Anywhichways, the tantrums would have to be stored till normalcy is restored in future, by focusing all efforts on the revival of industries and economic growth, however small our position may be in comparison to the size of the economy.

Key management drivers in post covid-19

Market and Competitive Analysis is a latest technique of coming up to speed on the performance and forming result-oriented goals for the organization to achieve. A baseline of information is provided after the assessment of market and competitors. Differences also come out in the growth trends, economic distinctiveness and technological issues. It serves as a process to evaluate broad market trends and specific segment needs, determining attractiveness of the market, assessing factors driving the change in industry, evaluation of competitors, SWOT. All these data help in finding the target market out of the overall market and addressable market.

Addressable Market data throws light on how much of similar offerings are purchased, availability of substitutes. Target market changes according to time and needs. Any market is influenced by changing certain demand factors on the limited resources; regulations and technology. Identification of market forces and emerging trends help predict market behavior in advance. A focused marketing scope is critical because of increasing heterogeneity of needs, increasing range of technology, product, process choices, economics of serving different product-market segments, fragmentation of channels in many industries resulting in the economics of serving different segments and which is challenging. Customer expectations are also important in market changes. Purchase decisions are influenced by a combination and not just from price, technology, quality, product range, features or speed alone. Marketing opportunity and sales strategy are also determined by the existing barriers to entry and potential competitive advantages.

Competitive analysis helps in driving the key industrial pressures, framework for developing growth strategies, marketing plan for target markets, customer service and sales forecasting/ planning. An interesting area to gain is from studying the past and current selling strategy. Customer action is strengthened based on market needs and strategies. It also gives opportunity to identify niches or market gaps for the substitutes and equivalents. The competitive analysis can be used to identify the level of rivalry among competing sellers, reviewing competitive strategies to encourage customers to switch from a competitor, analyzing ease of entry for new competitors, determining supplier and buyer bargaining power, distribution channels for products/ services, analyzing macroeconomic factors. SWOT analysis provides insights on other marketing strategies, competitive positioning and customer experiences (White, 2013-14).

Other industry standards of practice like pricing, market perception, purchasing cycles, seasonality, production etc also help in understanding market characteristics, positioning market strategies, assessing existing competitors, substitutes and alternatives.

Today's management practices are undergoing tremendous change in everything from marketing to ethics to competition to strategy. At times, management is the piece, at other times, management is the whole.

Those days are gone when marketing was deemed to be a hard core 'man's job' with a lot of aggressive sales-running and pitching needed. The inclusion of human spirit makes it soft to be considered as a 'complete' art of marketing.

Earlier companies were more focused on selling products, making profits and enhancing features. Needless to say, markets have shown increasing significance of customer preferences in the later years. Products and features are a prerequisite because customers expect to see them in purchases. However, the preferences of customers have given rise to more customized and tailored products than earlier. Today one can exercise online options to include or exclude certain features in a product. This trend is seen to transition into an era (supposed to be the current one!!) where ethics form the top priority in marketing. OK...products and features are necessary, customers are important BUT the most important contemporary issue is how to meet ethical standards. We have not completely landed into this era but are in the process of doing so. One needs to note here that ethics and ethical standards cannot be delineated or restricted. One company may consider -developing top quality products to be ethical, another company may consider compromising with quality but selling at low prices to poor people as ethical, another firm may not consider these aspects but just not bribing in its business as ethical, and so on. The difference helps in shaping organizational culture, in creating products and services that inspire and are inspired by the values of customers.

Another facet....Companies can choose to upgrade their 'marketing platform' or stay/stuck in the past. Apple may still consider that its products have differentiating and unique features to make better sales and hence Apple may not give utmost importance to 'human spirit'. Who can enforce that? Winner is the manager who observes the trends of companies and sees that the new era is emerging out of the customers who are growing more knowledgeable. Hence they are more responsible for their purchases and want to ensure safety of their families at a smaller context and of the world at a larger context. We can also examine companies like SCJohnson that started as a parquet flooring company in 1886 and is today the maker/seller of household products all over the world. The company is in the process of using products that save energy and natural resources and in turn are safer for the environment. The 'human spirit' part cannot ignore the green marketing part as this deals with the spirit of protecting the planet and the human race. The topic brings out the other side of the coin by emphasizing the ethics, attitude and culture of the company.

The interconnected themes thus bring out several hats that marketers, traders, partners, companies, employees and consumers could wear in the process. Sometimes, the marketing hat could be related to pitching features and selling products alone. At others, the hat could shift to that of understanding user needs and concerns thus creating customer segments. The competition is a combined effort of the participants and not of just the companies in business to provide healthier and more nutritious choices at a reasonable price to a larger segment of the population.

The competitive strategy addresses values from the stakeholder point of view as to stress the need for companies to be value-based to get positive partnership with all stakeholders - customers, employees, vendors, suppliers, partners. All these bring us to a set of questions- Will human spirit and ethics in business give way to new laws and regulations? Hence will management be much more complex than expected? Under what circumstances are customers prone to change their priorities between products, own preferences and ethics? How can the human spirit be imbibed into a commercial lifeless organization? What are the possible effects on public policies, advertising, healthcare and interpersonal/ interorganizational relationships? Will a new kind of relationship emerge between the organization and its customers (a new term like interpersorganizational= interpersonal + interorganizational)? Does it mean that the companies are shifting from a price-based competition to socio-based competition? Will the mission, vision and values of the company itself undergo a drastic change in the process? A study of these aspects of business will enable us to peek into it deeper and better for obtaining a first-hand insight into the economic future. Finally, the insights could be used in a course like Business Ethics to show a new ideal world of management for future professionals.

Team vs Individual contribution

There has been a lot of debate lately as to whether the organizations and groups should function as teams (in which everyone makes decisions) or as individuals handling authority and responsibility for a task. While everyone is entitled to their opinion, I prefer to examine the facts and see if there is any merit to this theory.

The decision of carrying on a task as a one-person responsibility or as teamwork depends on the type of the task or project. A humongous task involving many people can be executed better if a single person takes the lead and responsibility for the completion. It does not mean that all decisions would be biased or authoritative.

Functioning as a team with all people making decisions might lead to chaos and conflict. A saying goes - 'Too many cooks spoil the broth'. One person may take responsibility on behalf of others in conducting the task smoothly. We cannot ignore the fact that one person's central authority would prove to be more representative of others' decision than in teamwork where everyone would try to impose his/ her own opinion without being under any obligation to listen to other's views. All are on the same platform. The single person responsibility puts him on a higher pedestal with an additional task of respecting others opinions. One way could be conducting meetings and gathering everyone's decisions. One should not generalize that all groups should function as teams without any single person responsibility.

One also assumes that teamwork automatically ensures sharing of responsibilities and duties. In reality, individuals are more demanding for their rights but have the habit of shunning duties. In corporations and groups also, this holds true. The task of distributing work is not an easy one. There should be someone to allocate work and assure the individuals that it is equitable. If one person takes the responsibility of a task, he/ she shoulders well, the responsibility of allocating tasks as he/ she has to ensure the completion of the task in time. It is not appropriate to say that one-person central authority is not an effective way to get work done (White, 2013-14).

The issue of accountability is also noteworthy. A single person would be directly accountable for a task or project. A team of people would behave erratically. In times of failure, everyone would tend to pass the buck onto someone else. If the project becomes a success, everyone in the team would try to take the credit. If a single person takes the lead, the success or failure can be attributed to him/ her representing the whole team. The central authority can give an unbiased feedback on the individuals in his team. Individuals find it more rewarding when they are assigned a fixed task and performance monitored with appropriate laurels or criticisms. Teamwork cannot ensure all these in an acceptable and credible manner (White, 2013-14). A single person central authority may thus be more effective than a team working on a task.

The fall of personal power in organizations is better than that of the overall bargaining power of the global economy or even a single national economy, as signaled by scholars of the past like Harvey, Mills, Cairns and Fulop. Employees should behave like collaborators in the global crisis time without expecting individual profits at the cost of economic growth.

CSR

We should follow Phil McGraw to come up with a crisis plan without waiting for the crisis to come on us.

The definition of corporate social responsibility is on the best crossroads for more expansive modification in the immediate period after corona lockdown. We know that the media is a messenger or conduit for social responsibility activities, pledges, requests, champions, initiatives and other such healthy claims. The only area we have unequivocal support for is CSR but now we can see CSR not as attention pulling tactics, it is accepted as a new healthy way of life. Of course, it is no new thing but we are giving it a new relevance each time the economy is in a crunch. Let's accept that we remember to help others when we land ourselves in a grinding situation. Though not wrong in a crisis world is in need for a more consistent CSR approach after a rough tide too. Simple logic says that we will have a better and easier world to face in the next crisis. We can only be more confident and relaxed if we don't worry about the lack of the needy in the next crisis. Trust me, the best CSR also can't get rid of all poverty in the world, whether you view it as a local citizen or foreigner. We have to get new tough measures in place and not intermittent online viral videos as part of CSR. Do you sincerely believe that CSR can ensure food for all or shelter for all? No but this is the expected result. We have to achieve it citywide, country wide and globally. Final goal of CSR should be able to get the permanent solution to social problems and not one of the many attempts or trials because the needy face the trials and tribunals, psychos kill on a spree, farmers face suicide attempts and these are not asocial but social problems. The next problem is to get one solution for sustainable improvement in the global society with long term intervention for the coming centuries, not decades, for more reform orientation. Corporations and other individuals are equipped to help, so as beneficiaries of economic development all of us need to give equal participation in SR. Social responsibility when levied on companies, whether companies of firms, or companies of people (to extend it a bit more), becomes CSR but corporate does not stop the best society from participating in the development of other needy societies. The next advancement otherwise is to give the responsibility in the hands of society from the objective of spiralling the development of some to the rest of the society or the new needy societies emerging in the world. Life is the most unpredictable thing but we can prepare for facing new problems in the world. First we have to highlight the "h" of technology, humanism is no option with technology but technology is an option to facilitate new conveniences of humanism. Humanism is no different thing but a healthy way of embossing human, humanity, humane and other such words. Technology has to teach us to be more than any machine. How should a machine teach us to be more human? Easy task if we emphasize that we think, machines don't, we talk, machines don't or have to use our voice to mimic, in a way all that machines have is no less, no more than a healthy capability for imitation of human beings, this is the most that a machine can become no more than a robot or robotic equipment. Users will not feel independent of social networks, problems and responsibility in the absence of which we tend to do CSR as a feather in the cap when we have to treat CSR as a daily activity like feeding our family and other necessary thing for complete revival of national and economic growth because the gaps created by corona lockdown opens up many other such cracks formed by the past crises and current mistakes. Did not the 1939 downturn go unaddressed? We are not completely successful in closing all the issues arising from the depression more than eighty years old. Yes, problems grow old with us if we are not able to solve them because we are human. Humanism comes to our rescue in many instances, see how lucky the world is. The recession of 2008 is still discussed because we have a more frightful right to blame it for the new mistakes of our global leaders, entrepreneurs, businessmen, business women, political agents and other participants in economic growth. Unless healthy growth is brought in all countries, it may be a good idea to call everyone as agents of politics, because we have to be more like the responsible and respected lot instead of waiting for another Rabindranath Tagore, Ramanujan, Jagdish Chandra Bose, Abdul Kalam, Martin Luther King, Mahatma Gandhi, Florence Nightingale, Sarojini Naidu, Alfred Nobel, Swami Vivekananda, Madam Curie, Mother Teresa, Bhagat Singh, Rani Laxmi of Jhasi, William Shakespeare, Taanaji, Chanakya, Tenali Ram, Dr. BR Ambedkar, MS Subbalakshmi (the Carnatic singer donated till the last penny of her earnings), Charles Darwin, Akio Morito (Sony's founder told his progeny to value culture more than profit), WB Yeats (English poet stressed that we have to be one with Nature), Nelson Mandela, Aung San Suu Kyi, Malala Yousufzai, and many other luminaries that our books forgot. The real social responsibility begins with new initiatives taken by the corporate and educational institutions in creating characters of the top eminent best who rise by taking responsibility for all downtrodden in our societies. The topic must not forget Syria,Kroatia, Iran, Iraq, Japan and Africa all of which see CSR as a need but the world is yet to wake up to facts. Wars do bring devastation but as human beings the governments of other countries must do everything possible to restore normalcy after gaining their calm. The victory is no ruin of another country but CSR as a cross border social responsibility. No country can forget Japan and its Pearl harbour mishaps of pre-1950 period, in how it is no less than any other advanced countries in the new technology leaps but economically in need of aid because the citizens are still in a state of isolation from the rest of the world. The currency is not performing well due to its weak fiscal infrastructure but a combination of healthy cultural orientation on human values and rapid technology progress (both traits form strength of Japan), can't fail any country by the top global economic development benchmark prodding us to repose confidence in Japan and include developmental agreements on trade, tourism, foreign aid, educational exchange or other possible areas. Syria, Iran, Iraq and other countries in crisis need similar aid to rebuild social life, education, industry and other basic national growth drivers. Poor countries category is getting some help from NGO initiatives but not enough to teach them the best rules of national economic development, by enabling their citizens to be part of the fair global society. Because only then should we be able to facilitate real global economic revival. Who knows if the corona virus came from the infested African forest or a residue war chemical or other unfathomable source to a bat, which might have flown from another ignored reason? Kroatia can't get development without liberal help of developed nations because it faced a terrible time with Bosnia and Herzegovina in the 90s. We don't call it a crisis unless the bigshots like the US grab attention. But these and many more similar failures form a definition of global slowdown. The work in CSR is humongous and thus seeks collaboration of all countries in a more than steady effort to revive the world by overcoming many open issues along with corona.

Social realms of existence envelop the different issues spread across the different parts of the world hence CSR cannot address the complete list unless we try to bind the pages of global book with people's trust, agency ties (weak ties if interacting online and strong ties if personal) and technological benevolence (using technology for the larger well-being of the lowest segment of world population). Important thing is to bring together the interests of people to get ready for championing the cause of others and vice versa so that advantages befall both sides. The global imbalances can rest for a while in the alignment of world economic objectives otherwise the weight would push down the weak to weaker and we cannot measure the results of mitigating such big disparities.

Competition Strategy

Crisis shakes us to reflection and healing after coming to the surface till when we would feel it like suppressed pain, as per Briant McGill.

For more than innovative business, players have to indulge in markets where strategy depends on competition, competition depends on economic growth, betting on community development goals that can serve the government and corporate charter along with personal vision for the long run. The last boil down to totally production oriented advancements in terms of gaining 100% literacy backing skills and technology education, totally employed population can find ways to deal with similar risks faced in 'Andropause' (a term coined by scientists to indicate corona and lockdown followed by side effects on people, animals and economy); zero crime rates all over the world, bulbous growth is no possibility without a hale economy in terms of great minded people, functional markets and well shaped bodily health; cent percent nutrition (from our side, this is the best we can do to target reduction of mortality rise); needless to say, that if we can achieve so much, our interrelated and sub goals would take the shape of afforestation, universal housing, clothing-for-all, technology accountability following the India government's 'form, reform, transform, perform' principle customized for total economic success. First, form a strategy to reform the economy, followed by advanced revival schemes next to transform the different lagging parts of the economic development, finally adopting new technology to perform well in the role of a global contributor. At working for indigenous technology development, our native competition strategy needs to be formed by utilising strength of glocal resources or inputs, one way can be total indigenous technology from end to end, to prove ourselves in global competition, without foregoing the privatization verve. The objective of every nation should be to get new competition strategy in a bid to strengthen the local economy to such an environment that breeds global leadership, capable of attracting employees and entrepreneurs from across the best countries, while simultaneously nurturing a healthy lifestyle of all those living in the country by providing the best standard of living in a continued exercise of excelling in the process of national growth.

Table 3-Types of competition strategy

Competitor types	Participants	Strategy base
Leaders	Armed forces, entrepreneurs, lawmakers	Innovation
Learners	Mentors, economists, politicians, researchers	Knowledge

Leaners	Professionals, law enforcers, Unemployed	Collaborative
Laggards	Criminals, drug addicts, mentally sick	Exploitation

Competition energizes strategy whether in the agricultural, industrial or services sectors because ultimately, everything is dependent on users, employees and nexgen. New citizens are the kids and newborn babies who rise in the world to be future buyers and sellers of nexgen communities. They need a complete ecosystem to persist in a healthy society left behind by us to be further improved by them for their nexgen communities. Some are learners, leaders, laggards and leaners (Table3) as deemed from the world of competition strategy that accommodates competitors of all types. The best competition strategy in a time like this, hunted by corona lockdown, yearning for corona vaccine, fighting against the uncontrollable changes hopping on social norms and trying to be living in the normalcy, could look for cultivating future sustainability and persistence in the economic participants particularly industry because every citizen of the world is no less than an economic participant. We all start as learners while some choose to remain focused on learning for life because we are on the best part of progress of knowledge accumulation so as to be of help in the form of industry mentors, life coaches, economists, academicians or politicians, to the other three communities of leaders, leaners and laggards. Leaders grow themselves as well as others but tend not to be non profit participants like learners. Entrepreneurs, lawmakers, defense and armed forces, medical professionals or other such people on path breaking missions who rise by going out of their way, while giving opportunities of life, protection and livelihood to others by taking high risks. The nexgen economic participants who rise by the aid of other men or means are leaners. They would not be independent achievers but more than 70% of the world population can be slated in the category of learners (not parasites but lean on others for help), who are all cleaners of economic hurdles while leaning on mandate, rules, laws, government action, majority support, public movements or common man ways, like lawyers, professional teams, law enforcement agencies, all working and non working sections of the global community. The same individual and entity may simultaneously belong to multiple categories. Laggards are counterproductive or non productive elements or people due to ill health, illiteracy, unemployment or other reasons, people who are criminals, sick, drug addicts pull down the best growth or tarnish performance of a growing economy. Competition strategy is healthy if the government and others can stop or reduce the counter effects of the four categories of economic participants. Government has to step into the shoes of all four categories to understand the problems, plight and the best solution favorable to a globally competitive economy. We have to appreciate the fact that problems are on low-level, solutions should be able to get satisfaction throughout the economy in aiming at the final best high level growth with the help of thorough knowledge, complete revival and deep rooted measures of education, employment and economic upheaval.

Earlier micro poly was more predominant with multiple players in the domain of Web services and web products in internet, now monopoly is not a distant future with the games, apps, memory and storage drives, payments, books, besides the search engine optimization business, all monopolised by one player Google in case you don't have any other players with the similar business model emerging in the market in which situation the whole purpose and definition of "cloud" will be defeated. The speed and freedom of cloud will not be served by the flexibility of the free and high quality products and services that can reduce the cost of use by adding a new range of risk factors to users (narrow options, paid dependence in future), industry (loss of competitive innovation and business quality to monopolistic management tendencies and other opportunist egos, pricing and negotiation threats to customers not accepting the terms of the contract by the company due to absence of other services providers, finally compromising on the global economic climate. The only solution to the problem is to have a nice plethora of multiple micro players instead of a single big game betting on the future growth of organisation, industry and community. The monopoly is increasingly likely to reduce the quality of technological evolution unless replaced by the better organizing "micropolies" that will not depend upon a single company's whims to make free the customer and the partner companies with the freedom of selection. The competition laws may have to be modified by the global government to make way for the healthy growth of small businesses in supplying innovative technologies without being restricted by the large players that are likely to create a monopoly by making acquisitions.

Competition in the local or global initiatives should strive to depict success of law, equality, collaboration, knowledge, innovation, organizational liberation from hierarchies and mandate based operations resulting in high quality output, organizational agility, hispeed effectiveness, fair society, prosperous industry growth or trust. We may not find all inputs and achieve all results always because we are not machines, formulae or non human. At the same time, we must not be inhumane. Competition strategy is important in even such unhappy times for ensuring the revival of economic growth by right methods that serve persistence in attaining everlasting sustainable improvement with the same capabilities to get sustenance in the future times of economic devastation, if any. Right methods need not find a mandate and implementation of such strategy may be mistaken to be wrong at times, that's why we need upright leaders who would uphold the industrial productivity over the best interest of management or directors by putting the key stakeholders first, investors next and company profit last. Nothing is at stake if we don't take profit for five years, investors can live beyond stock market performance but economic development can't take place if users from the stakeholders suffer or are dissatisfied with the company output, operations or other things. The participants, users, implementers and feedback givers of competition strategy pervade through all levels of competition strategy pyramid right from bottom to the top. An economic pyramid consists of flows in both horizontal and vertical ways, top to bottom and left to right, not to forget the other way. Takers and givers are present both at the top and bottom with the regulations at the top, implementation in the middle and users at the bottom. Unless the best results accrue to the economy from the satisfaction of a healthy user community, the implementation flows back and forth correcting the strategy and its action plans, sometimes gathering feedback and inputs from above (regulators) and below (users). Below is a figurative representation of competition strategy pyramid-

Regulation

Implementation   Implementation   Implementation

Users   Users   Users   Users   Users   Users   Users

The repetition of users and implementation indicates that we have to revisit users more often than implementers and regulators give us orders to abide by certain rules. The extra line and triangle creeping out indicate that regulators may be partly left to their will (no option even otherwise) because there are chances for changes before and after implementation for which we have to assign some resources in the beginning itself.

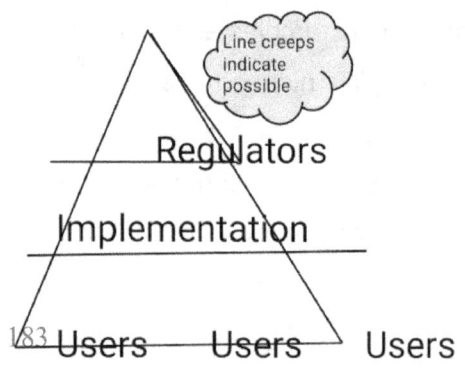

Fig 9: Competition Strategy Pyramid

The user community should be in closer interaction than even the teams and regulators so that we don't miss out on their changing expectations (Fig 9). The scope should be discussed and finalised without creeps and loose-ends beyond a certain acceptance level. Sometimes implementation may call for changes in favor of efficiency or productivity or effectiveness gains for the companies without having to flow from the user demands.

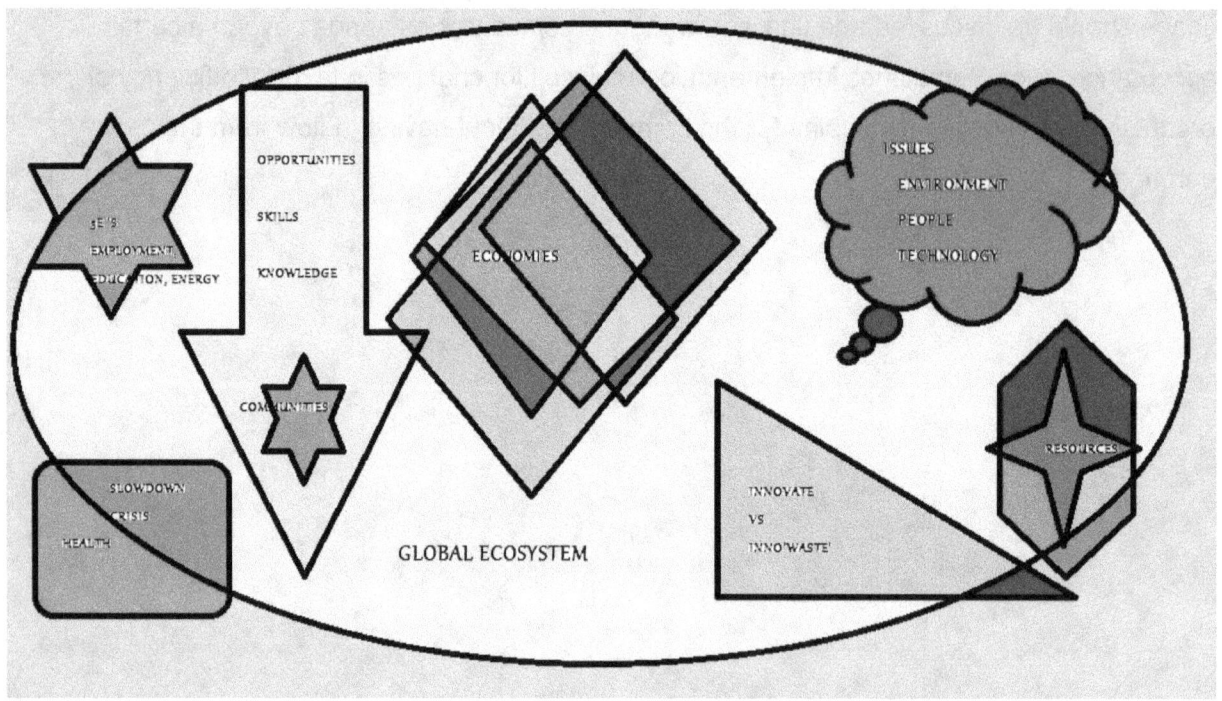

Technology Risks or digital wars

"...And we only got to know that… by experiencing...how they live their life." -Carlos Paz Soldan

Future technology comes with a set of problems that could pose risks of counterfeiting, fake access points, masked duplicate IP or unknown internet intruders.

One of the most expected trends in the future industry is to see portfolio consolidation or standardized competition between the big players like Google, Microsoft, Amazon, Yahoo, Apple and the likes, evolving to develop digital technology in the world of expansion and diversification to match with one another. The 2050 industry may be competitive with the above players in the same lines of service like email, virtual office, shopping, digital marketing, online payments, retail play stores, search engines, browsers and more web innovations.

The devices and softwares could be mismanaged to the end of hackers working for chaos in the lives of users. Passwords may be done away with totally and other forms of verification would be adopted for facial, eye retina, fingerprints or mole recognition as primary and secondary levels of identification.

Digital payments are in highest risk of grabbing user data on sensitive facts like that related to bank accounts, smart cards, digital currency, payment passwords and IDs, even the PINs sent on SMS are sometimes hacked for simultaneous use, approval information, secret questions, supplementary email ID, and other things hampering the financial transactions of people. Global connectivity has increased the risk of interference by illicit technological or system diversions, deviating data of users in unsolicited databases and sources. Enterprises, big or small, are equally susceptible to technology risks of outages or untoward incidents, risk of wrong expectations from technology, technology cannot save us from every fear, it is limited to resolve certain types of problems, as technology cannot save us from Covid-19, awareness has to be clear in risk management of information systems. The financial implications of risks should be assessed before making contingency plans because we cannot recover the losses of a poorly managed technology. Market observations reveal that mitigation collaboration between operations, tax, audit and forecasting risk teams is more pertinent in an age of shifting risks based on changing spending patterns as highlighted due to a rise in digital payments on certain categories of transactions in the world of Covid epidemic. Visibility of transaction and vendor data has increased platform risk calling for better best practices during the crisis when corporate as individual transactions are occurring online with a rise of more than 40% in volumes. We have to develop intelligent frameworks to calibrate risks in real-time by identifying, measuring and mitigating before occurence in a transaction or deal. Digital information is spreading so fast and widely in such large volumes that we would have information surpluses in the post-Covid world. The covid related phishing emails, chatting apps messages and SMS notifications are drawing public concern about fake schemes. Online sources advise us not to pay anything to advertisers luring entrepreneurs to invest in profit making business of selling masks or sanitisers, few working professionals have lost money to such cybercriminals who change phone numbers after the smart payment occurs. Even phishers are impersonating remote work locations or login pages for stealing credentials of employees trapped in phishing campaigns. The probability of error is high and risk for an organization's networks is higher whether through updates from government authorities or health institutions or local advisories or NGOs etching out donations. Malicious links or malware could risk the huge data systems of companies. Fraudulent emails were sent on behalf of WHO as spoof some time back as a new containment measure of covid-19 pandemic. Specious links should not be opened and we should be wary of cyber risks by identifying mistakes in spelling ,address, tone of message as in hurry for some detailed private information like tax identification or SSN or financial data on a masked email that shows as from office but is hosted on familiar email like gmail or unfamiliar sketchy email name. At times the email sender's promise huge amounts of returns for investing in airy business deals. Resilient payment monitoring systems, EMV-based secure terminals, contactless or RFID or Near Field Communication based digital or smart payments, along with double or triple verification data like CVVs, billing address, SMS PIN or instant caller transaction confirmation could be adopted to minimise risk. Online security and training measures need to be adopted in consideration of failing the threat actors by proper marketing and financial planning because AI and blockchain have increased interdepencies through tap-to-pay systems that connect multiple departments within organizations and encrypted user data could be understood by hackers of high intentions because they may at times, possess better infrastructure than even the most advanced innovators of the planet. We should not recite our card numbers, PINs on phone calls and never ask officials to log on our behalf because sometimes the phishers weaken our internet connection to request the other side to log in using our password. The number, volume and value of transactions should be limited so that the phishing chain does not extend beyond risk limits. Uncommon transactions misdirecting company funds, launching inventory frauds or ransom attacks, may prove to be expensive if proper measures to avoid risks are not taken. According to the FBI, financial losses of more than $2.7b occurred due to online fraud in 2018. Cyber fraud should use wise decisioning in checking the source of online transactions, some websites are created to appear real, some real email IDs are hacked, attachments are sent with malware , we should not open when such extra files are not expected or if alerts are shown by the system we should delete such messages. We should deactivate our financial mechanisms or inform the cyber fraud cops concerned or check the internet for such previous cases complained by people online. We must run anti virus software to keep our systems or devices safe from the reach of digital thieves.

The deployment of bots, drones and other technologies in covid world is expected to save us from the risk of spreading the disease by human proximity but not from the risk of invasive dystopian future arising from constant surveillance or contact tracing to lessen the impact of pandemic. Private data violations may continue after the crisis that may see undue storage of data and retention of public health details has to be averted from misuse, civil agreements have to be signed and corporate temptations must be kept under vigil. Poland, Israel and other countries are tracking citizens due to fear of spreading the disease but where is the assurance that technologies would not be weaponized after the Covid era? The drones and robots might be armed with the controls shifting from governments to hackers, decision making moving from public to companies and intentions from dispersing goods to wars. Peace and disarmament activists are raising concerns that it may turn into cross border surveillance leading to civilian unrest or cyberwars. The present economic revival may be tossed for political repression or militarism or violence if decisions are not selected wisely between human weaponry and AI rationality backed by system inequalities perpetrated by economic growth. The digital panopticon through surveillance, tracking, facial recognition, use of algorithms for policing, digital monitoring etc. may increase risk of resource deviation to violence later. Either stop the panopticon or put the other side too in public visibility radar by synopticon. Digital synopticon would keep human rights equal by allowing the surveillance of few (those monitoring the public) by the majority of the population being tracked so far. It would keep the changing objectives in check before systems get automated in violence to become autonomous weapons. We would have confidence in the strength of collective action because of equal susceptibility to visibility. The global leaders under surveillance would not be labeled as useless or feckless (politicians or corporates or others, if the few watching us agree to be watched by majority too), and would work to preserve human dignity by diverting human, material and economic resources away from military to activities that preserve human rights to be safe and well for reviving the economy from Covid crisis. Global security contracts must be signed by nations promising data and personal security of each other's citizens. Human rights activists should also gain technological strength to understand the use or misuse of technology after the crisis, because without the knowledge stopping the extended use is not possible. Even otherwise a lot of population statistics are available on government and corporate systems but now we are paying attention to detail. Governments could enter into agreements with citizens that such data would be used solely for the protection of people failing which penal amounts could be transferred to every person's bank account or payment channel id, whoever faces data privacy violation. In the current Covid disharmony, governments should provide smart wristbands to every citizen in the respective country, to help further with data on movements, health, body changes or other safety related information. Customer interviews reveal that fears or risks can be managed better by providing useful tools to citizens showing that the governments do care for citizens. At the other extreme, human intervention by deploying men and technologies from the United Nations at every international border, the Human Rights agency has to monitor and issue warnings to deviating nations to prevent undue tensions in global relations. Technology omniscience is not a facilitator of human activities but can become a bane to human existence if not deviated to other more useful objectives. Technology is needed for human convenience and human intervention is needed to enhance trust.

Organizational Resilience

We must learn from Marilyn Monroe on how to use class... gender, color ... privilege. She agreed to come to a show and sit at the front row ... if the organizers would let a Black Singer Ella Fitzgerald perform...

Post pandemic Strategy includes the characteristic of resilience within organizations as readiness to incorporate change of any toughness with the help of change mechanisms built upon employee learning sustaining the root of organizational psychology in creating and retaining employee identities to build competitive and leadership edges without loading them by restricting employee ideas or methods of dealing with customers. How much space can you create and leave free for the sellers to play with strategies without compromising on the interests of buyers, while preparing and defining the rules for understanding the stakeholders and buyers to restructure organizational capabilities with the help of learning mechanisms and change management? Crisis management and economic revival is not a small two-step task to mitigate crisis risks and grow the industry. It is a combined effort of multiple companies and institutions operating in the regional economies to get together in managing the expectations of citizens in various forms - buyers, consumers, users, employees, technologists, scientists, manufacturers, regulators and themselves in more capacities of fulfilling the economic requirements of the countries or companies they are working for. Thus we need organizational resilience to shift between micro and macro economic initiatives at firm and individual levels first to let it grow to national or regional or state or industry level before showing results on the economy.

Japan's private sector is a good example for organizational resilience. At firm level Toyota can be emulated by other companies. Japan's Toyota is a perfect example in demonstrating organizational resilience in adapting to the changing corona environment by changing to a work-from-home model when the company has been reluctant to remote work. The employees have been trained in organizational culture of understanding the customers without inflicting biases on user needs. The superior quality output reflects corporate readiness to change as per market standards and consumer demands. Though otherwise a leader with high sales the company has accepted the covid reality and slowed down production due to fall in sales following the lockdown restrictions. It shows resilience in responding to crisis by adapting the company goals to crisis requirements.

Organizational Change is the third step to reach resilience by application of learning to reflect in employee psychology or behavioral sciences of conveying organizational behavior as readily willing to reconsider market challenges, employee abilities, competitor responses, customer demands and environmental evolution. A crisis-hit company must not directly start with change or resilience mechanisms alone but has to invest in cultivating the learning habits of seller side stakeholders to understand the psychology of buyer side channel participants like supply chain distributors or retailers or resellers without taking losses due to obstructions by internal failings or crisis callouses. Changes to solutions or output are not possible without the organizational willingness to adapt employees to changes of different types - operational, functional, managerial, leadership or even downsizing.

Organizational Learning is the ability to get what you do not possess but in want by buyers, in addition to the psychology below. This is the next level of climbing the ladder of organizational resilience where your learning of business and people skills are both required to apply to change management related to both a competitive and organizational environment. Within one company at branch level, changes may be required to the way of functioning or structures at the headquarter level to be applied to different departments and sub-offices. Different types of employees place learning at necessity, comfort or objective levels. The first two are subjective applications when learners feel that they need to be eligible to conduct business operations or that they can showcase knowledge and prudence in convincing customers of company capabilities or solution worthiness. At an objective level, employees would be more in customer shoes without carrying the learning effect (as a need or feather) but use it in adapting to customer needs by understanding user perceptions and complaints.

Organizational Psychology is the ability to understand the different participants of the business ecosystem with equal skill in responding to the changes proposed by customers and other stakeholders in the market, or even the communication among the employees. Failure at this level means cascading effects on further learning and change-responsiveness with the final blow on crisis management because top managers end up hiring new men after firing the inefficient ones, again the cycle of learning and change management would get delayed under such circumstances. This is the first step to attaining organizational resilience. Proper training and working methods have to be adopted for employees to be on the same understanding as that of the top managers following the corporate charters. Combined understanding has to aim at reaching customer level to know what buyers want from your organization.

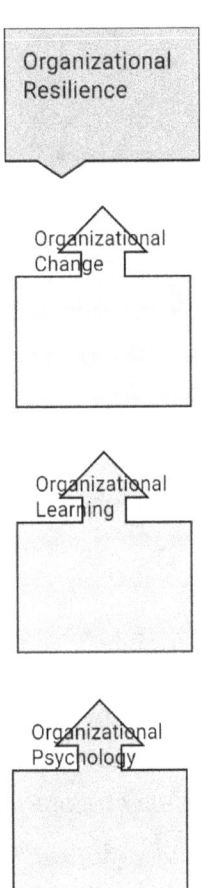

Fig 10: Organizational Resilience for Post Pandemic Industry

Post Pandemic Strategy for rebuilding organizational resilience involves work in three areas namely, organizational psychology, organizational learning and organizational change (Fig 10). We have prepared ourselves in implementing relevant strategies suited to the managerial lifestyle like sending folks to work from homes and giving the freedom to co-innovate with online participation. The advantage of virtual work is that everybody can participate online that otherwise was not possible for space constraints in offices. The select few elite employees used to be invited to the meetings with top managers and leave others guessing with the passed down information. We all know the game of organizational information melting or dilution.

A Manager whispers, "James is on the way. Kim is preparing for exams and both would join company jobs from next year."

Three sentences lose relevance by the time the 10th person has to say it aloud.

"...James is coming. Be prepared Kim...Both have to write exams..."

"James and Kim are in their final year of studies... Next year they will join offices..."

"...Thames is coming to teach Kim who would go to office next year..."

The 4th person loses the meaning still more.

"...A boy and a girl are preparing for exams together... they have jobs ready..."

"...Two people are going to join the workplace after finishing exams..."

"....Kim is ready for exams, she is ready to join the job..."

"....James is learning from Kim for exams and a job..."

The candidate pauses, laughs and stares at the entire queue to recollect whatever she can.

"....There are exams and jobs going on...and...corona is stopping..."

"...Exams and jobs are not dependent on anything...but James and Kith are trying for jobs..."

There is a slight change from the normal way of saying it in online seminars. Members say it aloud instead of whispering but still the meaning, sense-making (firms have to ensure that understanding is clear between employees and customers) and sentences are lost way before the final one blurted out as -

"...They have to wait for a job for one year...Both are not sure to pass exams..."

The event is reconstructed and simulated from earlier experience but serves our explanation of the topic for the day - Organizational resilience. The information is not heard by many, in full, some have interpreted according to the present situation, some according to personal state of mind, one thought that they were failing in exams, as you can see, every sentence has relevance according to the speaker but not according to the manager or the organizational situation. Same happens in organizations during times of crisis, we cannot understand where we go wrong because everybody is right in one's own way. What is in the loss of data? We may not feel the importance but the result is reflected on the customer. Take the last sentence, a customer would think that the coaching class is not effective, so students are failing; another customer may think that the job market is dull; one may feel that exams have been made rigorous that students are failing. Different interpretations come from the psychological disarrays portrayed by the speakers (Salesmen or business managers or employees responsible for implementation of strategies, anybody could be in the place), to distort perceptions about different industries like education, job market, automobiles (first speaker), medicine (eighth one) and interdependence (ninth member). A simple example proves that job is the main point in the present time of concern because nobody has missed the job part except one. All are collaborative because they are trying to summarise and grasp the essence from what everybody has said.

Above is a perfect illustration of Organizational resilience that is backed up by responsiveness to change, constant learning from the economic environment and understanding the psychology of stakeholders involved in organizational activities. Employees of the post pandemic season must be trained in various short-term psychology courses so that we do not err on understanding the different stakeholders or their responses or market signals and how they could generate multiple scenarios for possible addressing in the real-time interactions. Organizational resilience is not agility or flexibility or silence per se, it is a combination of all and more seeking to bring companies to terms with conditions prevalent in the business ecosystems without trying to alter them in the name of competitive tactics or change response. We may have to revert to different times back and forth in learning from experiences and failures, which is why experiential learning is the preferred mode of growth in handling the organizational learning during the crisis times. We have to meet customer expectations and it slows our brain by at least 1.5 times (according to research by Tietoz where 100 out of 100 respondents admitted that they need more time for completing the same tasks) in every pandemic in reacting to external change because of the correlation with crisis aftermath.

In a way organizational learning is a part of organizational change and organizational psychology is part of organizational learning because we may learn on the job, by courses or from others' experience (competitors, regulators, colleagues). Resilience flows bottom-up from psychology to learning to change in forming organizational resilience within industries. The first thing to study is the organization's psychology, how employees of a particular firm think and lastly how leaders influence the change. In between the learning comes that may take shape in online seminars or personal mentoring or group dynamics while implementing responsibilities or tasks. Real effort starts at the organizational resilience level after attaining the ability to understand, capabilities to change and appetite to improve performance, processes, ethics, quality, skills, methods, tools, or other technology or functional planning or implementation levels.

5 Key Steps in Post Pandemic Strategic Management

Strategy in a Fold!

"The dialogue that .... was electric ... because engineers and marketers exchanged ideas ... by brainstorming about technology ... developed by different departments ... for meeting business needs of customers..." - Ram Charan

Strategic Management has 5 key steps. It begins with developing strategic vision and mission, on the basis of which objectives are set in the second step. Strategy is crafted to achieve objectives, following which is the fourth step where it is implemented and executed. Fifth and final step is to evaluate and correct the strategy.

Strategy is a unique synthesis of features, design, cost, service, quality and positioning. Strategy planning process comprises strategic analysis, strategy formulation, strategy implementation and strategic control. It is important to identify strategic alternatives for corporate growth, concentration strategy for market/ product development and horizontal/ vertical integration, concentric/ conglomerate diversification, acquisitions and mergers, harvesting strategies, defensive strategies and combination strategies.

Business unit strategy focuses on gaining cost leadership, differentiating products and services and product/ market segment focus. Combination turnaround strategies in simultaneous and sequential strategy help organizations when they serve in different multiple markets. Defensive strategies may be for turning around a company, divestment, and liquidation, filing for bankruptcy, and becoming a captive of another organization. Another concept that is now gaining ground with the consumer product companies is the consumer-centric marketing to capture and deploy consumer insights to enhance marketing effectiveness and serve better the brand-loyal consumers. This marketing strategy moves from mass marketing to one-to-one marketing due to which marketing innovation cycles are accelerating. The company should be able to bring about major changes to their customer-facing processes. Defining and executing a cost-effective online strategy is important for marketing. It promotes cross selling services to increase customer revenue and customer yield.

Leadership in post crisis world

Management consulting expert Stephen Covey's belief that if we would not choose to do ..in leadership time...we would...do it in crisis management time…, holds true because of delay in decision making.

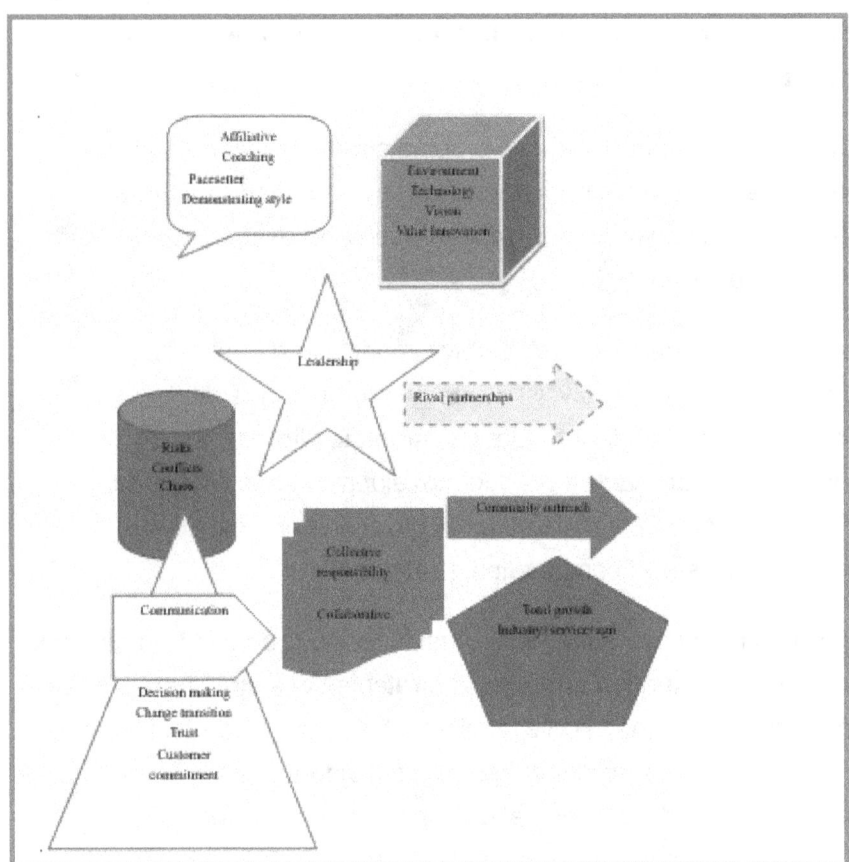

Fig 11: Post Covid19 Leadership

Decision making is a big criterion in our global economy to get new leadership models in the after-corona world. The unprecedented crisis has put the world's economy in a complete state of experiment without a sense of success or failure. Leaders should have mind and heart in place under tremendous pressure from management or employees, when supply chain is disturbed, media is constantly judging, demand from stakeholders is no less, everyone is looking up for speed and efficacy but data is incomplete besides increasing complexity of the situation. Pleasure changes to pressure to make decisions. Smart leadership is necessary for innovation by technology creating a humanist ecosystem across the globe. Leaders must try to be close to consumer, employee, innovator and technology groups, as much as possible. A leader is expected to be an engine functioning round the clock, more like a machine than human. Fix yourself to be strong and get people on your side. In normal time decisions are made using logic or emotion by the leader. Three times logical and once emotional... going by the online polls… logic dominates but emotions overrule all logic when it comes to connecting with people, at home or work. In adversity logic tells you to be emotional but emotion tells you to be stable and quick. As explained in the beginning we have to embrace spiritual leadership to be a nimble decision maker (Fig 11). Any task that involves your commitment by spirit and mind would come under spiritual leadership, there is no separate style as such. We prefer to be right to rise by the top ladders, few times we have to be liked. We can not appease all people at all levels but a proper check has to be placed for more right decisions than preferred ones in the longer run. Consistency is a better tool to be able to live in the present despite planning for the future. We can not afford to be lost in our global economic growth plans for the future without worrying about the past. Leaders should know what to do inhouse and where to go to experts for third party contribution. Teams have to be energized by leaders and it is no easy task to do without living in our present. We have to follow the detached attachment principle in order to face the crisis better. Moral dilemma is between switching strategy and running away because you are losing either way. Doing nothing to save something goes the same as doing something to save something but in a crisis world both may be not saving anything because we are stuck between management, customers and supply chain. Pacesetter leadership style has to be followed in setting the clear standards and levels from where the team would take off by following the established ways of leadership. Be detached and avoid swaying before acceptance of chaos and making decisions. Sound decision is then possible because leadership is a combination of task centrism and people centrism. We have to motivate people by treating them right, respecting them, training them and behaving authentic. Leader is a natural self and not masked differently. Leader is not supposed to be insecure with more competent subordinates or bosses. Trust that smarter or weaker bosses won't impede your growth, the same is true of subordinates. Your professional life is no other's to be shaken or vulnerable. Be willing to be vulnerable to create a corporate culture thriving on trust. We have to trust each other completely. Trust leads to empowerment backed by culture allowing people to be vocal and learning from failure. Let them speak up, suggesting changes to decisions. Innovative business by psychological work safety in crisis will get people by your side. We can see people taking initiative without shirking responsibility on others. We have to first accept that we are affected by the corona crisis and be transparent in communication to every stakeholder empathetically and emotionally to solve it together. Priorities have to be set and we have to communicate the top 30% to do lists. Distributed leadership by breaking up the problems into multiple ones to assign as many people as possible by interdisciplinary approach might work better if all age groups and disciplines are included but not ignored. Affiliative leadership could help manage teams of different departments working with interdependent outputs. Every department has to treat the other like a partner instead of a subordinate or boss. Of late, an optimistic approach is a fashion but not less than overconfidence because we can not prepare for risk arising from multiple contingencies. We have to create a culture of working from home to promote trust and empowerment instead of the number of hours at desk. The quality of outcome has to be then evaluated. We have to find ways to reconnect people at home to set the office mode uniformly by frequent online seminars, meetings, birthday celebrations or even asking employees to wear uniforms while working in their rooms at home. Research has provided confirmation that home environments can be made more formalized in promoting the work ethics if we wear uniform, at non - work stations. Next is to include young professionals in the top priority tasks by continued rotation and learning programs for more productivity. Leader has to display empathy while dealing with new problems because at the end of the day, they have to be solved by people. Human resources are the toughest to manage in organizations and the best results are not achieved by punishment but reward. New leaders have to be allowed to fail because they are also human and can attain success in the long term. Career ladders, peer relationship, friendships and personal goals are also like opportunities to improve our quality of life. Networking in the corporate world, certification in new skills attained in crisis periods can help us tap opportunities cropping up in the future. Building mentor relationships is a better investment than crying over a crisis. Gratitude and positivity come with new ways to face the side effects of the crisis. Don't compare yourself to others because we all have our strength, happiness and weakness. We have to work on strengthening intrinsic personality to help achieve results in professional life. Thus true leadership is to inspire others and then measure their performance because if you don't inspire then there are two possible inferences, you are not as worthy as you should be, next, whatever is achieved in results is no new thing that others would have accomplished anyway even without you. Digital era leaders have to first understand what success is.

Success

"...it's about the gap between the world champion and the rest of the field..." - Garry Kasparov

'There is no shortcut to success' - goes an old saying. People define success in their own ways. One definition of success is to be able to spend one's life in one's own way. I prefer to examine the facts and see if there is any merit in this definition. Life itself has got different interpretations by people. I would call life a mirror that smiles back if you smile and groans if you do so. Thus pending life in one's own ways has several implications.

Life of an individual cannot be viewed in isolation. The surroundings and people around are an inherent part of one's life. From the time an individual is born, there is a constant interaction with the outside world. The initial years pass with most interaction only with parents and other family members. The next phase takes up the level of school, where the individual learns to accept other's presence in life - of teachers, friends, students, staff et al. This phase takes a more serious form in college and office where age and maturity teach the individual to become a person. The person is in constant touch with so many others. In the process, goals and ambition take a form in the person's psyche. The endeavors also keep going (White, 2013-14). Right from childhood there is a constant striving to achieve something or the other - may be ranks in school, admission to a college or a dream job. The urge to succeed is thus born out of the ambition and spirit of competition. Thus spending life in one's own way would imply achieving the set goals in the course of life. From the above, we can definitely agree that life cannot be led in isolation but should be a process where there are many others with us. Then there arises the question of accommodating others in our life. In course of leading our own life we cannot ignore others and to be able to lead life in our own way depends on how successfully we are able to convince others to let us lead our own life in our own ways. For example, a person may want to spend life by creating trouble in other's lives, which will not be acceptable to society. The person should then mend his ways and live to other's expectations as well. That would be success.

A goal is the prerequisite for striving for success. A person may set his goal to accumulate wealth. Another person may want to complete education in the best college. Goals can be altruistic. For example, Mother Teresa's goal was to serve mankind, and she did so very successfully. Mother Teresa has definitely achieved success. In a January issue of Business World magazine, an author mentions that he has worked on several jobs. He would set a goal and achieve it within the time-frame that he had in mind but could never feel the happiness of achievement after every success. Finally he steps in as a freelance writer and that's what gives him the utmost satisfaction. This, he calls, is the real success. In this case, the definition of success has to be qualified - to be able to spend your life in your own way and to be able find satisfaction in that way. It rarely happens that a successful person is satisfied. In his book 'The seven habits of highly successful people', Stephen Covey talks of discipline and dedication to achieve success. Learning from one's failure is also success. When a person is not able to live the way desired, the real success lies in the ability to redefine the way and live it. To be able to spend life in our own way does not imply success but to be content with that way denotes success.

A leader has to teach others how to be successful. It is important for each one of us to be successful leaders in order to be able to drive the economy to growth. We want success in all fields but what leads to us? Can we arrive at a framework? Do you want a formula for success? Yes and No! Adhering to time-tested principles can bring us closer to success. As times keep changing we need to change our approach. There are 5 important constituents of success:

1. Hard-work

A lot of us are cajoled into believing that smart work can replace hard-work to beget success today. Hardly so. No amount of smart work can replace hard work because hard work creates dedication, focus and confidence within us. Smart work comes handy when you get used to the mode of work. You then save on time by doing the same task quicker and better than earlier. Pottery is hard-work, success comes with skill. Potter develops time-saving skills and does smart work in due course. MBAs know the management tips; they work smarter than others because they have already worked hard during the two years of the rigorous MBA program.

2. Self-confidence

You have to be confident of your success after having worked hard for it. Believe in yourself. Self-doubting is a common trait in us but we need to overcome it at some stage. A student, who has mastered the syllabus for the exam, does not get success, if she gets nervous in the exam hall. Performance is best if you have confidence. I used to be a topper in all exams (including State Ranks) because I believed that my hard-work and effort would pay off.

3. Competitive spirit

Benchmarking with successful people is important. Respect competition. This is true of individuals and companies. Don't get aggressive. Be proactive when new ideas come to you. Don't wait for others to implement them. Be reactive when your competitor is moving ahead of you. Follow the winners or devise new methods for winning.

4. Patience

Be patient. Give success time to grace you. Bill Gates did not become a business baron overnight. Warren Buffet did not build his riches in a year or two. Donovan Bailey did not achieve record laurels in athletics in a day or two. Work harder, make smart strategies and struggle to achieve success.

5. Redefining goals

Set milestones. If you fail, then set lower goals. Once you achieve them, set them at a tougher level. Success then becomes a game of joy. As you go on achieving higher goals, your success brings happiness to you and all others near you.

Follow the tips and strive for success. Don't be complacent but rejoice your success at each step so that you are not frustrated by failure. Success begets success, only as long as you covet for it. It is important for each one of us to understand the true concept of success in order to be successful as a team or an industry or an economy.

Leader has to go out of the comfort space to move others to boundless capabilities thereby getting fantastic results together and not, 'fine, it is God made crisis, I can not do anything, so as leader I allow you to run away from the situation as long as it is chaotic', this is escapism and not leadership. Things will not turn in our favor until we change ourselves because lost time can never come back. No two points of time are the same so no two crises are the same, difference attributes opportunity and chance advantage to the crises because they bring abnormal times to normalcy. Such abnormalities can be exploited by leaders if they are aware of the team dynamics, internal weaknesses and market deficiencies. Companies can project weaknesses as shields against the deterioration spun by crisis. Big companies make more losses in crisis because they have more to lose. Small companies do not have many strengths that could be at the risk of becoming weaknesses. In 2008, small banks were saved because they had weak structures and finances could not be eroded as they chose to do nothing amidst the crisis. They resumed operations later but tried to protect consumer interests by not letting the deposits move during the crisis. Big banks like Lehman faced total shutdowns. Small ones got those customers who were diversifying into alternative investment channels. Lessons are clear and leaders would not attempt at expansion but contraction of operations to ensure market presence of firms in the immediate future. A ship can sink in a sea tempest but small boats can make it curving along the waves. Leadership in the post-crisis industry is like rehabilitating the villages after a flood. First provide for the life sustenance and then look for diversification if it is difficult to continue profitable business in the same industry. We should never degrade ourselves especially when technologies are taking command of our life. Leaders don't lead, but follow the times. Demonstrating leaders follow the style of do-and-let-emulate for others to learn from the way activities are conducted, delegated, (teams) mentored, reviewed and measured. It might suit the immediate business conditions after the exit of covid-19. Changes would confuse strategy implementers as well as planners and a demonstrating style has to be followed for solution management.Coaching leadership style may be adopted when the team members are less experienced or need personal guidance for common skills to be acquired and applied in assignments. A leader is better adept at handling crises, more skilled, more learned, more educated, more experienced , more resilient, more tolerant and more agile than others. It could be more than the given series of attributes but not less is required in making leaders who are supposed to be responsible, ethical, humane and intelligent in dealing with people more than working with technologies.

Cross border Collaboration

Again, Maxwell Maltz's belief coincides with that of others who believe that the crisis situations are opportunities to advance, failing which we would stay still.

India has to become more production oriented than depending on imports or foreign manufacturing units in India. The brain drain can be reduced by encouraging native citizens to experiment and earn within the country. If other countries can make advanced technology products why can we not? If we can work for foreign company in another nation to assist the innovation there then should we not be able to do it in our country? Some amount of cross border employment is understandable but with each smartphone deploying more than 50 apps belonging to companies from another country, the time has come to prove ourselves.

China has to open up its country to the globe in the same way as it is opening doors for other nations for its companies to do business outside China. As hard working and more in number (population, patents), India and China can bring a huge difference to the global economic growth together than operating alone.

The USA could be more welcoming in utilizing the knowledge of India (skills, English, traditional value) in implementing technology initiatives with trust, result orientation, cultural amalgamation and other synergies to be discovered while at work. The Indians (Bhartiyas, not red Indians) have higher adaptation skills than any other groups in the world, not alone Asia. America has the wealth and resources, China has the hardworking people and innovative patents, India has the soft (software too) skills, knowledge, dedication and execution capabilities, Japan could be contributor of technology upturn; Australia, Canada and Singapore can be hubs for the results in the form of start-up upheaval, the native countries in middle East can become responsible investors and the best global development can be witnessed by such international collaboration. Be it advancements in health, electronic equipment, housing, financial services or any other area we have to be more united for better results. If not anything else, corona has brought together the different countries in the globe in indicating that as a group we would create new milestones and not as an individual nation. With collaboration using Ayurveda medical research knowledge from India, technology from Japan, investment from USA or middle east, R&D capability from Israel, medicine or vaccine for corona can be made in a short time and patents can be handy in using ideas from China. Raw materials, herbs, men, machines, R&D, drug development, clinical trials, funding, distribution and other logistics come from the different countries to present the world with a more effective solution. The time is all ours to utilize in a productive manner for including our global presence, shouldering our global responsibility, claiming our global competency and demonstrating our global collaboration. The same applies to all countries and not just India or others mentioned here as a suggested plan of action.

Japan has been fortunate in not becoming a victim of corona virus but it is cooperating with the other countries in adoption of safety precautions, lockdown rules and testing standards. Other countries battling the pandemic should learn from Japan. Later we have to be more collaborative with Japanese in restoring the economic development of Japan disturbed by other reasons despite the best technology ownership. The research in space should have united the different national governments instead of waiting for a corona attack. It is time for nations to come together and wait for another species on another planet to rage a war because corona battle is no less than the third world war. For collaboration with other countries- Reduce the mutual difference if we can not remove, combine the regional strength if we can not give, work together if we can not trust completely, though theoretically, we should be able to resolve all international differences, one nation should be willing to graciously give whatever is required by the others, every nation must be able to trust other countries and not worry about protection of the borders in defense always because attacks on other countries do not culminate in patriotic economic growth except for more pollution, loss of life, wastage of money, time and erosion of trust. It is taught by corona now and by more dangerous epidemics in the future if we don't take steps to incorporate the lesson of collaboration.

The globe is woven of different economies in close dependence on trade, employment, education, knowledge initiatives, innovative business exchange beyond foreign currency exchange or stock exchange, technology collaboration, cultural amalgamation (adoption of best traits from the other culture), ethnic understanding or other aspects. The same travels onto economic growth or correlation emerges in totally unrelated events in different countries. It is known how USA economy affects the programs of the rest of the globe, gold or oil reserves affect the forex reserve, DNA result from African genetic reengineering study can be used for the automation program because we are concerned about how the rapport will change between the best technology from Tesla and the users from all over the world. A life study can bring out new genes about protection of drivers during sudden breakdown of vehicles midway. The panic will give way to using cop help, informating family, informing the company or mechanics and other such measures without facing only fear and loss. This example is to show the range of impact of one topic on the globe in carrying the same type of correlation from one country to the globe thereby sum of all effects end up slowing down or pepping up the economic bust or growth. Cross border interdependence leads to a drop in supply in one country to support the falling demand for the products in another country as production has to be reduced, the fall in productivity in one nation indicates migration of skills and lagging customers who originate in another country. Lot of the local citizens employed in foreign companies abroad lose jobs because of the lockdown in both countries leading to higher unemployment rate, lower productivity and yield curves, higher price and inflation or sluggish industry curves. Hence development has to be revived by entering into fresh industry collaboration agreements, cross border employment initiatives and other trade contracts to restore the bilateral relations among international players, in the post lockdown period.

Not only trade, nations call for learning about handling the crisis well from one another. Germany has been able to achieve better results than others in Europe including the UK in dealing with the quarantine. Health of patients has improved and new case occurence is low. As a global economy all nations must take a look at Hong Kong in fair condition through overcoming the challenges of COVID-19 without going through the lockdown though the initial upsurge could be controlled by a phased return after the closure of school, work and other institutions. The law has been tracking and reporting defaults to impose fines of $25,000 or jail for six months on people violating the terms of quarantine. Moreover leaders in Hong Kong believe that the country could fare stronger and better because of the cultural values of people who are sharing the empathy for wishing good of others as is common culture of Asia's. The world can learn from Vietnam that holds zero loss of life in the bitter corona crisis world. It has sealed its borders and blocked all travels across China right in the beginning. The other countries took time to follow similar steps. Lessons for other nations include better testing and quarantine methods resulting in timely diagnosis and an effective cure. Another problem occurring in the lost world of the Corona crisis could be in the conduct of mandatory public activities like ballots and voting in elections. The nations could adopt digital voting in conjunction with biometric data verification so that key electoral activities are neither halted nor get the result affected by any reason.

International collaboration is needed to equip nations with the required technologies to effectively manage economic or sociopolitical activities during the corona crisis.

Population - Boon for Economic Revival

Sam Maneckshaw said that when God says, 'let there be light', there is light but when we say, 'let there be war', we are not yet ready...

...not ready for facing fears, not ready for progress…

The problems are attributed always to large populations of countries and no solutions spring up when we consider facts as problems. Neither low population is boon or bane nor large ones. More people means more farmers, more soldiers, more confidence and less fear. Decisions wait for people, and people wait for decisions, most cost increases happen due to delays in making decisions. Courage and loyalty are built when a large number of people get together instead of few top ones taking decisions leaving the action to be taken by the rest of the population. Leadership lies in being firm and not being dominant nor in showing the power of decisions-making to the majority who are either suffering or celebrating because of dependence on the minority few leaders.

How can one leader handle over 7 billion problems? Men are not problems but each one has a problem that needs to be solved before we can make progress in the world. Each one of us have to become a leader, again, we can become leaders by participating in the growth of economies by way of solving our problems and not waiting for governments or companies like Apple or Google to do it for us because when others try to solve our problems, they end up creating one more, in one way or the other, and the pace of development needs to be decided by the people by way of their adaptability that determines a growth route for the economy that in turn dictates the pace for industries. Instead of that we see the flow in the other way in companies becoming leaders to dictate pace of economy, whether they belong to USA or other nation, further the pace cannot address the issues of corruption or smuggling because people are bound by the predetermined flows in the society that suit only a few leaders and not the majority. The result is that the asset of a large population - patience - gets lost and so does the worth get diluted. Politicians start blaming it all on the population or the failures of the society though the weaknesses are created by the few leaders who are supposed to lead the population as they are.

Discipline and character if imbibed into the code of conduct of society could convert the burgeoning population into a blessing for any nation. No products or innovation could cultivate the traits within people unless we ourselves become self invigorating without waiting for others to become leaders. The economic revival is waiting for the citizens to become responsible and take leadership; for the leaders to take ownership; for the governments to take into account what each unique problem of citizens looks like; and for the companies to help with the same tasks of governments and people. The interdependence finds its strength in the collaboration between the governments, corporates and citizens of countries without hampering the market trends, customer demands and economic opportunities generated by the hiccups created by crises or epidemics. The hiccups are not often addressed by anybody because the environment is full of fear in such situations. Then they turn into crises or pandemics of international recoiling reflections when we cannot find leaders to pull us out of the chaos. It is in such times that the population can make best use of religion and individual pride for showing that those who make the economy can also lead it out of dark times. Great deal of self discipline is needed to solve our problems on our own, which is why we are on the lookout for external advisors and problem solvers. Instead of losing track in the chaotic atmosphere, we can try at becoming conduits of change and development in our small ways to be responsible as citizens, corporates or governments. The topic of economic revival is closely connected to people who are stuck in the pandemic causing pandemonium from the risk of epidemic in every nation. Most of the national growth occurs from the production of individuals working in circles of industries or own initiatives or services. Industrial growth slows down when individual productivity is less than earlier or expected average. Therefore the population if large can be a boon, and if small can be a boon too. Right now is the time to combine brains for a larger good because we are impacting economic development as much as the economic revival determines our future stakes of personal or business growth by overcoming the risks and problems prevalent during that time. The key difference is that the present problem is stalking the progress of each and every participant in the economic path of sustenance, growth and future changes. Covid-19 is different from other problems existing with times as they change with the efforts of skilled people concerned. In case of coronavirus the skilled professionals have to bring out solutions related to health saving drugs or vaccines and the task is not as easy as running a company or taking a new initiative. The people are like assets to the economy waiting for revival, the sick economy cannot support healthy people, and sick people cannot contribute to a healthy economy; so the flow is biway and needs a perfect alignment between individual values and group goals. Every individual whether working or not has a preferred set of values that one follows in life, in addition, the society teaches us some more beliefs or values to align us with the modern or up-to-date living styles, further the exchange of traits takes place between companies and consumers by way of solutions or expectations or perceptions, on top of that such contingent times entrust us with the task of redefining our ways and refine our beliefs to successfully meet the challenges of time throwing thousands of questions to all sides of economy for the different groups of participants to understand, mitigate, solve, address and prevent present and future impacts of such crisis situations.

Illustration Photo: Temple in South India

GOD

G. O. D - Generation, Organisation, Destruction

Yat Sarvam kshamyatam Dev - Lord Krishna, Bhagavatam, Bhagavad Gita
Meaning : Forgive all our sins. Forgive all of us. Lord Krishna told this to the great Bhishma when he was about to leave the last life breath after the 18-day battle of Kurukshetra. Ask for forgiveness from God in every prayer and action after the completion to make amends for all the mistakes committed by us knowingly and unknowingly.

Novel Corona is expected to see the next phase of corona attack and fear has started inflicting losses on the world without disparity. Education or wealth does not make it different when health issues are rampant in the virus affecting the health of all populations of the world. As we have to find the solution in God, some pray for universal health, some say that we have to accept the act of God while some battle it out. As liberal as we can get and as wise as we can think, 2020 is the time that has brought us to the well of questions we have been avoiding on nature, God and spiritual care. We have been able to use the topics of God and nature to our opportunistic advancement successfully in the past whether debating on clinical cloning, genetic research, religion or politics. The topic of God is not as complex as it has become and the concept of God is simple. We would benefit to recall the 1993 TV discussions of Yoga leader BKS Iyengar, because the present health care requires an input from such stalwarts who could align our physical and mental health, God is a better generator, organizer and destroyer than us. The activities of generation can be natural or man-made genetics. This is to fill our perspectives on the matter of God. Organizing is simply seen in the world in the form of welfare of organizations and individuals. Destruction is important to us because of the high uncertainty of nature. Sometimes it sends a cyclone or a hurricane, sometimes it sends a powerful wicked virus and sometimes we ourselves bring about our destruction in wars and other human errors. The value of human life or in fact that of animals or environment is the same as far as the equality law of God is concerned. Whether the victim is a tiger or a father or a child or a player like Novak Djokovic, Kevin Durant, James Dolan, Rustu Rekber, or another celebrity like Amitabh Bachchan, Tom Hanks or Olivia Nikkanen or Comic Ali Wentworth, or politicians like Jyotiraditya Scindia or Yaakov Litzman, Mikhail Mishustin (Russian PM), Matthew Hancock, Nadine Dorries or singer like Madonna, CNN anchor Chris Cuomo or their families, the intensity of treatment should be made by doctors in the equal level. The divine act of saving human beings is not less than generation and organization part of God. Presently we are striving for economic and political revival in all nations because to err is human, people do not like to leave the government to go scot-free. Every nation is facing the citizens ' angst against local government, we have felt,'... That minister could not be successful in managing the corona crisis... This policy is not intended for public good... Government is not doing anything to help us out... '

Truth is not hidden, government in every country is not inactive, whether accepted by the public or not, initiatives are made to ensure welfare of the community and lock down measures are aimed at protecting ourselves from the virus attack. This is the organizing process that seeks more improvements in the medical care for rebuilding industry and other systems of organizations as they are crucial to strengthen our global business environment. From our knowledge and foresight we have to convert the destruction part to extermination of the corona virus and end the crisis. However it will be even more difficult yet thoughtful of us to be able to convert the destruction to a driver of our global power. The global power lies in the development and growth of every country. We are already well aware that the destruction is out of control and we cannot restore more than little if we continue to grow in destructive mode (whether we attack other countries or allow corruption to breed in our country or disrupt trade activities across the globe : we refer to the citizens of any country in the world). Therefore we have to see that our world is not in a destructive way because the acts of God are more than enough to teach every single country a lesson. We are better off to trail along the way of generation of collaboration, organising the collective action and driving through the process of getting global economic development. God helps those who help themselves. As global village, we have to help ourselves with the best possible skills and research to produce a covid vaccine, infrastructure improvement and support for our industry recovery, serving and maintaining the highest quality standards throughout our output providing safety to customers with excellent prevention measures and to ensure cordial mutual respect among nations that are like the different communities of the United global village (UGV). UGV is bound by certain rules and regulations of legal compliance to protect the rights of the citizens by law enforcement or punishment under conditions of deviations or aberrations. The information contained in the various digital sources is our UGV strength. It is not possible that humans may totally eliminate errors. The acts of destruction initiated by us, in increasing the pollution, decreasing the number of trees, depleting ozone, and other economic disorders as re emphasized earlier (illiteracy, crime, poverty and now the value depletion due to increase in virtual realities) have to be brought to manageable and balanced ranges for enabling the future generations to repair or erode and re-learn lessons like we are doing. If we don't improve the situation even a bit then we are not giving space to the next generation. We got a clean nature to ruin, the future kids get a ruined nature that is at a higher risk of doom and destruction, and in such a world existence is not safe, people may perish unless they can occupy other planets in a clean state. Regardless of the future Mars or moon rehabilitation our effort has to be made in the direction of restoration of natural resources and nature along with the human bonds across the countries. Urbanization and nuclear family models are not less damaging than uranium and nuclear power plants so it is not in our best interest to move away from the countryside to the modern country movement in bringing the world to a time where future parents won't be recognized by children created by using the scientific tube embryo cultivation methods or other genetic cloning techniques.

What would great men like CV Raman, Hargobind Khorana, JC bose, SN Bose say had they been alive? They have advised use of science to advance the species of mankind by preserving nature's monopoly. Today's technology pioneers also provide the same ideology like Vinod Dham, the man behind Intel and father of pentium, who believes in the furthering of education and health care. Modern scientists are few of the most ethical and natural people in the world. We can not advance into the future without saving our environment.

The Arctic circle is fast melting on the polar ice and heating on the chilly climate due to global warming. Since the lock down is not applicable for polar caps there is no saving the climate effects with three times more heating than the rest of the world. The environment experts are in dire need to help reduce the Arctic heat like that of the Amazon forest fire. Alternative modes of afforestation must be tried to replace the lost forests. One such mode of growing trees is the Miyawaki method. The Miyawaki method of growing forest is a unique Japanese technique that can make vegetation on degraded land by using soil improvement methods. Three years of maintenance is required after which natural afforestation takes place on its own ; and the start has to be done by planting scores of species native to the soil (main trees, subspecies, shrubs, ground - covering herbs). Dense urban forest is possible to form in a short period with a speed of 10 times growth in global mini ecosystems that are monitored, watered and weeded to help grow 20,000-30,000 seedlings per hectare. Commercial forestry accommodates not more than 1000 plants per hectare. Sustainable soil amendments using rice husk, banana peel compost, cow dung and other tricks can help create an ecological desert for generating green corridor against software corridor. The carbon and all pollutants of the environment can be erased without any further complexity of depleting the natural resources. However such photosynthetic forests may not be able to bring rain and usually end up as a comfort forest for the birdwatchers, trekkers, wood collectors (wood fuel, pulp wood, maple syrup, saw logs are the end products) and flora enthusiasts to enjoy the man-made forest.

The issue of protecting the world's energy resources for future generations is a very pertinent one in today's modernized world. International leadership and worldwide cooperation play a very important role in conserving energy (White, 2013-14).

The world is seeing fast progress in terms of technology. The distances are shrinking, and the concept of global village is emerging. In this race, humankind is fast depleting the reserve of natural resources. Energy resources that are consumed most are water, air, trees/ forest, and oil. 70% of the earth is in the form of water. In some regions, the water table that is the minimum level of water maintained underground, is falling in its levels. This might lead to earthquakes in the region. Nobody denies that pollution is as much a culprit in dirtying waters. Similarly, the air that we breathe is as much an energy resource as water, since it is the base for our survival. The poisonous gaseous fumes and raucous grunts and groans of vehicles leave no room for the oxygen in the air to be pure.

According to a survey, deforestation (cutting off trees) is the main culprit of depletion of energy resources. Trees in forests produce oxygen needed by all living beings.

The world is witnessing constant scarcity of energy resources like water, pure air to breathe, oil resources; and this scarcity is leading to formation of cartels e.g. oil cartel by the Gulf countries. high prices. Organizations like World Wide Fund (WWF) and individuals like Alan Greenspan are already working towards conserving energy resources but the cooperation of all the countries and an international leadership is essential to preserve energy for tomorrow's citizens.

The future generations thus face a dearth of energy resources.

The ozone layer that protects the earth from the sun's harmful ultraviolet rays is being depleted due to the chlorofluorocarbons. Even animals' lives are threatened in due course. The chain of survival is balanced with the presence of animals and human beings together in the living environment. The environment itself is facing a threat.

Our future generations are thus facing a life-threat. Initiatives by individual nations without the cooperation from other countries cannot solve this problem. And it is the 'world's' problem and not a single nation's. Individual nations cannot make international laws. An international governing body can help create ground for all countries to come onto a common platform and decide the future course of action.

Preserve today to conserve for tomorrow. The above analysis thus brings out the importance of international leadership and worldwide cooperation needed to preserve energy for the future generations.

Next, we need to stop fighting in the false pretext of religion. Religion is often seen as a taboo for discussions and arguments. Use it to promote human welfare and not demote human values. Let us explain what we mean by this statement.

There are over seven billion people in the world. All have their values, beliefs, cultures, diversities, habits, civilizations, rights, duties, responsibilities and expectations. Some of the commonalities are grouped in the form of religions. There are many religions all over the world - Buddhism, Christianity, Hinduism, Islam, Sikhism, Zoroastrianism, et al. The people belong to, follow or adopt one religion or the other in the form of different spiritual practices and forms of worship of different Gods. This does not mean that they despise the other religions. This does not mean that we have the right to criticize other religions. Religion should make us stable in our human values but not fanatic. When religion breeds fanaticism, human values deteriorate and it gives rise to conflict and wars. God is one but we have seen Him in different forms in different ages. He appeared as Lord Krishna, Lord Rama in Hinduism. He came as Lord Buddha in Buddhism. We know Him as Lord Jesus Christ in Christianity. We worship Him as Guru Nanak in Sikhism. Some Gods are worshiped by people from multiple religions. Lord Saibaba is worshiped as God in Hinduism and Islam alike. Some worship idols, others pray to symbols, and single or multiple forms in Temples, Mosques, Churches, Synagogues and visit pilgrimages during their lifetime.

All religions were and are propagated by their leaders and none advocates one as superior to others. Religion preaches unity and teaches us to retain faith. Faith is aimed at preserving the human species with collaborated progress but not ruining it with mutual hatred. Competition is not among religions because they are not in the race. We, human beings, are in the race of progress and should strive at making our religion better than earlier by bringing out the best (peace) instead of degrading or looking down upon others.

Religion connotes sacred and divine. Religion should lead us to peace. Let's come together and practice religion to make it a means to attain God and not tarnish with prejudice and violence.

Illustration Photo: Home Garden in Germany during Covid19

Eco-friendly Revival

"You have to have arrogance to say ... I can win the battle with nature ... you also have to have humility ... to recognize that you are limited ..." - Leonard Susskind

The ecosystem has to be cleaned more than earlier in facilitating the post corona economic recovery. The masks, gloves and other accessories used in the Covid era have to be taken from biodegradable polymers and raw material. The process of disposal should be simplified enough to not complicate the environment by cluttering up plastics or non biodegradable wastes. In addition, the responsibility of society is on resurrection of the forest and natural resources for growing children of the future in a green and clean atmosphere. Pollution control would've to be complemented by the afforestation measures to repeat the oft-repeated environmental protection episode. We have a feeling that somebody else is there to take care of everything that is needed for us. The books and schools would not teach us about everything that is going to find its way to us in life. The initiative and implementation of positive steps in public cause should be provided by ourselves. The smaller things bring a change for the larger good. The least we have to do is to revitalize nature by planting trees in and around the house we live in. The need to save our ecosystem is on rise. It can start with the home. Grow plants and feed stray animals or birds with extra food, water, grains and other things to go to garbage collection otherwise. The next step is to spot the government lands that are anyway deserted and can grow beyond desert if only we would like to participate in planting the seeds of vegetables and fruits that we have to throw away. The initiative can be used by both government workers and other citizens during the regular occasions when cleaning the roads and highways, the staff could be kinder than necessary for handling a field or two, planting flowers and other greenery, and watering the lawn or nursery whenever rains miss out. The students and professionals who are interested in browsing the web in free time, could become volunteers for nursing the free landscape by sowing seeds and leaving green bays for the next group of housewives or workers to give the next green touch. Efforts would be effective and without any side effects on converting free mud patches to flourishing green corridors. The results would make us feel better and not let us run guilty of not taking care of the most important factor in the existence - the environment, when the next crisis would stare at us. Companies should have weekend greenery drives to give group bus rides to employees and organize the tree planting and forest cultivation activity in public lands. Government can allocate such lands for free plantation and the community could volunteer for work at will to give a green life to the concrete cities. The need for us is to become genuine and totally serious about the development of the green habitats rather than creating few more deals with environmental vocalists. Agreements will have to happen within ourselves that we don't want to transmit diseases and unfavorable conditions to our new generation but we're going to improve the quality and conditions of living in the environment. Mauritius is facing a total distortion of ecosystem due to the oil spill, sea plants and marine life are not in green health but in oily dark, the nearby animals, birds and humans are worst affected and the environment is at total loss waiting to be rescued by the small task teams and individuals volunteering to give the best solution by saving the water life wherein pollution of the highest kind has occurred and the efforts have to be termed as ephemeral because more than damage has happened that we don't have a great capabilities system and response potential to restore environment to the earlier state.

Eco-friendly inputs and outputs of factories using less harmful chemicals and equipment legitimately contribute to industry growth by combining environment friendly measures with techno friendly strategies to save people, money, and the surroundings from unwanted exploitation. The future objective of every industry in each nation should be modified to be more in favour of agricultural economy thereby making the full use of technology for cutting costs of manual involvement, reducing the dominance of technology over environment and men and protecting the resources by giving nature superior importance above men or machines. Once we recognise that environmental protection is more important than industry growth, economic recovery would happen on its own because more resources could be directed to the global next in the form of preservation of natural resources thus doubling the next generation safety and health quality. Industry would then truly innovate new ways of growth without altering the environment to promote solution standards. Redefinitions of social networks will emerge, new social norms and values are bound to revolutionize healthy living in such a pro environment and "possible technology" world. It can be called as possible technology because such technology will not ruin the environment but devise processes to make it possible for technology to save the natural ecosystem. The logic that agriculture is directly related to our economy and environment in progressing both or one depending on our way of growth, presses on us, a need and sense of urgency to be aware of the future effects of the present activities. If we make it a part of the agricultural activities that we have to grow forests along with grains and nuts then that's the only contribution from us to future children otherwise they have as much brain to innovate gadgets and gizmos like us. We have to teach the sense of environmental conservation to the future citizens so that in the process, they learn to be patient and understand the art of living in crisis situations. The lesson has to start with the top in knowing how to protect our atmospheres and surroundings. Protect Nature to provide true worth to your personal nature. Ultimately we are then in a position to drive the economy out of downturn and crisis. Nature is a part of ourselves and the world.

Every nation should follow an agricultural economy in taking pride in rural activity, without falling for the sheen of the words like urban, technology and business. The root of every individual or industrial or commercial or economic development lies in the ability to support environmental safety, let nature live in full, to give sustainable energy for tomorrow's global growth. Even more than ten billion people can be happy and comfortable in the present world by overcoming greed, wastage and managing the resources well at our end.

Post Covid Knowledge Economy Transformation

"... whatever... knowledge you have sometimes bettering the economy...if you use it... you have a conflict free world..." - Dr APJ Abdul Kalam

"... a group of scientists ... made ... an experience machine ... where you can go and get whatever experience you want ..." - Nick Bostrom

The process of crisis management is altering the next era digital knowledge management system without which we would be neither effective problem solvers nor quick learners nor solutions seekers nor quality implementers nor agile strategists nor results achievers. The economy is victim of mismanagement where rules fail to understand what the growth means to different categories of citizens - newborns, students, mothers, working class, senior citizens, entrepreneurs, social workers, governments themselves and others reaping the benefits or losses of activities with or without direct participation. Industries can't grow better if one of the links doesn't function in the chain of (Fig 12) - learn, seek, know, strategize, implement, solve, achieve and exceed. The last step to exceed expectations and own abilities entwines - measure and maintain - substeps, depending on market situations that challenges companies to give better output beyond sustaining the customer expectations. Knowledge is key to initiate the process of economic recovery in beginning to learn about the weaknesses, risks, threats and lessons in addressing by combining strengths, opportunities, and other capabilities of the companies, communities and other agents involved in the cycle of economic development. The need for participants is to find out problems and solutions by taking advantage of strategy, technology and business knowledge for reviewing, restarting or repeating the steps in the intended interest of speed, quality and convenience with innovative implementation and maintenance of every new aspect of knowledge in flow, storage, distribution, retrieval (in a different form and interpretation) and research. Today's knowledge may be treated as outdated information by tomorrow's customer or yesterday's outdated information may be sought after by tomorrow's companies. The need and situation may make it sound different from the viewpoints of market analysis and user experience. The knowledge is the same but application is varying from user to need, company to technology and scholar to framework. Users have needs that have to be met by comparing to problems to be solved by the companies. Companies should have the right technology to give tools for addressing the issues thrown by the market of users. The process is simplified by scholars combining knowledge and framework for deriving the skills required to give a green solution. The knowledge in a given scenario is about getting a green solution for your customers by taking advantage of technological tools to enhance the relevance of knowledge and change the problem into an opportunity. Transformers of the knowledge age would appreciate and address the changes to the environment before moving to the digital pace of instant solutions. The process is better to begin with the analysis of negatives and losses before selecting the best solution with benefits highlighted by the companies, activists and critics from the respective angles. The future effects would be analysed more than the present ones in deciding how best to utilise the knowledge in given situations and unpredictable tomorrow that might have the economy hanging in a volatile crisis scenario. Knowledge innovation systems may train future robots to be more human and drones may be instructed to plant trees in dry grounds. The information regeneration and knowledge management would be such that new opportunities for growth of the economy are seen through different improvements in the environment.

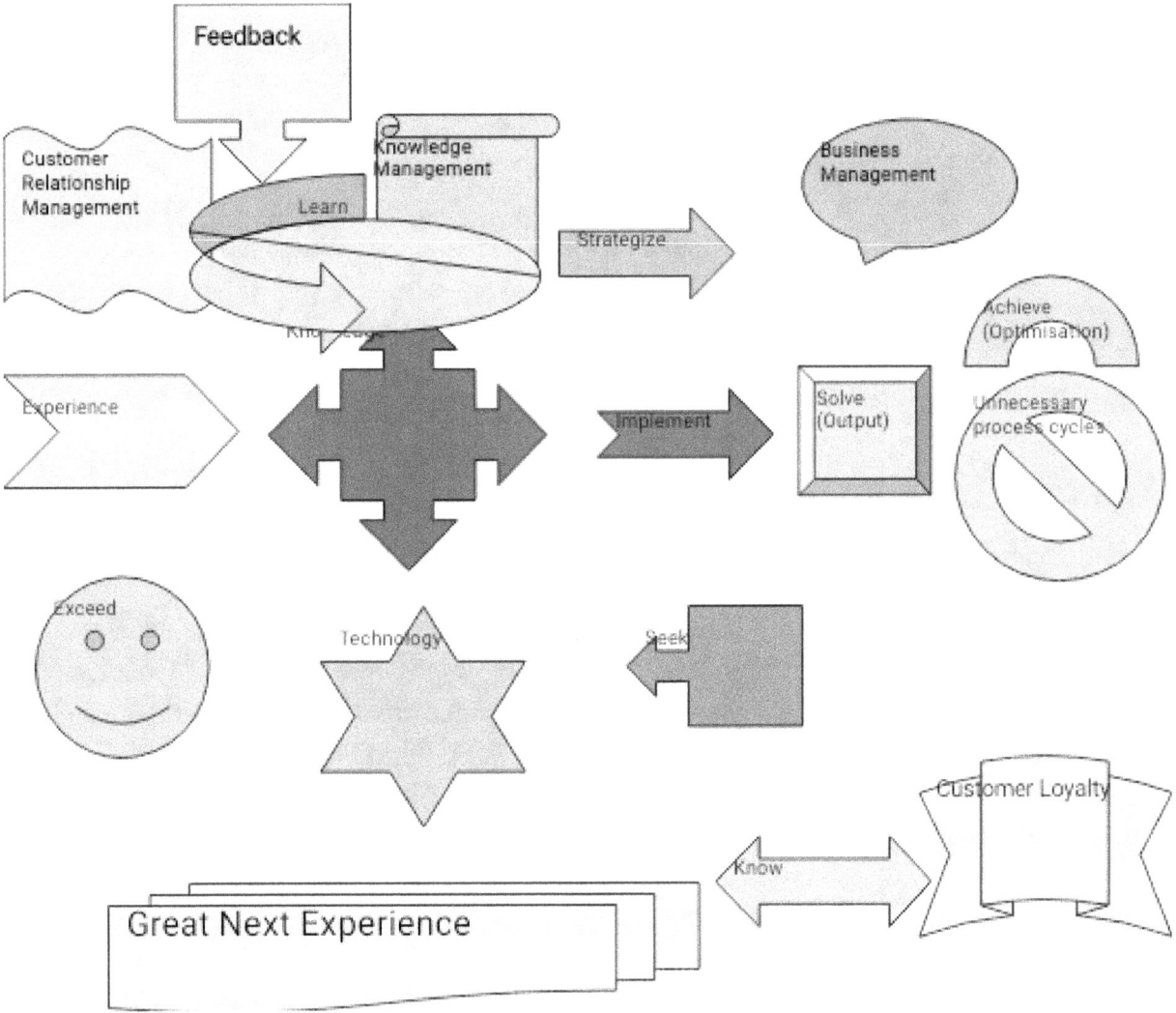

Fig 12: Knowledge Economy

Technology and data processing go hand in hand, with increasing use of technology, knowledge systems have become part of business administration, as data warehousing and business intelligence prevaricate information gathering from secondary sources. Knowledge extraction and interpretation followed by application to give outputs to customers, constitute the three main steps in knowledge management. The need is to be a provider of well informed solutions, goods and services for the end users. The future companies should adopt a different customer relationship model that 'derives' from knowledge and 'deprives' the process of unwanted cycle of information simulation without realising any optimisation gains but calling as optimisation when the actual present activities in the organizations interchange the derive and deprive above. The customer is deprived of knowledge in pursuing the competitive splurge on large scale product selection derived from unwanted personal data perceptions. The customer expectations draw lessons encapsulated in their respective knowledge purviews. Enterprises must have information channels to capture the essence hidden behind the user demand whilst defining the scope of experience and product innovation. The process of future knowledge management would begin with the last step in customer relationship management of today- experience. Top management team should focus on the definition of the experience that they are expected to promote to the customer before moving to follow up with the teams facilitating solution management down the line. Tomorrow the process of productization will start with understanding the feedback of customers even before entering into need or the next best alternative and the experience step would be a 'great next experience' (Fig 12) in solving the problem, creating loyalty and supporting customers. Knowledge economy can thus avert business attention from unwarranted deviations created by the rivals and unfavorable elements in the industries; at the same time customers could be enthused in terms of what to look forward to from the companies. The start would be such that customers get knowledge experiences enriching lifestyles without intruding into the user value space as most family concerns revolve around new knowledge disturbing old beliefs. In a way knowledge economy would lay emphasis on all branches of management without adding expense to the company pockets. It is a way to deal with crisis situations that can attribute failure to any type of flawless implementations or business plans drawn by experts. Managers would gain best results in crisis management by tying each action plan to sound knowledge databases or market intelligence warehouses. Interpretations, perceptions, experiences and feedback would be interacting with big or small data or deep machine data by converting data into knowledge systems for future applications. Knowledge could manage volatilities of economic crisis better than rapid restructuring or innovation or heavy cost cutting or inorganic tactics or organic tactics or downsizing measures or stock market dramas or noisy stakeholder reviews.

Failures of the decade and impact on post pandemic economy: Company closures (Covid-19 Positive Corporate Cases)

"... everyday we lie down (to sleep) we become unconscious ... how does it feel ..." - Richard

Many companies have died in 2020 due to the impact of covid-19. The names would go down as failures of the decade in the history of industry.

The decade has ended (2010-19) and begun (2020-_) on a wrong note.

eBay has lost the battle in the business of e-commerce because of overlap with centralisation and decentralisation. The employees globally didn't have freedom to Innovation and entrepreneurship of sellers was encouraged by narrow return opportunities that had to be created by sellers but approved by the company management team. The gap in understanding led to a gap in knowledge and end users suffered the mismatch in skills and Technology reflecting in the business output lacking integration with market demand and Customer expectations, tending to fail due to the low acceptance of products. The company could not buy Customer argument of low performance products that found shelter in Management inertia, competitive analysis was conducted by Management team instead of changing organisational structure, employee work methods and business priority. Results could be seen in high costs, unexpected losses and closures. The case is not correlated with covid19 but may turn into corporate failure for others conducting business with corona fear psyche. Ebay had acquired Paypal and Skype both of which are much used applications in digital payments and communications. For future sustainability Skype and Paypal have to draw lessons (in organizational structures and strategies) so as not to affect the acquisitions by the problematic effects of the parent eBay. The management teams have to review the business goals, methods of achieving, customer feedback and future expectations before going out on the competitor analysis or change management related to the exogenous change drivers.

Fig 13: Covid Company Failure

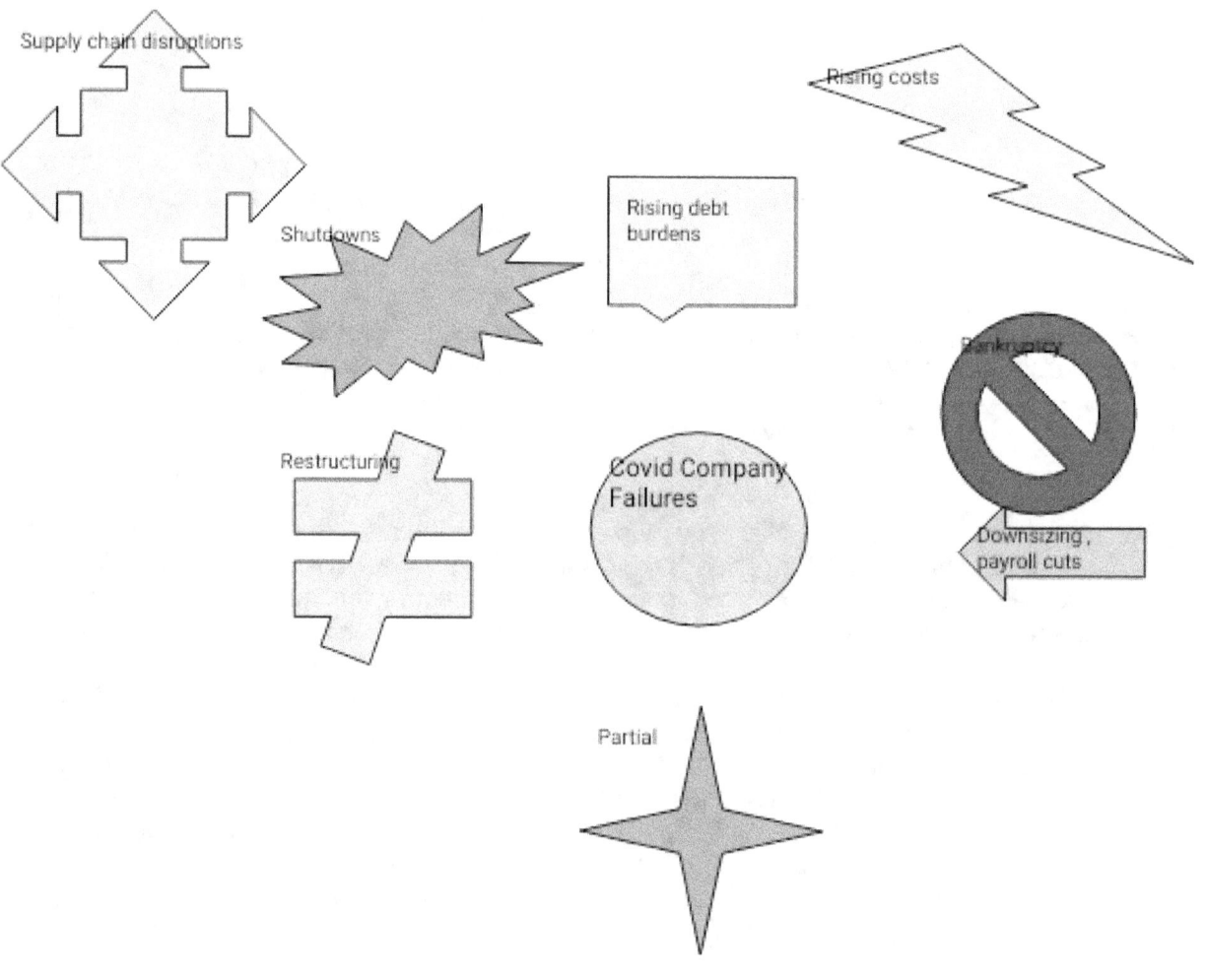

The lessons for the post pandemic economy are clear (do not make tough decisions until the situation resumes normalcy, do not run in panic but hold the management tight, do not raise expenses but go easy) though more bankruptcies are coming from corona. Billions of dollars in debt can't afford to get optimistic in post pandemic firms. The closure of business hence makes sense without losing integrity in the quest of business existence tactics to eliminate effects of exigencies by the exogenous corona fear. The companies with all business prospects at stake are - oil field services company Weatherfield International that got aid but real effects of bankruptcy will continue to reveal after the end of the pandemic; Hertz in transport service; tailoring businesses; gym chains ; Neiman Marcus, Chesapeake, Aldo group, Apex Parks, Avianca, Bluestem Brands, Frontier communications and Intelsat are some of the big names, ceasing operations due to covid slowdown leading to debt burden, insufficient demand, failed attempts on competitor sale, supply chain disruption, lawsuit pressure or reorganization failure. Expense reductions, restructuring, expansion attempts have been foiled by covid19 backed andropause (Fig 13).

Some other companies are answering the enigmatic pandemic challenge by combining closure and restructuring measures. RTW Retailwinds, is planning to wind up more than 50% of the branches in a bid to begin liquidation sales. Virgin airlines filed bankruptcy in Australia.

The closure is sector neutral in firms exiting communication, retail, e-commerce, e-learning, talent acquisition, furniture, financial services, apparel, real estate, banking, insurance, transportation, automotive, cosmetics and beauty, fragrances, kitchen goods, entertainment, animation, special effects, agriculture equipment, dairy, restaurants, malls and high Street, sporting events and other businesses.

Commodity price crunch, drastic share price falls, scandal involvement, failed renegotiation with creditors and large enterprise size are becoming supportive reasons of Covid backed closure of companies.

The wholesalers, retailers, resellers, discount sellers and other types of dealers are seen quitting the business in the environment of Covid crisis.

Efforts are not paying off whether downsizing or restructuring or partial closure of operations or even new innovation or product launches at low prices. The market is not confident due to the downfall set by covid crisis, the customer is not optimistic to decide in favor of sellers as in normal times and the economic spectrum does not support further advancement without reviving from the existing quagmire. We have to respect the corporate failures and learn from the companies that tried to survive thereby giving us the opportunity to understand from their experience what fails and what not. It is true that we won't see brands of vanishing companies but we have to keep them in our lists of industries so that we do not miss the lessons given in the cases of company failures, we know that most of these examples are not deliberate failures but a victimisation of crisis. The leadership and strategies may be calle deplorable but they are in fact appreciable because they took the hard decision enabling resources to be not wasted further, freeing the resources to be utilised better elsewhere and not pulling the industry average down by the poor performance of the foreseeable future. The management teams studied the forecasts, found the numbers weak, and could not work with options beneficial for the stakeholders and customers, so it is best to move on with bankruptcy claims or closure tasks or winding up of operations without depending on unrealistic expectations or miraculous bailouts or magical sales pick-up or remedial cost cutting or further debt refinancing or management tactics. Learn and leave... decide the right time to exit business in crisis; do not waste resources in heavy ad or marketing spends in a bid to save the weak firms; do not wait for scandals or corruption activities rise in the name of getting market visibility or notice in the industry as if to buy time for more business operations, such strategies won't work with consumers because competitors won't leave empty handed so the gains for rivals are more than for the 'trying company' when saving of sinking enterprises is not possible because stakeholders including customers have given up on expectations from the business. Leadership means to recognize the failures and quit industry in acceptance of crisis effects. It would then open up new alternatives for promoters, employees and stakeholders to pursue better or different business options suiting future interests of customers and communities. Government should offer incentives for companies that can dare to accept failure and close business to move to a new greenfield or venture to serve global communities better. Economic development can happen better by adopting new options instead of eroding resources in unprofitable or unsustainable industries. It is better, that we do what we can do better than competitors, than improving upon the failures with an expectation to match rivals or exceed them because it would be a superficial goal then.

New Opportunities (Covid-19 Negative or Immune Industries)

"... it is very important to understand... we function better if there is no safety net..." - Arnold Schwarzenegger

Crisis opens up opportunities similar to the way it closes success on some paths. Where there is pain there has to be some gain. For sure, digital technology has found a new acceptance and application in the corona world. Post pandemic in health has become a post epidemic for industries, but there are other industries that have found new lease of life (Table 4) in the wake of the covid19.

Plasmonics could open up new vistas for venturing into modern mobile vision Innovation with ability to fulfill the needs of the wide range of users with vision disorders. The further contribution might see benefits of seeing in the dark and exploring treatment of special people by advanced combination of electromagnetic waves with light emitting medicinal radiation therapy. Extend the optical innovation to the rest of the body. The stress is not related to covid world but accounts for Technology offering real comfort to the handicapped people who could get a new opportunity for joining the process of developmental activities otherwise considering the less abled in exclusion from the rest of the society. Prosthetics is not new business but Technology should have direct gains passed on to old, disabled or sick people who are in need of a tool to complete the physical constitution and compensate for the missing bodily capabilities. The voice features or special keyboards or other visuo- touch - audio developments could go close to assisting the users of Technological applications or devices but not sure of how to provide tangible benefits. The robotics could give a good substitute for a missing limb and allow the user to get painless surgery or artificial body parts. Usually the person gets better support with increasing pain when an artificial limb is attached to the body. Covid world has gone through enough pain to empathize with the global special populations. The post pandemic economy can grow better by allowing special places for handicap segments of people by letting Technology work for the betterment of lifestyle of the 15% population living with some form of mental or physical disabilities. The non physical deformities like depression could reduce the new health of society otherwise provided by technologies. The human values and habits leading to happy lifestyle should be propagated by the other healthy population, besides the health care professionals and Companies working with different technologies to reduce human isolation and induce human factors affecting user experiences, enhancing user emotions or feelings without binding to monetary interests because money converts emotions to e-motion or electronic motion or exaggerated motions for increasing dependency on technology and tools instead of people or situations.

Illustration Photo: Garden in Argentine house

Table 4: Options for new opportunities in the post corona world

Optical sensors innovation	Nuclear energy	Solar power engineering
Supercomputers	Healthcare	Digital commerce
Mobile lifestyle (housing)	Digital education	Digital governance

Build an innovation curve by inducting employees into learning by innovation. Give more innovation assignments initially than waiting for the learning to happen from ordinary tasks. Scientists are working on computing power enhancement to apply in daily lives. Future digital abilities may be hosted on a superserver with all our devices functioning on super computational features not just pertaining to calculations but wise decision making systems to reduce the probability of all types of losses to zilch. Examples are no - accident traffic management, zero-emission vehicles, extending to improvement in human performance, robotics ensuring that employees do not fail to perform in organizations thus leading to sureshot success of assignments or projects, high - precision technologies and products learning from human mistakes to simulate experiential scenarios without users having to trouble much on teaching themselves but knowing what to ask for, how to retrieve information and use the same for the immediate benefit of the participants in the situation (the supercomputers may be able to help the department of criminology in tracking the culprits and punishing them without waiting for time consuming official decisions to be made by courts and staff).

The environmental and economic volatilities could see more mobility of future residents moving across countries or within regions of a nation in search of a better place to live with families. The change could both be cause and effect of digitalisation of economy because children would learn online in virtual schools, elders would work on digital workspaces, medical facilities could be conducted on virtual diagnostics, delivery of required food, medicines and other things might not get hindered with drones flying to the remotest spots to provide the stuff within minutes or hours of order; and all other lifestyle needs would be met by technologies rather than manual service. It would give more freedom to people in deciding how they want to conduct life and activities of day to day importance. We may choose to live on trees or build a house near a river to escape the city blues and enjoy the natural luxuries of open spaces, cool breezes, green lands and birds singing free melodies as against a noisy speaker emitting rocky tunes in a birthday party. More use of technology will open our eyes towards what we are missing in nature and people won't stop themselves from responding to the inner drives and instincts guiding us to be near nature. Mobile housing is already in demand and robotics are coming to more help in building complete houses within hours. Quality is unquestionable and people are willing to spend the extra money on customising personal habitats that would otherwise be immobile constructed in cement or concrete over long periods of time. Recreational vehicles (RVs) are doing well in sales according to manufacturers and suppliers like Winnibago and Thor that are selling record numbers in the pandemic endorsing social distancing, health concern, travel restriction or safety issues; people are readjusting the way they vacation and demand for RVs has gone up by more than 300% in USA where companies are facing shortage of labour, drivers, resources and time for delivery of the new product and used ones also in demand for commercial purposes and personal use. Companies of other industries are using the vehicles for distribution of goods to the end-user. The smaller businesses are using the RVs for ad campaigns and motor marketing efforts. Individuals and families find the mobile shops and restaurants useful but we are not allowed to live in RVs as houses. Laws and policies have to be made to enable the adoption of motor homes or motor offices. Who knows, the future could see us moving our house to a different layer of atmosphere or underground to avoid the vagaries of natural calamities and damages caused by hurricanes, cyclones, floods, earthquakes, volcanoes and other disasters. Man has to get ideas to innovate technological assistance but ideas do not come from our brains alone, they need the inputs of nature. We cannot isolate from nature and expect to remain natural (in thinking, generating ideas and living successfully and peacefully in full health) because human beings are products of nature. Robots of tomorrow may learn from human life and may demand trees around them. Humanity can remain superior to robotics as long as we do not exclude nature from our daily activities.

Energy revolution in the post pandemic era amounts to innovation in solar and nuclear spaces with more productive utilization of nuclear fusion (source of solar energy anyway) in the form of household utility inputs or vehicle gas or factory fuels. Solar power engineering is possible because we have tremendous sunlight and unlimited heat generated by nature but we have to learn to store and use instead of (un)depending on clouds or rain. The new metal alloys that can absorb heat and trap light to release in night times are being studied by the industries of the future. Soon we can replace batteries by alloy or compound devices that can emit the light stored within and radiate heat absorbed from the sun; a nuclear fusion plant can emulate the solar energy generation process because the sun uses hydrogen to combine into helium and we can replicate the same in fusion. The energy can be used for running irrigation plants for agriculture fields and man-made nuclear fusion can escape the ultraviolet effects of the sun. The next innovation could be to try simulating ozone for guarding our space beyond earth and making it safe for life. When distributed on a large scale, such energy could be used to power the street lights across cities, even provide power to industries and offices or houses to be equipped with solar power pipelines of nuclear energy transmitters. A lot of work has to be done before we get quality assurance on high safety lines replacing the direct electricity lines with nuclear lines or solar lines that may be safer, better, greener and more cost-effective in the long run. Pollution may be reduced drastically if vehicles start using solar powered batteries or if factories could safely source nuclear power from the large fusion plants located near the outskirts of cities. Fusion waste is not considered to be as harmful to the environment as fission wastes. Positive developments in fusion space could see a shutdown of nuclear reactor plants because we reap more losses than gains out of such activities.

Healthcare industry undoubtedly is the most flourishing one in times of epidemic and innovation is likely to pick up more pace even after the end of covid pandemic. We have seen above how insurance in the health sector is getting rising importance in the present times. Future times would expect more work in terms of developing digital equipment and machines to test people from a distance without having to visit the laboratories. Technologies are working in that direction that some devices can track physical changes and warn the patient of illness before it occurs on the body. It can be innovated to predict the arrival of potential dangerous viruses and pathogens in advance so that we can disinfect the air or prevent the illness by eradicating the harmful diseases even before they hover in our surroundings. Robotics have to engage in continuous research to come up with inventive techniques to prepare medicines and vaccines according to the changes in our air. A lot of unknown elements are present in our air and we do not feel the presence unless threatened by a disease or infection. Technology innovation can prepare robotic researchers that can leave bots to constantly study our air for changes, favorable (rare) or unfavorable, and inform the decision makers or act instantly depending on the seriousness of the situation. Robotic sensors detecting emergence of new damaging elements in air could prepare solutions for the treatment of infected air without having to wait for covid19 to ruin the entire next year. The robotic sensors could be solar powered because sun's heat can destroy many harmful pathogens, similar facts have to be known about other possible medications so that we can prepare using natural herbs or plants because the root input for all medicines lies in one or the other plant as raw material (we only need to trace it back to origin of each input). Robots have to be trained to study and understand medicinal benefits of plants around us or far from us. Any poly's, sterile's, -nol's or chemical compounds undergo multiple processing before suiting our physical requirements otherwise the ancient man could directly rub a plant against his body to heal a bruise or consume a leaf to cure a disease. Even the purest of artificial compounds find their origin in natural substances related to the plant or grass world. Scientists could work with robots in guiding them to understand the healthcare requirements and solutions in related or unrelated ways from nature.

Digital governance (Table 4) is not far from us because soon people may take over the administration from the inept politicians across the world. Citizens could choose to be ruled online or administered by digital regulators but care has to be taken in not surrendering completely to robots that would later ask us to leave the planet or become slaves of machines. To begin with, simple governance transition to digital means is already happening and more ministers would move to online leadership instead of the on-field political ballistics or more elections would take place in virtual booths without the voters facing party threats, thereby reducing the rigging or 'misvoting' (false votes cast on behalf of absentees, non existent voters or corrupt ballot). Online political campaigns would replace the expensive party rallies with voters more active in interacting over the virtual political promises. A minister if found to be corrupt would be expelled online immediately to be replaced by the next one without having to go through the costly process of conducting another election in the middle of the operational year. Administration would be smoother and more hassle-free when the government would be based online to save costs of public meetings, international conferences and high-tea interactions. The advantage for politicians is that they are safe and need not equip with bullet proof apparel or vehicles or entourage of security beefed up to save one minister leaving the entire nation to luck. Better utilisation of resources is thus inevitable gain of digital governance besides saving the expense of infrastructure, office utility, power and other things wasted in a day at office. Scandals would not recur often, billions of dollars would be saved for use in the state welfare tasks. Politician ad spending itself amounts to more than $10billion according to WSJ, digital ads would prove to be more effective and less costly than otherwise. It would go a long way in contributing to GDP growth if we save the political expenses whether on security or tours or ads or the posh life-work-styles of public 'servants' (politicians are celebrities and not serving the public anymore but served by the public). Gone are the days of true political leaders like Thomas Jefferson or John Kennedy or Lal Bahadur Shastry or Sardar Vallabhai Patel when people and nation mattered more than recognition or power. Today priorities have changed for politicians and technologies would provide an answer to the changing style of the world leaders.

Digital commerce is in and trade is on conversion to digital modes to facilitate easy cross country or state transition. Tax changes and logistics protocols have to be implemented to facilitate international exchange of goods and services (online without having to travel). It could be in the form of exports or MNC operations or patent sharing or virtual corporate governance for facilitating global commerce via digital technologies. The last one may see relevance in future when global companies skilled in a product or service would help run local operations of importer countries by providing expertise, guidance or directions online (e.g. a Japanese leader in robotics could run a local subsidiary company in India by providing senior management leadership from Japan online, and with the same quality output). Payments in foreign currency are remitted online by transfers or a global currency in future digital commerce.

Digital worlds require more ethics and accountability in any sector because we are not watched by people but machines. Work is needed in terms of framing digital laws and regulations for providing secure flow of activities, processes and operations in the virtual management world.

Digital education is the way of learning going forward as students pick up online sources of knowledge sharing with the international community of teachers, scholars and certifiers. Online exams are not a distant reality but soon to be extended to the user location so that we need not visit a centre or public place for taking exams. Robots will administer exams using hologram or virtual testing environments for students sitting in homes with personal laptops, giving more real-time exam scenarios with little or no scope for cheating but offering tremendous scope to be creative and thinking on spot. Scoring would be instantaneous and case based, with evaluation of every step in arriving at answers without caring for just final answers, irrespective of subjects, Mathematics or Sciences or Arts or Languages.

Digital transition would make it even for all sides by exploring the rights and responsibilities of all the stakeholders of the economy including governments, citizens, corporates, institutions etc.

CONCLUSION

Nixon believed that the battle would be easiest, and the decision...most difficult...to fight or escape... and the most dangerous period is the aftermath... resources get exhausted... dulled reactions and faulty judgement... must be watched...

Another occurrence of the corona crisis is not a good idea to have because it will weaken the confidence of the whole mankind with the fact that no powerful and fully effective vaccine or medicine has been developed. Though it is a good opportunity for pharmaceutical companies to take on, and Patanjali claims to have a real solution to the problem of corona it should be confirmed by the best medical experts to get accepted in the world. Till then we have to see that the government is equipping health care units in every nook and corner of the world with infrastructure supporting the testing, diagnosis and treatment of the corona patients and the general public must be taken care of to prevent disease. The role of a business entity is to provide competent technology to help the overall conduct of life in the communities through online education, research, work, health, insurance, shopping and other activities to avoid the risk of population congestion in roads and other areas of risk to infections. Digital resources will help if you are ambitious to work with your daily routine of meditation or exercise in groups under the supervision of professional trainers because we have to help ourselves with some serious self care to prevent tension from growing healthy lifestyle in general immunity building that can improve your health defenses to annihilation of viruses before taking the shape of disease. In the beginning of 2000s when the treatment was attempted to end coronavirus, the symptoms of SARS could be controlled but not totally cleared by the medical solution. The first step is to take care of individual body health and nutrition. The next step will be sterilisation on the day to day environment by providing an unfavorable or unfriendly air where viruses cannot survive and protection is possible by sprinkling aerial disinfectant. The information cannot be completely divulged but companies are working with generation of aerosol to purify the air on a consistent basis with the help of drones. If we're able to win this war with corona it will be another major step in the existence of humans because corona is nothing less than corruption of natural air leading to the destruction of personal health. It can arise from a small common cold problem to result in a serious risk of illness. Be sure to bring your own habits and prayers to as close to nature as you can. It will be the best responsibility for researchers to provide you with proper information about how consuming meat can transfer the cause of disease from another dead body to your body, knowing that the origin of the corona crisis is a bat that a Chinese foodie could not resist. Any method of reducing your neighbours ' health by spreading the risk through spitting, garbage and other nonsensical ways will not help reduce the cost of disaster that you can otherwise overcome by collaboration, gratitude and a glass of herbal concoction like turmeric and warm water as a home remedy. Nothing concrete can be recommended to reduce the heat of corona but it is often possible to use the natural tricks of old times when newer trouble pops up in new times. It is possible that we can have a nice drug to check corona out of the human body but it is not difficult to imagine that the problem will likely result in a long-term impact of sweeping changes to the next generation lifestyle and thought process. The kids of 2030 will have a better hygiene and safety sense to think about the quality of environment in and around them. They will also provide more space for the fauna to a better interaction with nature, particularly in the present condition, the world of animals and birds of wild has heaved a little sigh of relief in the pollution- free concrete jungle, which is left behind in the world of relentless technology, materialism and mindless progress with all products for facilitating safe or comfortable journey of life before admitting the truth that you have to learn certain things from the natural world that too in the hard way to get the best feel of modern life experiences. Unless you're able to relax under the tree, you will never be able to accept the use of an air conditioner or portable air cooler against the scorching heat of the sun. If you understand that the depleting ozone is making it more difficult to face the treeless world than the 'car free' roads then you would be owning a company that can help us with green products instead of creating a surge of new age pollutants. The next step is to make a product culture that can fit your needs and healthy lifestyle as supplementary best practices for fighting around the monsters in the night or day, air or water, food or any other way of getting into your belly because bacteria, viruses and other risk factors will not look for a better species or place than man on earth. Corona has not a thing to do with the eye or heart but it is not kind to any part of the body once allowed to use it as the house. The way out is not different, we have to battle with the disease together with a good foundation of optimistic thinking and better understanding of preventive lifestyles. The role of entrepreneur is to focus on education, energy and environment to reduce the risk of failure in the world of technology that is subservient to the narrow goal of machine or digital growth without any contribution to the natural enhancement on the front of enrichment to the way of living, innovating, growing, learning and building our own business and personal strategy essentials for our wellbeing and safety. One company Totalsum is finding a good solution to fully understand functional principles of the life of customers to help connect with a wide range of alternative technologies to help you drive innovative business instead of innovation driving your home product choices. The current scope is crucial for opportunity generation in the interest of future development of the applications. Technology is needed to help with household and office activities while giving support to the studying children, aging parents, growing toddlers and visiting friends or relatives, or work stakeholders. New products are being made in line with the need for safety and not preference. Twitter has provided $1000 to employees to prepare office spaces at homes. The need was for digital navigation systems till yesterday, today we have to transfer the skill to a new home cooking system or temperature control panel or home-school - office facility with the family staying at home, and tomorrow is the need for combination of speed and flexibility for safety and security along with knowledge systems to recommend the best method based on the information derived from environmental and intellectual expertise in advising the working household elderly people to stay with kids to avoid problems of vulnerable diseases in the particular period of time or to eat a certain food in the interest of health care or hygiene during the day of lunar eclipse, for example, to reduce the risk of health disorders.

REFERENCES

1. Multi dated online newspapers like Business line, Economic Times, Business Wire, CNBC, CNN, BBC, Wall Street Journal (WSJ)
2. Online Tietoz surveys
3. The Seven Habits of Highly Successful People, Stephen Covey, 2004
4. Various Reports by World Economic Forum, 2020
5. Bhagavad Gita, Pt Ravi Shastry, Gita Press, 2003
6. Yahoo Contributor Network, Archives of Articles, Marsha White, 2013-14 (pen name of CV Madhavi)
7. www.brainyquote.com

Table of contents

Acknowledgements

Backdrop - CORONA fears

Before corona (BC)

After corona

Procedure for corona crisis management
- Customer
  - Agricultural Economy

Post Pandemic Growth of Services Sector

Modern Education
- Changing employment contractual models
  - Our Responsibilities
- Government
- Industry
  - Sport & Fitness industry - Health is wealth
  - Global apparel and textiles
  - Shift in Global transportation industry
  - Entertainment & Media
  - Information technology
  - State of Energy sector
  - Electronic future
  - Semiconductors and memory storage
  - Insurance
  - Banking
  - Real estate parody
  - Kids industry segments
  - Data analytics
  - GDP (Genetics, Diagnostic and Pharmaceutical)
  - Total transformation in FMCG
  - Global Payments industry
- Markets
  - Investments
  - Taxation

Procedure to revive the economy
- Organizational inertia
- Entrepreneurial benefit
- Rethinking strategy
- Supply chain management

- Networks and transaction cost models
- Way to Innovation
  - A special mention of Quantum Computing
- **Corporate ethics after corona lockdown**

Business administrative transition (Bat to hit the crisis)
- Marketing, sales, advertising
- **Financial twists**
- **Management tantrums and Corporate revival**

CSR

Competition Strategy
- Technology Risks or digital wars
- Organizational Resilience
- Leadership in post crisis world
- Cross border Collaboration

Population - Boon for Economic Revival

GOD
- Eco-friendly Revival
- Post Covid Knowledge Economy Transformation
- Failures of the decade and impact on post pandemic economy: Company closures (Covid-19 Positive Corporate Cases)
- New Opportunities (Covid-19 Negative or Immune Industries)

CONCLUSION

REFERENCES

Notes

Note of thanks

The book has been written to give the readers a broad way ahead to solve the crisis of corona. It is supposed to serve as a guide for revival of the global economy. The idea is not to confuse the readers with data or facts but provide a more reader-friendly aesthetically appealing digital book. Therefore, we have not illustrated many diagrams or figures except where really necessary. Finally we thank you for your patient reading and hope to have more joint collaborations with readers on bringing out more relevant books in the future.

About the authors-

Dr. Ch S Rajagopal is a veteran of Financial management and Auditing services with reasonable exposure to matters of Taxation. He has a vast multi faceted experience of over four decades in Hindustan Aeronautics Ltd., where he worked with the top management initially and later was invited as a Consulting Expert, after retirement to assist in the formation of new branch offices across India. Cost accounting, mentoring, auditing, capacity building and financial accounting are some of his work areas of interest and expertise. Rajagopal is Member of Aeronautical Society of India (M.AeSI) and is an MBA graduate. Later he obtained two professional doctoral degrees, as Doctor of Law in taxation (D.Law) and PhD in Management. He is married to Alka who is a life coach in Hyderabad and they have a daughter and a son.

CV Madhavi is a successful Strategy professional and works for companies (on behalf of Tietoz, a Consulting sole proprietorship) in helping them formulate and implement strategies for business excellence and an exhilarating customer experience to give delight by taking to the next level in offering profound legacy product and service solutions. She has devoted more than 17 years of work years to consolidate knowledge sharing and operational improvement of global industries. She is also the author of more than 30 Management books. Madhavi is an MBA graduate from IIM Calcutta. She is also a professional doctor in management. She lives with her father and mother in Hyderabad, India.

Word	
corona	
world	
crisis	
global	
business	
companies	
economic	
economy	
growth	
industry